CAPTIVE
OF THE
LABYRINTH

CAPTIVE
OF THE
LABYRINTH

Sarah L. Winchester
Heiress to the Rifle Fortune

Mary Jo Ignoffo

To Tom Enjoy Mary Jo Ignoffo

UNIVERSITY OF MISSOURI PRESS   COLUMBIA AND LONDON

Copyright © 2010 by
The Curators of the University of Missouri
University of Missouri Press, Columbia, Missouri 65201
Printed and bound in the United States of America
First paperback printing, 2012
All rights reserved
5 4 3 2 1   16 15 14 13 12

Cataloging-in-Publication available from the Library of Congress
ISBN 978-0-8262-1983-1

∞™ This paper meets the requirements of the
American National Standard for Permanence of Paper
for Printed Library Materials, Z39.48, 1984.

Cover designer: Susan Ferber
Text designer: Stephanie Foley
Typesetter: Foley Design
Printer and binder: Thomson-Shore, Inc.
Typefaces: Bodoni and ITC Garamond

Cover photographs: Sarah L. Winchester's enormous, labyrinthine
house, which she designed and had built on the outskirts of San José,
California, between 1886 and 1906, when its seven-story tower and
other tall portions collapsed in the San Francisco earthquake. This
photograph, which predates the quake, was probably taken from a water
tower. After Winchester's death, the house was transformed into a tourist
attraction, the Winchester Mystery House. Courtesy History San José.
Inset: Sarah L. Winchester, circa 1872, portrait by Isaiah Taber of San
Francisco. Courtesy History San José.

For Pat

The labyrinth of her days

That her own strangeness perplexed;

. . . what her dreaming gave

Earned slander, ingratitude,

From self-same dolt and knave.

WILLIAM BUTLER YEATS,
"AGAINST UNWORTHY PRAISE"

CONTENTS

Author's Note *ix*

Preface *xi*

Acknowledgments *xxi*

Introduction *1*

Chapter 1 New Haven's Daughter *7*

Chapter 2 Marrying into the Winchester Family *22*

Chapter 3 "The Gun That Won the West" *39*

Chapter 4 The Winchester Fortune *66*

Chapter 5 A California Dream *83*

Chapter 6 Labyrinth *106*

Chapter 7 Daydream or Nightmare *123*

Chapter 8 Guns, Guilt, and Ghosts: The First Commentaries
on Sarah Winchester's Odd House *138*

Chapter 9 Health and Welfare *166*

Chapter 10   Changing Fortunes *179*

Chapter 11   Trapped in a Mistaken Legacy *196*

Chapter 12   Capitalizing on Spirits: The Mystery House *206*

Notes *215*

Bibliography *233*

Index *239*

AUTHOR'S NOTE

Although named "Sarah" after her mother and a deceased elder sister, Sarah Lockwood Winchester was always called "Sallie," nicknamed for her paternal grandmother, Sally Pardee Goodyear, who died just months before Sarah Winchester was born. "Sallie" stuck, and even late in life Winchester was called "Sallie" or "Aunt Sallie." Nevertheless, for this narrative, she is identified by her formal name.

Winchester Model 1876 rifle, larger and heavier than the Model 1873 and designed for larger centerfire cartridges to take down big game like grizzly and buffalo. It became a favorite of hunting enthusiast Theodore Roosevelt and the official weapon of the Royal Canadian Mounted Police. This model is sometimes referred to as the Centennial Model because it came out the year of the nation's hundredth birthday and because it was featured at the Centennial International Exposition held in Philadelphia the same year. Courtesy Buffalo Bill Historical Center, Cody, Wyoming; gift of Olin Corporation, Winchester Arms Collection, P.20.1877.

PREFACE

―•― ⛭ ―•―

FIRST SAW A WINCHESTER REPEATER WHEN I WAS TEN YEARS OLD. My brother Mike had been given a 1966 Winchester Centennial .30–30 for his eighteenth birthday, and as he took mock aim and cocked the lever, the hallmark of Winchesters, I thought he looked like Chuck Connors in *The Rifleman.* Mike pointed out the gun's distinctive design features—the octagonal barrel, the fine walnut finish, the gleaming gold receiver, and the intricate, eight-cartridge magazine. His enthusiasm did not convince me, though, and I was afraid of the gun. But even as the gift attested to his interest in hunting and his coming of age, it was largely symbolic. The Centennial Model 1966 rifle was a collector's item, a modern replica of the 1866 Yellow Boy, so called because of its brass-colored receiver. The Yellow Boy was the first repeating rifle manufactured under the Winchester name.

The Winchester repeating rifle is legendary, and when my brother received it in the 1960s, it conjured images of cowboys and Indians, bandits and marauders, reinforced by television and Hollywood movies like Jimmy Stewart's *Winchester '73* and John Wayne's *Rio Bravo.* Today, few people are familiar with either those movies or the rifle. Gun collectors and sport hunters may know that the Winchester Repeating Arms Company was sold in the early 1930s, and that products manufactured under that name today are produced by other firms. For most of us, the Winchester is an antiquated icon of the sometimes questionable development and mythology of the American West.

A decade after my brother's birthday, when I lived in the Santa Clara Valley fifty miles south of San Francisco, Mike visited me. By that time he had become a bona fide hunter and sportsman, and had added to his gun collection. He also possessed a substantial store of Winchester trivia. When Mike went to see the valley's hottest tourist trap, the Winchester Mystery House, he gleefully reported back the odd traits attributed there to Sarah Winchester, the one-time owner who had designed the home. He gave chapter and verse of a tour guide's account of Winchester's gun guilt, superstitions, religious practices, and unaccountably weird house. For my

A "witch's cap" on Sarah Winchester's house in San José, California. Photograph by Mary Jo Ignoffo.

A distant view of Sarah Winchester's huge San José, California, house before the 1906 earthquake, with the farm operation in the foreground. Courtesy History San José.

part, I was as skeptical that people paid money to see the Winchester house as I had been about the rifle Mike had received ten years earlier.

The Winchester house has been a tourist attraction since 1923, the year after the widow's death, when it was reportedly transformed into a haunted house. Over the years the business has subsisted on tourist dollars and during the 1970s and 1980s was spruced up to attract a more discerning traveler. The gangly house is touted by huge red-and-black billboards along California's highways and beyond, luring the curious with a silhouetted house superimposed by a human skull. The signs suggest that visitors may encounter an apparition from another realm. The Winchester Mystery House has emerged as a major California tourist destination, where trade groups and conventioneers are often booked for tours. As the house has become more well known, the person of Sarah Winchester has receded further and further from reality, her real life story obscured by a highly successful advertising campaign.

Almost thirty years after my brother visited, I happened to be conducting research at San José's main library one day when the librarian, who knew I often worked on local and California history, suggested that I write a biography of Sarah Winchester. I laughed. Who in their right mind would want to spend years researching and writing about this imbalanced, ghost-obsessed woman, and furthermore, who would read it? Besides, it was often reported that Winchester had left only ghosts behind, no real life records. "I am asked for information on her every single week," the librarian insisted, "and I have nothing to offer."

He pointed me to a local museum, History San José, saying it "might have something on her." Sure enough, History San José houses a collection from Sarah Winchester's attorney, Samuel Franklin "Frank" Leib, that contains twenty years' worth of notes, letters, invoices, canceled checks, and magazine subscriptions that paint a picture of a woman far different from her quirky mystery-house persona. The Leib collection led me to one of the same name at Stanford University because Frank Leib had also been counsel to Jane Stanford and had served on Stanford's board of trustees during its first twenty-five years. Stanford's archives also hold correspondence between Winchester and Leib. Both collections surprised me with her handwritten directives and legal questions there. I was intrigued by little things in the collections such as a Christmas list, receipts for a succession of automobiles, subscriptions to *Architectural Record,* and canceled bank drafts. Here was the stuff of a life—a business life at the very least. Was there more?

Another collection at History San José offered me an even more personal side to this unusual woman. A Winchester employee, John Hansen, and his wife, Nellie Zarconi Hansen, lived and worked for almost twenty-five years at Winchester's San José ranch, where they raised two sons, Carl and Ted. In the 1970s, their descendants donated photographs, letters, and scrapbooks to the museum. More recently, Carl's son, Richard Hansen, gave the museum a collection of daybooks, one for each year from 1907 to 1922, in which John Hansen had made notes about operations at the ranch and the comings and goings of "Mrs. W." The daybooks and Leib's letters document which of the five Winchester-owned houses Sarah Winchester happened to be visiting on a particular day or week or decade. This group of records sheds considerable light on Winchester's day-to-day life.

Other records reveal the public's perception of Sarah Winchester. She was the subject of scores of newspaper articles beginning in about 1895. Initially these articles introduced her as a bit unusual because she was building such a large house over such a long period of time. Before long, she was being described as superstitious and guilt-ridden, and in later years, she was presumed mad. Rumors piled on top of each other almost as fast as she added rooms to her house. Time has woven the multiple story lines into a tight and complex web of intrigue.

What was it about Sarah Winchester and her (arguably) odd house that elicited such a judgmental commentary? Why did anyone care what she did to her house? The crux of the Sarah Winchester story is the gun. The awesome and deadly power of the repeater, most often used on the frontier hunting down buffalo or against bandits or American Indians (or, when the tables were turned, against the cavalry), stimulated outlandish stories about Sarah Winchester and how she dispensed her fortune. As the Winchester repeater became an icon of western expansion, a symbol of an indomitable pioneering spirit, it also represented raw power—against man or beast—and it became clear that this power was much more than symbolic: this one tool had participated mightily in the subjugation of the West. Toward the end of the nineteenth century, the American press began to seriously acknowledge the brutality used against American Indians, and the American conscience began to be bothered by Indian atrocities. Sarah Winchester's reputation suffered scathing attacks of insult and ridicule beginning at the same time. As the most visible woman associated with the Winchester Repeating Arms Company, she was deemed its conscience.

Newspapers pinned the burden of guilt for Winchester-induced deaths on the widow, but there is no evidence that Sarah herself felt guilty about the repeating rifle or about earning money from it. Yet her connection to the rifle made her a scapegoat for the sins of its destruction, and people assumed she would have to face an ultimate spiritual reckoning with God or with ghosts at some point. She was not targeted simply for being rich;

it was the fact that her fortune came from the repeater that made some convict her. If she had not been a Winchester, if her wealth had derived from something other than a firearm—a sewing machine, for example, patented at about the same time as the repeater—the rationale for the huge, odd house would have followed an entirely different tack. No one would have suggested she was guilt-ridden by sewing machines or feared ghosts of garment workers. The themes of superstition, guilt, fear of death, and communication with the netherworld are due to Winchester's connection to the rifle. In other circumstances, they would have been displaced by some other (possibly equally fanciful) speculations.

Ghost stories are hard to resist—and easy to embellish. In the case of Sarah Winchester, they have been embellished masterfully by successive and successful marketing strategists. But like all ghost stories, this one is hugely suspect. In some ways, my quest to demystify Sarah Winchester may have begun with my brother's long-ago birthday gift. Here are ghosts of a different sort, the kind that lurk in the shadows of our memories and appear now and then to remind us of our pasts. Decades after that birthday gift was opened, I was reminded of my brother by a cache of Winchester letters, and something mysterious nudged me to look for more. I was astonished to find substantially more, enough verifiable data to give Sarah Winchester a place at the table of history, to enable us to hear her speak in her own words to those she loved and those she battled. I was hooked. I could not resist the story of this small, infirm, brilliant, apparently introverted woman and her unwieldy house. This book lays out the results of my research odyssey to flesh out the ghost of Sarah Winchester.

A few writers have attempted to chronicle the life of Sarah Winchester, some more successfully than others. One claimed to have channeled messages from Winchester from beyond the grave. Needless to say, most of that information does not square with the historical record. Ralph Rambo, the nephew of one of Winchester's first employees in California and a noted calligrapher, made the best effort. His sixteen-page booklet *Lady of Mystery* (1967) divulges many facts about Winchester's life, but it also includes all the far-fetched stories, giving the reader a confused dose of fact and fable. Rambo's booklet continues to sell very well in the Winchester Mystery House gift shop.

In 1951, a student at San José State College, Bruce Spoon, chose Sarah Winchester, her house, and the legends as a topic for his master's thesis. He interviewed people who remembered Winchester and collected

Sarah Winchester's houseboat, often referred to as the "ark," which she docked at land she owned on San Francisco Bay in Burlingame, California. Dozens of similar craft were commissioned and occupied by wealthy San Franciscans in the early twentieth century. Courtesy History San José.

newspaper clippings and magazine articles. Spoon's conclusion was that Sarah Winchester built the big San José house for two reasons: one, to keep craftsmen employed with good provision for their families; and two, to give expression to her artistic vision. He asserted that the legends about Winchester were less compelling than the real story, but that "through time, and by various means, some quite intentional, others pointedly purposive, the legend has grown." When those who knew Winchester die, he believed only the legend will survive.[1]

Although Burton Klose (1915–1979) did not write about Winchester, he collected scores of documents relating to her life and properties. Klose grew up in Burlingame at the foot of Oak Grove Avenue, and he went in Winchester's houseboat as a child. Every evening of his youth, his elderly grandfather ventured out on the footpath of Sarah Winchester's old "Pasture" for a walk. One night, the grandfather did not return; he had fallen dead along the path. After the death of his grandfather, Klose remained intrigued about the houseboat property and wanted to find out more about it. In his retirement years, he collected copies of every public record relating to Sarah Winchester that he could find. He tape recorded interviews of former neighbors or others who had come into contact with Winchester or her niece, Saidee Ruthrauff. Klose gave his collection of clippings, documents, maps, and interviews to the San Mateo County History Museum Archives, which proved very helpful in this research.

Some people who knew Winchester tried to denounce the burgeoning mythology. In the 1920s, after they had grown to adulthood, Winchester employee John Hansen's sons, Carl and Ted Hansen, tried to refute the stories of an obsessively superstitious Winchester. When their attempts fell on deaf ears, each made a strict policy not to grant interviews about the deceased widow. They believed ghost stories would always win out over facts, and they did not want to contribute details that would only be used to embellish the false stories. In a private letter in 1972, Ted maintained that the "fantastic stories, . . . many of which were published long before her death, have become so popular that any attempt to refute these is more or less futile." Underscoring his late uncle's opinion, Richard Hansen, Carl's son, even as he generously shared photos, letters, and documents with me, doubted that anyone would believe or buy this book. "The truth doesn't sell," he warned.[2] This daunting challenge to a would-be biographer appears to ring only too true, as thousands pay to tour the "haunted" house and patronize the movies, stage plays, and art exhibits that keep Winchester bound in a strictly marketable costume.

Up to now, Sarah Winchester has been left to stand, all fifty-eight inches of her, devoid of the setting, scenery, characters, and events of her actual lifetime. It is no wonder she comes across as odd when she is so one-dimensional. During her life and since her death, she has been consistently viewed out of context. When she first arrived in California, she could not have been more out of place, a wealthy heiress who had left her home of a lifetime in the urban East and planted herself in the middle of a rural valley, the proverbial backwater. From that point right down to today, she has never been allowed the company of her roots, her family, her culture, her class, her time and place, her servants and workers, her homes and gardens. This book uses primary source documents to place her in real life. She emerges as far more compelling than a mere comical anecdote to the Winchester rifle story.

＊＊ ▬◆▬ ＊＊

My brother Mike's 1966 Winchester Centennial .30–30 had a rough life and so did he. Through the years the rifle had been kept in pristine condition as he used a variety of other rifles for hunting. He died young, at age forty-eight, of colon cancer, and within weeks of his death, before anyone could collect his belongings, his place was robbed. The Winchester was stolen along with some other rifles and a few pieces of art. After almost a year of sleuthing, our younger brother tracked down the thief

Entry to the William Wirt Winchester Hospital in New Haven, Connecticut, once a tubercular clinic, funded and endowed by Sarah Winchester as a memorial to her husband, who died of tuberculosis. Photograph from *General Hospital Society of Connecticut Centenary,* published in New Haven in 1926.

and recovered the .30–30. During its time away, it was used and abused, and no amount of restoration will return it to its previous condition. But for us, it does not matter how it looks or how accurate it is in firing. It represents something larger, something difficult to identify, something that reaches beyond the rifle to recall a life. It is symbolic of our late brother. That anniversary-edition Winchester struck a personal nerve with us, we who are by no means hunters.

It is not so difficult to understand how the Winchester repeater came to be a potent symbol of American culture in the West. There is something about when it arrived on the scene at the beginning of an American adulthood, a harbinger of progress and death, violence and life. Its sleek design lent it a distinct identity. Although the history of the West is tarnished and bruised with violence and exploitation, it is a part of our national identity. To admit that the Winchester repeater is an icon of this is not necessarily to idealize it or what it represents.

Sarah Winchester's identity and persona are also born of the ambiguity surrounding the repeater, and she remains an enigma. She continues to be clothed in a mantle of idiosyncrasy and madness for a public that remains conflicted about the role of weapons in our society and skeptical about the notion of life after death. Her connection to the repeating rifle has elicited a sort of gallows humor, making her the standard-bearer for those wishing to communicate with the dead. This quirky assignment comforts an uncomfortable public, and allows people to make fun of her without implicating themselves in any such beliefs. Winchester never spoke directly to these timeless challenges, but her life story tells, as the Yeats verse at the beginning of this book describes, how one woman's strangeness and dreaming earned slander. Some highly credible sources have relegated Winchester to an eternal madhouse. One was the long-time director of the San Mateo Historical Society, Frank M. Stanger, who declared that she was "demented," and even when author Ralph Rambo wrote to him, saying "I saw her often and remember her well" and that he believed she was sane, Stanger was not persuaded.

More troubling than a single opinion, though, is that the Historic American Buildings Survey (HABS) bought the legends hook, line, and sinker when it added the San José house to the National Register of Historic Places in 1981. Documentation for this states, "This extraordinary structure is *sui generis*. Constructed over a period of 38 years because its owner, Winchester Rifle heiress Sarah L. Winchester believed she would live as long as construction continued, the house contains 160 rooms and covers six acres. The original portion purchased in 1884 contains 12 rooms. Some of the 40 stairways and 2,000 doors lead nowhere."[3]

Historians who gather information for HABS applications are supposed to offer objective analyses of particular properties, not merely parrot the claims of their owners. They failed in this instance. The HABS survey was undertaken at the behest of Mystery House manager Keith Kittle. His motivation was not pure self interest, although the National Register status garnered significant publicity and brought more tourists to the house. Kittle appreciated the house's historic character and the role that popular culture assigned to the Winchester rifle in the West. However, Kittle had very little knowledge about or understanding of Sarah Winchester.

A quick look at county records shows that the property was not even purchased by Winchester until 1886, two years later than the survey states. Second, HABS does not take into account that the house was substantially damaged in the 1906 earthquake. The blocked stairs, doors, and chimneys have simple explanations: they were not repaired after the earthquake. The house was constructed and remodeled between 1886 and 1906, reducing the years of construction from the HABS record of thirty-eight years to twenty. After 1906 there was no extensive construction, and only simple repairs were undertaken. Furthermore, there is no evidence that

Sarah Winchester pinned her existence upon the construction project. In fact, she put far more effort into estate planning than house building.

Those who are the most mocking of Winchester, her most strident accusers, have based their definitive opinions on a mythology that does not stand up to historical scrutiny. It is a disservice to the facts of her life to dismiss Sarah Winchester as a superstitious madwoman. It is time to set the record straight. If Winchester's San José house had not been turned into a tourist attraction, her memory would have been relegated to the annals of local history as an eccentric dowager who spent a fortune in equal parts on frivolity and philanthropy. But as the house draws thousand of people each year and represents details of the widow's life to them, it becomes imperative to give the other side of the story.

ACKNOWLEDGMENTS

S ARAH WINCHESTER IS AS BEGUILING A SUBJECT AS ONE CAN IMAGINE.
Her simultaneously secretive and public life called for such a wide
spectrum of sources—ranging from archives to zip codes—that
as I acknowledge those who helped I am afraid that some will
be left out. I offer gratitude and admiration for many, many friends, colleagues, professionals, and strangers who helped map out this life story.

The idea for this work came from Bob Johnson, librarian (retired) at
Martin Luther King Jr. Main Library in San José. He planted the seed
and over the years has asked about its progress. Other librarians and
archivists have also been essential to this work, including Barbara Austen
(Connecticut Historical Society), Allison Botelho (New Haven Free Public
Library), Lisa Christiansen (Stocklmeir Library and Archive, California
History Center, De Anza College), Mary Hanel (Santa Clara City Library)
and the staff at the Mission Branch of the same Santa Clara library,
Margaret Kimball (Stanford University Archives), Thom Peters (Hopkins
School, New Haven), Carol Peterson (San Mateo County History Museum
Archives), and Sean Campbell and Mary Robinson (Buffalo Bill Cody
Museum in Cody, Wyoming).

The most important sources for this book were found at History
San José, a regional museum and archive. I am grateful to the former
archivist, Paula Jabloner, for initially showing me the Leib papers and
the Hansen Collection. The current archivist, Jim Reed, was remarkably
accommodating over a period of a few years, even through the relo-
cation of the archives and a thunder-and-lightning storm that took out
power and Internet service for over a month at precisely the time I
requested images and permissions. Thank you, Jim, for your good-natured
and professional help.

Richard Hansen, grandson of Sarah Winchester's ranch foreman John
Hansen, sent copies of pictures, letters, documents, and references to
me. His kindness is a warm reflection on his parents and grandparents,
who made a home at the Winchester place for more than two decades.
Likewise, the great-granddaughter of Winchester's attorney, Frank Leib,

Marian Leib Adams, agreed to be interviewed. She provided detailed family background and access to an unpublished manuscript of a Leib family history. April and Hans Halberstadt rescued some Leib-Winchester letters from a Saturday morning garage sale and shared them for this work. The general manager of the Winchester Mystery House, Shozo Kagoshima, was very courteous in agreeing to be interviewed and helpful in explaining how the public views today's tourist attraction. Others who helped in sometimes very detailed ways were Bob Knapel and Charlene Duval; Dale Fiore at Evergreen Cemetery in New Haven; Katerina Rohner, who sent current photographs of New Haven; and architect Leslie Dill, who accompanied me on a tour of the Winchester Mystery House. She helped to identify the portions of the house lost in the 1906 earthquake.

I appreciate the people and institutions that loaned photographs with permission to this publication, namely, Marian Leib Adams; the Buffalo Bill Cody Museum in Cody, Wyoming; Richard Hansen; History San José; the San Mateo County History Museum Archives; and the Whitney Museum in Hartford, Connecticut. I am also thankful to LeeAnn Nelson of Nelson Design in San Ramon, California, for designing and producing the maps and family trees that appear in this book. I always get new insights from working with an amazing artist like LeeAnn.

The California History Center at De Anza College, where I teach, has welcomed me and inspired me. Tom Izu, Executive Director, and Lisa Christiansen, archivist, are both friends and colleagues who have apparently never tired of hearing or asking questions about Sarah Winchester. Lisa responded to many arcane requests, and Tom has a knack for seeing a much larger picture than most. The history center's class "Significant Californians" welcomed Sarah Winchester as a subject worthy of the title, and students who took that class in Fall 2008 rendered important insights and questions about our visit to the Winchester Mystery House. I am grateful for the support of De Anza College Dean of Social Sciences, Carolyn Wilkins-Greene, and History Department Chair, Margaret Stevens.

The nursemaid of this project has been Grey Osterud of Newton Upper Falls, Massachusetts. My one-time San José State University professor—turned friend—then editor has followed and cajoled this project with faith and insight. Despite life-threatening health challenges, Grey consistently encouraged and questioned at the same time. She is a first-rate critic and supportive friend, as well as an ardent advocate for women's rights from Afghanistan to Zambia.

I would like to thank those who read a portion of the early manuscript and commented on it, including the late Don Fuller, Susan Fuller, Emily Mace, and Bob Senkewicz. I am in debt to those who read a draft of the final version, including Kimberley Cameron, Lisa Christiansen, April

Halberstadt, Leslie Masunaga, LeeAnn Nelson, and Grey Osterud. I was happy to find a supportive community at Stanford's Publishing Courses Writers Workshop in the summer of 2009 and people who read and commented on this work, especially Jay Schaefer and Bonnie Solow.

I am grateful that the University of Missouri Press has taken on this project and managed it through every stage with professional facility, especially the Editor-in-Chief, Clair Willcox, editorial staff Sara Davis and Gloria Thomas, and marketing staff Beth Chandler and Jennifer Gravley. Each has been courteous and patient, elusive qualities in this fast-paced world. I very much appreciate their hard work.

On the more personal side, friends and family have often asked about the progress of this book, and each inquiry was appreciated. Bob and Susan Raffo have been unbelievably supportive, even calculating the present value of Winchester monies. My parents, Sandy and Helen Hull, who as this book comes to publication celebrate their sixty-fifth wedding anniversary, are remarkable in every way, especially how supportive they have always been. My brother, Sandy Hull, and sisters, Laura Sando and Debbie Hull, often ask after Sarah Winchester, knowing she has been a steady companion for some time. Sandy rescued our late brother Mike's Centennial Winchester and told me the harrowing details of that rescue. The rifle is currently in his possession. My sister, Miriam Hull, encouraged the genesis of this project before she died in 2005. The Ignoffo family of Vancouver, Washington, has also offered support, particularly John, with technical advice. I am grateful to my son, Joey Ignoffo, for research assistance at the Santa Clara County Superior Court and for consistent comic relief; and to my daughter, Lisa Ignoffo, for photographic help and fashion counseling. Sarah Winchester was discussed in our house for a good portion of Joey and Lisa's childhoods, and it would not surprise me if on many occasions they did not believe there was actually a book in progress.

Finally and most importantly I am grateful to and for Pat Ignoffo, my husband, confidant, and great friend. In considering the dedication of this book, there was no question in my mind. To Pat, with admiration, appreciation, and abiding love.

M.J.I.

CAPTIVE
OF THE
LABYRINTH

INTRODUCTION

S ARAH WINCHESTER'S LIFETIME SPANNED THE VICTORIAN AGE. SHE WAS born in 1839, two years after the teenaged Queen Victoria was crowned, and eighty years later, as death approached, Winchester could have been a Victoria look-alike—a stooped little lady, face veiled, in black silk mourning garb. Like the queen, she had seen profound personal and societal transformations occur during her lifetime. Winchester's attitudes and tastes were shaped as turbulent religious, aesthetic, and political seas changed America in the years just before and after the Civil War.

Winchester was born Sarah Lockwood Pardee in New Haven, Connecticut, at the peak of the Industrial Revolution and in the same year that the *Amistad* incident focused worldwide attention on New Haven. At the time, the underpinnings of America's religions were making seismic shifts, and belief systems such as spiritualism and transcendentalism entered the mainstream. Sarah was nine years old when the first women's rights convention was held in Seneca Falls, New York, in 1848. Before her death in 1922, the Nineteenth Amendment to the U.S. Constitution had established women's right to vote. She was witness to and the product of a magnification of women's roles in the world. But despite her financial and apparent social independence, Winchester was not able to live as she wanted. In California as well as in Connecticut, her days and decisions were highly circumscribed by the boundaries of traditional upper-class womanhood. She developed a sharp intellect, but had no prospects for higher education. She admired clever, time-saving inventions, but her gender and class kept her from engaging in work that was more than a hobby. She often ignored social, religious, and business expectations, but this gave fodder to labels of superstition, religious fanaticism, and mental illness. These judgments, although often rendered against women who ventured beyond the implicit confines of womanly behavior, overwhelmed any personal identity she may otherwise have achieved.

When Sarah Pardee married William Wirt Winchester in 1862, he was heir apparent to a large and profitable clothing factory in the center of

1

New Haven. At age twenty-five, William was running the day-to-day operations of the Winchester & Davies Shirt Manufactory, and there was no question that one day he would carry it to unparalleled production and record profits in New England's garment industry. But within four years of his marriage, William had relinquished his partnership and taken on a leading role in a rifle company. His father's aggressive investments in a weapons factory dragged William into this unlikely occupation. The younger Winchester's unexpected conversion from garment-maker to gun-maker changed the course of his life as well as his new wife's.

The design and manufacture of firearms had undergone a dramatic evolution, almost literally in the Winchesters' Connecticut backyard. Eli Whitney, inventor of the labor-saving cotton gin, established the Whitney Arms Company late in the eighteenth century in Hamden, Sarah's ancestral village. Whitney applied the principles of mass production with interchangeable parts (tactics that the Winchester firm later adopted) to appreciably accelerate the process of weapons production. In the meantime, Samuel Colt of Hartford invented the "revolver," a pistol with a revolving barrel, and Horace Smith and Daniel Wesson partnered in developing a repeating pistol called the "Volcanic." These sidearms were the immediate precursors of the "Winchester," a revolutionary advance from the traditional muzzle-loaded musket.[1] The Winchester was the first financially successful repeating rifle and the most sought-after long arm in the last quarter of the nineteenth century. It generated great wealth for the Winchester family.

Sarah and William Winchester, together with William's parents, built a palatial home on the outskirts of New Haven overlooking the new Winchester Repeating Arms Company factory. From 1868, when they took occupancy of the new mansion, until 1880, the couple lived in high style and traveled together, and William devoted himself to his father's rifle factory, which he planned to take over one day. Sarah's mother died in the spring of 1880, and William's father died at the end of that year. Just three months later, in March 1881, William died from tuberculosis, leaving Sarah his Winchester Repeating Arms Company stock worth $77,700, which paid dividends of $7,770 annually, and she stood to inherit another $200,000 worth when her mother-in-law died.[2] If those three deaths were not enough to cope with, Sarah's eldest sister, Mary Converse, died in 1884. The following year, she fled New Haven a grief-stricken woman of few words and even fewer companions, a practical, no-nonsense Yankee embarking on a quest to create a California retreat where she could heal from the loss of her husband. She purchased land in the warm and salubrious Santa Clara Valley and invited her assorted sisters with sometimes difficult husbands and half-grown children to come live near her. This extended family generated episodes that embroidered Winchester's early years in California with comedy and tragedy and headaches—common symptoms of complex family relationships.

Winchester's move to California came at a time when thousands of others were settling in the West. After the midcentury Gold Rush, there had been a steady stream of pioneers making the trek by wagon across the prairies and over the mountains to California. With the opening of the Transcontinental Railroad in 1869, the stream grew, and by the middle 1880s, people were flooding into the West to start life anew. At the beginning of her residence in California, Winchester was very much like others of her class who lived in the valley. She joined Leland and Jane Stanford, who, recovering from the death of their only son, laid the foundation for a great university. Another neighbor was the Pullman railcar heiress, Harriet Pullman Carolan, who brought her fortune into a marriage and set the social scene on the San Francisco Peninsula. Carolan's best friend, Virginia "Ella" Hobart Baldwin, was heiress to one of the Comstock Lode's silver barons, Walter S. Hobart. Like the Stanfords, the Carolans, and the Baldwins, Winchester owned several homes on which she lavished expensive decor and furnishings. She purchased a houseboat (others may have preferred a yacht) for summering. In this company, Winchester may not have appeared particularly odd.

The excesses of the Gilded Age were less apparent in California than in the East, however, and Sarah Winchester's display of wealth, although in step with a few of her neighbors,' mostly stood out in the rural and middle-class valley. Her house and ranch took on the look of a personal "exposition," a micro version of the enormously popular world's fairs held during that era. While the international expositions in Philadelphia in 1876, Paris in 1889, Chicago in 1893, and Glasgow in 1901 reflected the wealth and achievements of nations around the world, the homes of the wealthy during this era made public statements about the aspirations and sensibilities of their owners. Winchester's house, for example, displayed a collection of disparate styles and decorations in the building arts. She found great satisfaction in directing the construction and remodeling of the large, "rambling" (to use her word) house.[3] The landscape of the ranch was divided into carefully cultivated fruit and nut orchards, plus decorative gardens favoring Japanese-style horticulture. An English garden with French statuary accented the Victorian house. Setting Winchester apart from both neighbors and other elites was the fact that she herself superintended the construction rather than hiring a construction manager. She drew plans and directed implementation until 1906.

The ways that Winchester spent her vast income put her in the public eye and the society pages. Like a modern soap-opera star, she was often the target of far-fetched newspaper stories. In 1895, a San José news-paper writer wondered why Winchester kept adding rooms, turrets, and towers to her already enormous house, suggesting that she must be superstitious. Perhaps, the story went, she was afraid she would die when construction stopped.[4] Several subsequent articles built on the first and specifically linked her building practices with guilt for those killed by Winchester repeaters. For the next two decades, increasingly complex reports declared Winchester superstitious, compulsive, obses-sive, and clairvoyant.[5]

Meanwhile, as Winchester withstood this ridicule, she supported sib-lings with monthly allowances. Three sisters had also moved to California, leaving a lone sibling, a brother, in New Haven. Of the siblings, Sarah's sister Isabelle "Belle" Merriman lived closest to her. She and her husband lived on a nearby ranch that Sarah had purchased. Belle was as outspoken as Sarah was silent. Involved in politics and Progressive Era social issues, Belle worked as California's first state humane officer. She rallied for kindness to animals and railed against child abuse. On a number of occasions she carried out citizen's arrests, causing street scenes and scandals reported in the press. She was ridiculed for speaking out, and Sarah was ridiculed for silence. Each sister was foil to the other and each withstood the burden of association. The Merrimans' daughter, Marion, who was called "Daisy," was Sarah's favorite among her nieces and nephews. In the early 1890s, Daisy left her parents' Mountain View ranch to move in with Aunt Sarah, where she lived for fifteen years, until she married. Sarah Winchester and Daisy Merriman established an unbreakable bond of affection and loyalty that endured hardship, tragedy, success, and disappointment.

The great San Francisco earthquake of 1906 wreaked havoc at Win-chester's house. The seven-story tower collapsed, and fifth and sixth floors dropped into the lower part of the house. A dozen chimneys top-pled and many walls crumbled. Winchester decided not to repair the damage, opting instead to simply have the fallen debris hauled away. Almost no one responded to the earthquake like she did; most felt it was in their best interest to rebuild. She demonstrated no such compunction, and in the years after the earthquake there was almost no construction at the old house, so the quake left lasting scars. The house's so-called stairs that lead to nowhere had previously led to an upper floor. Likewise, doors that now open out into thin air were once entryways to suites of rooms, and pipes protruding from the house's exterior once plumbed upper floors. The oddities of the giant house are easily understood when one takes into account the massive earthquake of 1906.

Winchester weathered more ridicule after the earthquake. She was presumed to be mad because she did not rebuild or adequately repair her mansion. At the same time, advancing age brought declining health. Although she kept social engagements in the years her niece lived with her, after Daisy Merriman's marriage in 1903, Winchester stayed mostly in seclusion. Rheumatoid arthritis took its toll, and her hands and fingers became disfigured and gnarled, so she kept them gloved whenever in public. She had very few teeth and opted to wear a veil to conceal her face. Her refusal to participate in society or be interviewed by the press cast her as a woman of mystery and superstition. Despite the fact that she owned five homes and spent most of the last twenty years of her life in the one in Atherton, California, she was never fully able to escape the old rambling house that bears her distinctive architectural signature. Since the turn of the twentieth century, she has been a captive of the labyrinthine house in San José, confined with its legends and mythology.

Winchester's life in California was not easy, but she remained despite many personal setbacks. She could have returned to New Haven at any time, but like her ancestors who transplanted themselves from England to New Haven, she lived out Connecticut's state motto, *qui transtulit sustinet* ("the one transplanted still sustains"). She died on September 5, 1922, at age eighty-three. It was a private death mourned by only a handful of relatives and employees. She did not presume to defeat death, but planned quite carefully for it, right down to the details of her funeral.

Upon her death, attorney Frank Leib told the local newspaper, "Mrs. Winchester was all that a woman should be, and nothing that a good woman should not be. . . . If there is a heaven, there she must surely be."[6] His comment points to a Sarah Winchester caught in the cross fire of her own inclinations of what were appropriate ways to spend her life and money against expectations of New Haven and rural San José society. She found herself living as her own frontierswoman, demanding a right to privacy and defending herself from defamation and libel while fighting off provincial and intrusive neighbors. She was also caught in a much broader cultural cross fire, one that echoes in our own day—an ambiguity about women's roles and about those who manage their own wealth, an uncertainty about how we relate to firearms, and conflicting feelings about religious beliefs. The supremely private Sarah Winchester drew extraordinary attention to herself. She kept her religious affiliation private, but she became a way for the public to perpetuate fundamental religious beliefs—a belief in the supernatural, for example—without putting it on themselves. The press placed squarely on Winchester's shoulders doubts, insecurities, and secret hopes about life after death without surrendering its own solid scientific ground.

Winchester's legacies fall into two categories: the intentional and the accidental. The bulk of her estate benefited the Connecticut General

Hospital Society's William Wirt Winchester Hospital (today part of Yale/ New Haven Hospital), a tubercular clinic that she began funding in 1909. Sarah Winchester's mortal enemy was not death. It was tuberculosis, the disease that stole her husband. Her life's work focused on funding the fight against that illness. When she created more than a dozen trust accounts to benefit nieces and nephews, she dictated that the principal from the funds would ultimately revert to the hospital.

Winchester's better-known but unintended legacy is the Winchester Mystery House in San José. Of the several houses that she owned at the time of her death, all sold except the strange San José house. The property was leased to an amusement-park promoter who capitalized on existing legends and transformed Winchester's house into a haunted house for the express purpose of attracting paying tourists. It has evolved over ninety years into a major California tourist attraction, and the house remains privately owned by descendants of the first renter.

The mythology surrounding Sarah Winchester is difficult to dislodge, since it has become as institutionalized as the tourist attraction. In fact, a visit to her house today is disappointing, since it has almost no furnishings and there is so little of Sarah Winchester to know or to take away (the only exception is the collection of art-glass windows). However, the public appetite for the macabre seems as strong as ever. The pull, the draw, the magnetism of the Winchester House is substantially prodded along by nearly ninety years of advertising. The bottom line that promoters through the years have understood very, very well is that no one can resist a good ghost story. Promoters may not have made up the Winchester story, but they have made absolutely certain that ghosts, rather than history, stay front and center in any discussion of the widow of the rifle fortune. It is ironic that the house was leased in 1923 rather than sold, which saved it from the wrecking ball. The bankers who wanted to be rid of it were certain that if they had been able to sell it, the buyer would have razed the old ramshackle house. It is very likely that Winchester would have agreed with those bankers, and would be amazed that her house has survived this long.

CHAPTER 1

New Haven's Daughter

————— ✦ —————

S ARAH LOCKWOOD PARDEE WAS BORN IN A CHARMING NEW ENGLAND TOWN.
At least that is how Britain's popular author Charles Dickens saw
New Haven, Connecticut, when he visited just about the time
she was born, a year before he penned his classic ghost story, *A
Christmas Carol.* The town's seventeen-acre Green with three beautiful
churches particularly captured his fancy. "The effect is very like that of
an old cathedral yard in England," he noted, " . . . a kind of compromise
between town and country; as if each had met the other half-way and
shaken hands upon it."[1]

Even the climate was widely admired. One account (written when
most of the present-day United States had yet to be explored) claimed,
"As to pleasantness of situation and salubrity of air, New Haven is hardly
exceeded by any city in America."[2] The whitewashed fencing of the
Puritan days had lately been replaced with black iron gating, and hundreds of elm trees had matured into leafy tunnels sheltering carefully
groomed streets. New Haven was, as Dickens saw it, one of America's
most beautiful cities, and the vibrancy and comfort of the Green became
a standard by which other towns measured their relative ambiance.

Sarah Winchester's ancestors had lived in New Haven almost since
its founding, making her American roots as old as the colonies. In 1644,
a battered and maimed twenty-year-old George Pardee tumbled off an
emigrant ship into the shallow harbor at New Haven Colony, a fledgling village on Connecticut's coast. Pardee was Sarah Winchester's fourth
great-grandfather, the younger son of an English clergyman descended
from a French family.[3] He had been chased out of his native Somersetshire,
England, for hard-line Puritan statements, and after a brutal beating, he
had fled for his life. His escape from anti-Puritan England was in the nick
of time, for he had been beaten so badly that he never fully recovered
and walked with a pronounced limp for the rest of his life. This marked

him as a man of unflinching religious convictions. Even his name suggested a lineage of churchmen:"Pardee" derives from an old French oath, *par Dieu* ("by God"). He found a probationary welcome at New Haven, and his name first appears in a court record apprenticing him to a tailor. "George Pardy shall dwell with Francis Browne as his apprentice for the terme of 5 years from hence forwards, dureing which time the said Francis is to doe his endevor to teach him the trade of a taylor."[4] Sarah Pardee Winchester came from decidedly Puritan stock.

As an unmarried man, Pardee was not permitted to live apart from a respectable householder, and Francis Browne became his patron and mentor. During his apprenticeship, Pardee gained practical knowledge as well as respect. He was assigned the fourth seat from the aisle in Center Church, a manifest advancement from his poor and bedraggled condition upon his arrival at New Haven. In 1650, after the prescribed five-year indenture, Pardee married Martha Miles, and four children came in rapid succession. The community discovered his latent talents, and in 1662 he was appointed the first rector of New Haven's Hopkins Grammar School, which thrives to this day. He must have studied or been tutored as a youngster to be entrusted to teach English and "to carry them on in Latin so far as he could."[5] Having learned scripture and obedience at the foot of his Puritan father, Pardee had a stern disposition that kept New Haven's boys orderly and pious. Soon he was living nearer the commons, another indication of his growing social status.

Like many seventeenth-century women, Martha Pardee died in childbirth. In 1655, George married Katherine Lane and had four more children. The youngest child and only male of his second marriage, Joseph, born in 1664, was the undisputed favorite son and, not unlike the biblical youngest named Joseph, was resented by his siblings for the important roles he was given in the growing community. When a new bell replaced the drum that had heretofore called the people to worship, Joseph was hired, for five pounds per annum, "to ring the bell for ye Towns occasions or ye Sabbaths . . . and allsoe to sweep ye meeting house every week."[6] Moreover, George guided Joseph to learn a trade. As a young man, Joseph took up carpentry and developed into a successful craftsman.

Joseph Pardee married Elizabeth Yale (a cousin of Elihu Yale, the benefactor for whom Yale College would be named) in 1689. By the time of Joseph's wedding, George Pardee had been in New Haven for forty-five years. The gifts he bestowed on his youngest son are a testament to his success in the colony. He gave Joseph his home near the Green (provided that the senior Pardees could live out their lives there), other town lots, and thirty-four acres on the west side of the Quinnipiac River. The generous gifts excluded all of Joseph's siblings, which was a fairly common practice when elder siblings had long since established their own families. But Joseph felt compelled to address the complaints of his eldest half brother, who believed the gifts were a particularly egregious insult. Joseph attempted to persuade his father to divide the worldly possessions fairly among the Pardee sons (evidently he was not so concerned about his several sisters). But in 1700, when it was clear that George was about to die and had not changed his mind, Joseph arranged to have the property deeds redrawn because "the just rights of my other relations are not answered and secured, but manifestly injured and invaded through the mistake of the scribe," meaning the senior Pardee.[7] Joseph Pardee demonstrated an unusual adherence to fair play.

Sarah Winchester's ancestry derives from George and his son, Joseph. Characteristics of these men, including a strict sense of justice, found their way down several generations to Sarah, who also possessed the Pardee appreciation for woodworking.[8] Joseph Pardee's descendants over the next four generations—Enos, Thomas, Joel, and Leonard—were all woodworkers and lived in Hamden, a small village bordering New Haven on the north. Sarah Winchester's father was Leonard Pardee, born in 1807 to Sally and Joel Pardee. After the early death of his father, he was raised by his mother and her second husband, Eli Goodyear (a relation of the patent holder for the vulcanization of rubber for tires). Leonard followed in the footsteps of generations of Pardees, perfecting his skills as a joiner.

The family's neighborhood in Hamden, which bordered New Haven, had a distinctly industrial identity. The famous inventor Eli Whitney, who revolutionized the cotton harvest with his gin that separated cotton from the seed, had established the Whitney Arms Company there in 1798. The Mill River, so named for the number of mills along its banks, ran through Hamden. Its water powered the jigs, drills, and lathes of a dozen small factories. Life in Hamden provided Leonard Pardee an entree into the inner workings of the Industrial Revolution. He perfected machining skills along with his traditional wood-joining techniques, and schooled himself to produce those small but vital parts. By age twenty, Leonard was living in New Haven and making a reasonable income.

⊷ ⊪◆⊪ ⊷

The young woman who would become Sarah Winchester's mother was born in 1808 in Milford, a town of about 2,500 residents that had grown up west of New Haven along the Wepawaug River. It was primarily a fishing village and, unlike New Haven, did not have an industrial base. At the time of the American Revolution, its population was large enough to require having a fort there, but eventually Hamden and New Haven eclipsed Milford, leaving it a bit of a backwater. Sarah W. Burns was the fifth daughter and seventh of twelve children born to Ralph and Polly (Morehouse) Burns. Her grandfather Burns fought in the Revolutionary War as a gunner at Fort Milford,[9] and her father was born at the height of Revolutionary skirmishes. Ralph and Polly fed their family alternately by oystering and farming, depending on the season and whatever could be coaxed out of Connecticut's rocky topography. The Burnses were different from the Pardees. They did not have a personal Puritan history, nor a long-established tradition as tradesmen. For them, making a living was an arduous perennial demand.

Whether Burns or Pardee, one immutable reality that all shared in common was the persistent and equal hand of death. The Milford cemetery holds the remains of infant twin Burns girls who died in December of 1821, a two-year-old Susan who died in 1828, and sixteen-year-old Jennie, who died in 1829. The most commonly held theology in New England at that time insisted that a wrathful God rejected those whom He had not predestined for salvation. Perhaps the deaths of Sarah Burns's sisters during her adolescent years inspired her to question tradition and venture to a Baptist camp meeting on the riverbank. Although the inspiring preacher maintained a belief in predestination, his brand of revivalism heralded a radical departure from Congregationalism's dismal, restrictive, doomsday message. She and hundreds of others were captivated by the preaching of the Reverend Benjamin Hill, a self-proclaimed "Calvinistic Baptist," who held forth on the banks of the Quinnipiac for the better part of a week in May 1828. Hill called out for converts to come to baptism. His invitation to salvation was so appealing that membership in his church doubled between 1824 and 1828.[10]

Hill's revival was just one example of modern denominations' vying with the traditional Congregational (Puritan) Church for members and for higher moral ground. Several distinctly American religions emerged as the Industrial Revolution pulled thousands of men, women, and children from farm to factory, and New England and New York provided fertile breeding grounds for alternative religious expression. Large Baptist and Methodist revivals converted hundreds, and other spiritualities were initiated by commoners rather than an educated (but out-of-touch) clergy. Among the radical departures from mainstream religious thought were Mormonism, transcendentalism, and spiritualism. Each offered a more personal experience of the divine. Joseph Smith, founder of Mormonism, deemed himself a new Moses, accepting God's code of conduct directly from an angel. Smith found ready adherents and ushered his followers to establish a western outpost. A bit later, transcendentalism gained many followers when Ralph Waldo Emerson and Henry David Thoreau articulated a fresh way of intuiting spiritual reality. Spiritualism, born of the upstart religions, supported a belief in the ability to communicate with the dead. It surfaced in New York after two young sisters claimed that knocking noises were directives from a murder victim. Kate and Margaret Fox's claims drew widespread attention to their Hydesville community, as the idea that spirits were seeking to speak to humans resonated with people who were overwhelmed by the relentless presence of death. Spiritualism became more popular during the middle decades of the nineteenth century, affording commoners a toehold in religious interpretation and practice.[11] Its practitioners were most often women, who overrode the authority of the pulpit by suggesting a life after death even for the unbaptized. The notion that one could hear directives from deceased persons lifted the dual yokes of death and damnation and captured widespread attention. Spiritualism took flight in America.

The great jostling between traditional religions and upstart varieties during the Second Great Awakening manifested itself in Connecticut in 1818, when the state declared that Congregationalism was no longer the official religion. At about the same time, as if to stabilize shifting theological ground, in an attempt to maintain authority stalwarts built three classic church buildings in a neat row on New Haven's Green. Center Church claimed an ancestry dating to the Puritans; Trinity Episcopal Church, the earliest Gothic-Revival church in the United States, stood as testament to the colonies' Church of England ancestry; North Church was the epitome of strict conservatism when it was constructed as a Congregational church. The stoic Yale College bolstered the religious stricture on the Green. Even though it hosted some of the premier thinkers and inventors of the era, it had been founded to educate a conservative clergy. Its very buildings had the look of restrained tradition. New Haven Green remains among the most beautiful historic enclaves in New England. It is also the most vivid picture that we have of the setting and scenery of Sarah Winchester's childhood.

Sarah Winchester's parents came of age just after the churches on the Green were constructed, in Puritanism's last gasp. Sarah Burns emerged from baptism in the chilly Quinnipiac River ignited with religious ardor, born again on the eve of her twentieth birthday in the early spring of 1828. As it happened, one Leonard Pardee was also swept up in the revival and proclaimed his faith.[12] Sarah and Leonard encountered the preacher, the divine, and each other at the same time, and were inspired to join hands into the future. The two young converts found common ground despite the apparent differences between their respective families. They were the same age, each was a Connecticut native, and both found hope in the more democratic and expressive Baptist Church.

Leonard Pardee and Sarah Burns married in 1829, stating wedding vows before Rev. Hill, a startling departure from the Congregational roots of both families.[13] Hill's simple brick-and-stone church on Olive Street, although modeled on Center Church, was no candidate for real estate on the Green. It was a house of worship for the more demonstrative, and the singing and public prayer that emerged through its walls would not have made a good neighbor to tradition. Leonard and Sarah established a lifelong friendship with Hill, whose message inspired a passionate spirituality. For the next four decades, even after he answered a call to lead another church, Hill often returned and presided at Pardee funerals and weddings.

— ⚏ —

The Pardees made a home at 12 Hill Street (an interesting coincidence, given their attachment to the preacher of the same name), near the Congress Avenue junction in the center of New Haven.[14] They began having children shortly after marriage, and in a pattern common for mid-nineteenth-century New Englanders, had a child almost every other year for fifteen years. They were luckier than most: all but the first survived childhood.

In February 1831, a daughter was born and they named her Sarah, adhering to the custom of naming the first daughter after the mother. The baby's first year progressed very well, but in the summer of 1832, she died. Although town records list scarlatina (scarlet fever) as the cause of death, it is likely that little Sarah succumbed to the cholera epidemic descending on New Haven that summer (neither cholera nor scarlet fever were treatable before the introduction of antibiotics). A local physician kept careful notes on the outbreak:

> The first case of cholera in New Haven, in 1832, occurred on Tuesday, July 10th, in the person of Mrs. N. She arrived the day before, from New York, with her son, six years old, at the house of her father, Mr. J., in Grand Street. In the house which she left in New York, there had been several cases of cholera and two deaths. She was attacked the morning after her arrival, and her son on Thursday, two days afterwards. Both had the disease severely, but recovered. On Friday, July 13th, Mrs. J., the mother of Mrs. N., and on the night following, Mr. J., her father, were attacked, and both died; one in eleven and the other in thirteen hours from the attack. No other case of the disease was observed in the city for more than three weeks.[15]

Then a new round of cases appeared, and it included eighteen-month-old Sarah Pardee. The child died on August 11, just hours after showing symptoms. The death toll in New Haven rose to more than thirty. While the doctor rightly believed the disease had been brought to New Haven on incoming vessels from New York, the public was confounded by the disease that struck so quickly and took life so promptly. Most looked to the heavens for answers, believing that cholera must have been sent by the hand of God in retribution for lax living. The Pardees lost their first-born, and the grieving parents held a Baptist funeral for their baby girl.[16] Not even the new Baptist faith offered salvation to the baby, who was relegated to eternal damnation. This kind of forbidding theology allowed spiritualism to chip away at Calvinist doctrine. The Pardees' Baptist fervor cooled, and when a schism divided the congregation after a new pastor arrived and his salary of $1,200 per year was announced, Pardee attendance at Sunday services was intermittent.

When the Pardees' first child died, Sarah Pardee was pregnant. Another daughter was born in 1833, and baby Mary thrived. Two years later, in October of 1835, Antoinette ("Nettie") joined her. The Pardees enjoyed relative health for the next decade. They were not so lucky financially. The troubled national economy of the middle 1830s was stretched beyond its limits with widespread speculation and an oversupply of paper money. More than a third of the banks in the country closed, limiting the capital available. Leonard Pardee teetered on the brink of poverty.

Andrew Jackson's presidency bolstered the hopes of the common man and reflected a nation more in keeping with citizens like Pardee. The president personified a shift in American culture toward decentralized government and fewer class restrictions. Individuals in every arena, from family to church to government, had the right and the power of self-determination. New Haven, with almost 10,000 residents living within its six square miles, was a microcosm of the nation. Young journeymen who were coming of age, men like Leonard Pardee, aimed to take economic power from the Whigs, the old-moneyed aristocracy. The Whigs were nervous and attempted to strengthen their grip on money and power but, in New Haven as elsewhere, were unable to hold back the new, young craftsmen, active players in industry who were ready to take their place. So not only was the religious foundation of the community in flux, with the likes of Rev. Benjamin Hill entering the scene, so too the economic and political hierarchies were shifting. The community was beset by a new rivalry between the upper class and those of moderate means.[17]

Leonard Pardee embodied the Jacksonian Democrat who by the skill of his hands and the will of God could improve the destiny of his family. Life did not play out this way. Money was scarce, customers unable

Sarah Winchester's Family

LEONARD PARDEE *(1807–1869)* ══ **SARAH BURNS** *(1808–1880)*

SARAH E. PARDEE *(1831–1832)*

MARY AUGUSTA PARDEE ═══ William W. Converse *(1834–1889)*
(1833–1884)

ANTOINETTE E. "NETTIE" ═══ Homer Baxter Sprague *(1829–1918)*
PARDEE *(1835–1913)*
    Charles Homer Sprague *(1856–?)* ══ Jennie L. Starbuck
    Sarah Antoinette "Nettie" ══ William W. Davis
    Sprague *(1858–1916)*
        Mary Converse Davis *(1882–1968)* ══ 1. Edgar R. Marsh *(1884–1912)*
                    ══ 2. Glover P. Prout *(1878–1918)*
            William Davis Marsh *(1907–1974)*
            Bryant Risley Marsh *(1910–1965)*
    William Pardee Sprague *(1860–?)* ══ Louise Velbert
    Goldwin Smith Sprague *(1869–?)* ══ Isabel

LEONARD MOREHOUSE ═══ Sarah H. Domkee *(1838–1912)*
PARDEE *(1837–1910)*
    Sarah "Sadie" Catherine ══ 1. Eugene Beecher
    Pardee *(1870–1956)* ══ 2. William T. McLean
        1a. Hazel Beecher *(1902–1991)*
        2a. Anita Sarah McLean *(1914–2010)*
    Louise Beecher Pardee *(1872–1922)*

SARAH LOCKWOOD ═══ William Wirt Winchester
PARDEE *(1839–1922)*   *(1837–1881)*
    Annie Pardee Winchester *(1866)*

ISABELLE CAMPBELL ═══ Louis A. Merriman *(1835–1908)*
PARDEE *(1843–1920)*
    Marion "Daisy" Isabel ══ Frederick A. Marriott III
    Merriman *(1869–1949)*
        Margaret Marriott *(1903–1961)* ══ 1. Richard C. Smith *(divorced)*
                    ══ 2. Donald Robesky *(divorced)*
                    ══ 3. ? Gale
            2a. Donald Robesky
    William Winchester ══ 1. Fannie R.
    Merriman *(1872–1959)* ══ 2. Chrissie W.

ESTELLE L. PARDEE *(1845–1894)* ═══ George Lyon Gerard *(divorced)*
    Sarah "Saidee" Louise Gerard ══ 1. Arthur Bugbee *(divorced)*
    (1868–1925) ══ 2. Henry "Harry" Ruthrauff
    George Leonard Gerard ══ 1. Grace M. *(divorced)*
    (1869– before 1940) ══ 2. Katherine Wade

to pay, and basic needs went unmet. Making a bad situation untenable, a horrific fire broke out in New Haven in the summer of 1837 on the south side of Chapel Street, between Church and Orange, just two blocks from the Pardees' Hill Street house. Despite a valiant effort by hundreds of townspeople forming bucket brigades, more than twenty buildings disintegrated into ash. The homes and livelihoods of the Pardee neighbors and customers were destroyed. Leonard Pardee was compelled to find alternative work to support his growing household, and by this time another child—the Pardees' fourth—was on the way. Even though he had doubled his efforts by combining machining with carpentry, the fire destroyed his last hope for making a living at his trade.

Leonard Morehouse Pardee, the first and only son, was born a month after the fire. Shortly thereafter, the senior Leonard took a position at the City Bathing House, a new facility built in the wake of the fire. The building at 27 Orange Street made bathing available to all citizens of New Haven. Heretofore, only the wealthy could afford regular bathing, but city fathers and the general public had recently recognized a relationship between cleanliness and good health, and the City Bathing House proved a worthy investment in public health. A modest fee purchased access to the men's or women's room, a water or vapor bath, or time in the steam cubicle. Iron slipper tubs could be filled with hot or tepid water or saltwater. In a desperate but practical departure from carpentry, Pardee worked collecting the toll and attending the patrons at the bathing house. The family took up residence in the living quarters at the adjoining 29 Orange Street. The job he hoped would be temporary lasted a decade.

Barely two years after baby Leonard's arrival, another girl was born into the family. In the summer of 1839, the Pardees' fifth child and fourth daughter, later known as Sarah L. Winchester, was born at 29 Orange Street.[18] The baby's birth came shortly after the death of her paternal grandmother, Sally Pardee Goodyear, so although the newborn was formally named "Sarah," she was always called "Sallie," for her grandmother, and she signed personal letters that way.[19] Little Sallie was given "Lockwood" as a middle name after her father's childhood friend, Lockwood Sanford, a wood engraver whose intricate designs for bookplates and other printable pieces earned both financial and artistic awards. Sanford became quite well-known throughout New England, and he maintained close ties to the Pardees. Undoubtedly, Sarah Lockwood Pardee Winchester's lifelong appreciation of carpentry and fine woodworking was more than a little influenced by generations of Pardee joiners, her father, and her father's friend and her namesake, Lockwood Sanford.

Sarah happened to be born the same year that worldwide attention was focused on New Haven because of the *Amistad* incident, in which fifty-three African slaves aboard the Spanish galleon *La Amistad* mutinied while the ship was off the coast of Cuba. After the slaves killed most of the crew, the ship meandered with the mutineers at the helm, until it blew into Long Island Sound, where the Africans were captured. While the Spanish and Cuban governments sued for possession of the slaves, local authorities incarcerated the mutineers in New Haven's county jail on Church Street, just blocks from the Pardee home. The debate over the rights or ownership of the Africans galvanized a quiescent abolition movement in Connecticut as the court proceedings became a cause célèbre.

Roger Sherman Baldwin, a New Haven attorney and committed abolitionist who lived on Church Street very near the Pardees, pled the case on behalf of the Africans. Baldwin pointed out that the slaves, while in their native Sierra Leone, had been free and therefore could not be the property of any government or enterprise. On January 13, 1840, the judge hearing the case ruled that the Africans "were born free," but the verdict was immediately appealed to the U.S. Supreme Court, where Baldwin was joined at the defense table by the elderly former president John Quincy Adams. After a lengthy and tumultuous court case, the lower court's decision was upheld and the Africans were freed to go back to Africa.

While in New Haven, the mutineers were a novelty, and although several black men and women lived in the city, New Haveners were intensely curious about and wanted to see the Africans. Long lines formed outside the jail as citizens waited to file past the cells, looking at the inmates in zoo-like fashion. Yale divinity students tutored the captives in English, and women made quilts and socks for them. The case brought the moral and political issue of slavery in America to the forefront. Slavery had often been characterized simply as a Southern issue, but by the early 1840s, New Haven was nudged to face its own complicity in the slave trade. Human chattel had been bought and sold on the Green, and local substandard crops were collected and shipped out as slave food to the Caribbean. Furthermore, slavery was not officially outlawed in Connecticut until the relatively late date of 1848, nearly a decade after *La Amistad* drifted into the Sound. The entire incident had social and political ramifications that lasted for decades. The *Amistad* turmoil sounded a prelude to the Civil War.

The story unfolded in the immediate neighborhood of the Pardee home in the first years of Sarah Winchester's life, and it would have been impossible for her family to ignore the social tumult surrounding it. Did the hue and cry have an impact on the child Sarah? Did the strident arguments she witnessed as a small child make her withdraw? Years later, when other Pardees went public with their opinions on progressive causes like abolition, suffrage, and kindness to animals, Sarah never did.[20] She played her cards close, growing into an extremely private adult.

While the Pardees lived at the bathing house, two more daughters were born. Isabelle, or "Belle," came four years after Sarah, and two years later, in 1845, Estelle was born.[21] The family was full and healthy—five girls and one boy, Leonard's livelihood improved, and the children could attend school. In 1850, all six children were listed in the U.S. Census as being in school, probably the Union School, just doors from the City Bathing House.

Orange Street was busy with carriages, hitching posts dotting the well-traveled street. Families lived at the premises of small businesses, livelihoods earned by a steady flow of New Haven customers. When the Pardee children ventured from the City Bathing House, they first encountered a "botanical physician," or herbalist, who had a small shop next door. Further along the street to the north, several tailoresses and dressmakers worked in the upper floors of dry goods stores. At least five single women worked as milliners, most living at one of the four boardinghouses on the block. A shoemaker on the street was black, as was a widow who lived at the tobacconist's. Leonard Pardee had a side woodworking business, and he found good company with the cluster of cabinetmakers and furniture makers just to the south. The stable and smithy at Orange and Court streets were convenient to the courthouse and the county jail, and they also brought patronage to the district. The Pardee family lived in the rear portion of the City Bathing House until Sarah was eight years old.

◆◆ ▬◆▤ ◆◆

In 1847, Leonard Pardee left the bath house and reestablished a full-time carpentry business. He partnered with a machinist and they set up shop, aptly enough, on Artizan Street. The partners produced small wood and metal parts for neighborhood factories and hardware for carriages. The Pardees rented a house around the corner from the shop, on Court Street, a main artery of commerce and civic activity linking Wooster Square with the Green and the courthouse (thus the name of the street). Court Street had a more industrial atmosphere than Orange Street, and it hummed with carriage works, clock shops, and carpentry mills, punctuated by overflowing boardinghouses.[22]

In a coincidence that had a profound impact on Sarah Winchester's life, the Pardees moved to Court Street at about the same time as another family. For a brief two years, from 1850 to 1852, the Winchester family, recently from Baltimore, was a close neighbor of the Pardees'.[23] The Winchester household was made up of Oliver and Jane Winchester; their

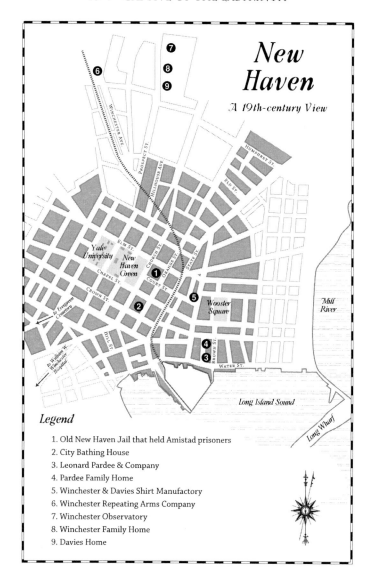

New Haven

A 19th-century View

Legend

1. Old New Haven Jail that held Amistad prisoners
2. City Bathing House
3. Leonard Pardee & Company
4. Pardee Family Home
5. Winchester & Davies Shirt Manufactory
6. Winchester Repeating Arms Company
7. Winchester Observatory
8. Winchester Family Home
9. Davies Home

teen-aged daughter, Annie; their son, William Wirt, called "Will," who in 1850 was thirteen years old; and three-year-old Hannah Jane (always called "Jennie"). The Winchester children paired off easily with the neighboring Pardees. Annie Winchester was the same age as Nettie, and just two years younger than Mary, the three on the verge of young womanhood. William was born the same year as Leonard Jr. Jennie Winchester, at age three, was the youngest, and she fit in with Belle and Estelle Pardee, who were five and seven in 1850. Only Sallie, at age eleven, was not matched with anyone in the Winchester household. Even in her own home she did not obviously pair with a sibling. The two eldest girls were very close in age, and the two youngest girls approached school at about the same time. Sarah and her brother, with whom she kept in touch over her life but does not seem to have been as close as to her sisters, would have been school-aged together. Precocious Belle was engaging, demanding attention, and quick to make her will known—traits she manifested throughout her life. Estelle, as the youngest, was always catered to. Sarah appears to have been on the path of a loner and independent thinker before she was an adolescent.

After just a few short years on Court Street, Leonard Pardee purchased a large family home in the exclusive Wooster Square neighborhood. The district dated from the 1820s, a time of great optimism, when a six-acre pasture was developed and named for the Revolutionary War general David Wooster. The large, classical houses made Wooster Square the most fashionable neighborhood in New Haven. The ability to purchase the home at 10 Brown Street indicates substantial success for Pardee. It affirmed his role as one of the city's skilled craftsmen who had risen to the upper middle class by virtue of the art of his work. He also purchased two lots contiguous to the house and established Leonard Pardee & Company, a large mill and wood shop at 39 East Water Street, fronting the harbor. The business advertised "sash, blinds, and doors," as well as decorative and practical accoutrements. Pardee fashioned pedals for organs and pianos, grave markers, finish carpentry moldings, and hitching posts. His mill backed up to the Brown Street house. His son and daughters had a front-row seat to watch skilled wood craftsmen at the busy workshop. Sarah Winchester's fascination with the skill of woodworkers never waned.

By the time the Pardee family settled at the Brown Street house, Britain's Queen Victoria had reigned about a dozen years and exerted profound and far-reaching influence. The attitudes she and her growing family displayed, everything from social etiquette and beliefs about moral propriety to specific styles in the building arts and architectural details, developed into the mark of the Victorian age. Her style transferred from the European stage to the American, particularly with the Crystal Palace Exhibition in London in the summer of 1851, sponsored by Victoria's husband, Prince Albert. The first of the great world's fairs, it offered a single venue for both art and industry. Newspapers reported on the "Great Exhibition of the Works of Industry of All Nations," which brought visitors from all over the world. The queen's attention and the number of times she attended helped highlight a budding Victorian style.[24]

Leonard Pardee's skills as a craftsman put him at the right time and place to reap financial benefits from Victorian trends. He produced the increasingly popular architectural details for Victorian-style homes and buildings in New Haven. He had orders for spindles and moldings, tracery and wainscoting. His personal wealth took a big leap during the 1850s. At the beginning of the decade he had assets of about $1,500 in both personal and real property. Ten years later, he owned real estate valued at $18,000 and claimed $22,000 in personal property. He was able to hire an Irishwoman as a live-in domestic servant and provide private music lessons and a French tutor for his children.[25]

A higher income notwithstanding, he could not ignore the daunting task of ensuring that five daughters married properly. Mary, the eldest at twenty-one, was courted by a slightly younger William Converse, whose father had been a weaver in a Massachusetts textile mill. Converse had an outgoing and cheerful disposition and was a sports enthusiast who competed in amateur winter sports.[26] Nettie's beau was Homer Sprague, slightly older and far more serious. His name matched his intellectual destiny; he, his father, and his uncles had all been named for literary greats: Milton, Virgil, Homer, Justin, and Cullen. It was as if Homer Sprague were predestined to embark on a literary career. He graduated from Yale in 1852 and was valedictorian. Two years later, he was ready to marry Nettie Pardee.[27]

Mary and Nettie were so close in age that it is not surprising that they shared a wedding day. The Pardee sisters were married in a double ceremony on a December morning just after Christmas in 1854.[28] The combined wedding was a celebration of the Pardee family maturity, of its financial security, and of the bonds between the parents and their children. Mary's new husband went to work at Leonard Pardee & Company, and he brought his brother into the firm as well. Both proved valuable employees. Nettie's husband was hired as principal of Worcester High School in Massachusetts. The position did not last long. It is unclear whether he quit or was fired, but his tenure at Worcester ended because of his controversial and outspoken abolitionist views. This incident was the first in what would become a pattern for Sprague. In most of the positions he accepted in academic institutions over his lifetime, he would be fired or forced to quit because of his vitriolic opinions. In his mind, he was standing up for moral ideals. To school boards and administrators, though, he was a difficult and unpredictable employee who, at the very least, was impolitic. Homer Sprague did not work well with others.[29]

Sarah Winchester lived at the Brown Street house from 1853, when she was fourteen, until her wedding nine years later. She and her brother and two younger sisters grew to adulthood there, roaming freely from the house through the yard to their father's mill. The comings and goings of wood craftsmen were simply a part of life for them there, making up a lifestyle that Sarah replicated years later in California. Houseguests at the Pardee home reflected the religious and political preferences of the parents. Rev. Hill often stopped in, and abolitionists found a hearing there. Henry Bergh, an advocate for animal rights and later child welfare, was often a houseguest.[30] As founder of the American Society for the Prevention of Cruelty to Animals (ASPCA), Bergh was dubbed by the press "the great meddler" for intervening at the sight of mistreatment of animals on the streets of New York. The Pardee family entertained some of the most progressive ideas of the day.

From the age of eighteen, Leonard Jr. worked in the carriage business, one of New Haven's most important industries. Perhaps it was just a matter of preference that he did not join his father's woodworking business, but he took up his own trade as a carriage trimmer, adding the necessary or attractive details to coaches. Remaining so employed for life, eventually he shifted with the market from coaches to automobiles. Belle and Estelle attended a new high school whose guiding purpose was a "devotion to the ideal of self-improvement" and to "constantly perfect [students'] knowledge for reasons both moral and practical."[31] When the school opened, Sarah was nineteen, past the age for high school. It was a social outlet she did not share with her sisters.

The blossoming of the Pardee family mirrored New Haven's maturity. Connecticut's largest city boasted several new buildings, including a government building with post office, a custom house, and a federal courthouse. Four sets of rail tracks transported passengers and freight in and out of the city. The Green had also reached a carefully prescribed elegance, with graveled footpaths and iron gating. Numerous elm trees grew large, giving New Haven its distinctive identity. The scenery, however, could not mask social ills descending on the city. Thousands of immigrants, mostly Irish famine victims, crowded New Haven, working at menial jobs while the established working class feverishly put out clothing, clocks, carriages, and corsets. Smoky soot clung to even the new building facades, and industry's hum came with a cost to the quality of life for all the residents.

Sarah Winchester was born both in and of New Haven, bred on the town's classic architecture and precisely manicured landscape, and attuned to modern industrial inventions. Her childhood and young womanhood bore the marks of Queen Victoria's influence as well as a distinctly American approach to religious thought. Her parents' willingness to entertain new approaches to religion, livelihood, and progressive ideals provided their children with a foundation to build lifestyle and philanthropic choices outside of the mainstream. Sarah Winchester's worldview, bestowed upon her by New Haven, her ancestry, and her time in history cast long shadows, across all the days of her life.

CHAPTER 2

Marrying into the Winchester Family

—•——• ⚏◊⚏ •——•—

·

S ARAH PARDEE HAD KNOWN WILLIAM WINCHESTER SINCE CHILDHOOD. William moved next door to Sarah on Court Street in 1850, and shortly after that, he graduated from the all-male Hopkins Grammar School, finishing there with eighteen other students. He went on to attend high school at about the same time the Pardee family moved to Brown Street, in the Wooster Square neighborhood of New Haven. The families would have seen each other at least at church, since Oliver Winchester acted as treasurer for the First Baptist Church of New Haven, and Leonard Pardee was its tithingman.[1] The two men guided the church's financial viability. In addition to being fellow churchgoers, it is likely that Pardee serviced machines at Winchester's shirt factory, as he did for other factories in town, so the two men had a business relationship as well. The acquaintance made between the Pardees and the Winchesters created a relationship that lasted into the next century.

The Winchester family's American antecedents had followed a more difficult route than the Pardees,' though they had been in America about the same length of time. John Winchester, to whom William traced his lineage, was born in Kent, England, in 1611 and came to the Massachusetts Bay Colony eight years before Sarah's ancestor set foot in New Haven. The Pardee occupational lineage followed a direct line, with the skills of woodworking passed down from generation to generation, while the Winchester path was marked alternately by success and poverty. In 1636, John Winchester was in Plymouth Colony, where he requested to be made a "freeman," a voting member of the community.[2] Two years later, he married Hannah Sealis, and the two went on to have five children. He married well: Hannah inherited land "commonly knowne by the Name of Connihassett or Cohassett." Her father also left her "one great brasse kettle, one blacke and white Rugg, one paire of sheets, two

Table Napkins, . . . and two pewter platters."[3] John and Hannah died in the 1690s and were buried in Brookline.

The Winchester name passed down through three generations to Jonathan Winchester (1717–1767), a minister and sometime professor at Harvard. Jonathan married Sarah Croft in Brookline. The inscription on his tombstone gives a clue to his personality: "The gentleman, the scholar, and the Christian were in him conspicuous. As a preacher he was acceptable, as a husband tender, as a parent affectionate, as a neighbor kind, as a friend sincere. For candor, meekness, patience and modesty remarkable. *Integer Vitae, Scelerisque purus.* (Honest of life and Pure of Crime)."[4] Jonathan was beloved by his ten children. One of his sons was Samuel.

Samuel Winchester (1757–1811) was a sturdy man, weathering much adversity. He lived in far more modest circumstances than his father. He worked as a laborer in Brookline and in Boston.[5] In the space of thirty years, he married three times and fathered eleven children. Hannah Bates was Samuel's third wife; they married in Boston in 1801. She bore five of Samuel's eleven children. Their youngest, born in 1810, were twins: Samuel Croft Winchester and Oliver Fisher Winchester. The firstborn was his father's namesake, and he carried his paternal grandmother's family name (he also had a great-grandfather Samuel Croft). The other boy was named for Oliver Fisher, a neighbor. Oliver Fisher Winchester would become William Winchester's father.

The infants were christened on Christmas Eve at Boston's Hollis Street Congregational church in 1810. Just four months later, the Winchester children were left fatherless when Samuel died. Widowhood forced Hannah and her four surviving children into poverty. Within a short time she married a Mr. Richardson, who was not disposed to raise another man's offspring. The twins were put out to work at an early age, an unfortunate but fairly common occurrence. Neither boy had much schooling; both learned carpentry skills. As teenagers, the two went to Baltimore to seek their way in the world. Remarkably, the twins kept in touch with their elder siblings and sent them money. Their mother reportedly died in Philadelphia.[6]

Oliver and Samuel Winchester were rough-hewn survivors who had been made to fend for themselves. Although christened in the Congregational church, they did not profess a particular religion. They came out of a difficult childhood, marred by poverty, hunger, abuse, and abandonment. The Winchesters had never been craftsmen and did not have marketable skills to pass on from one generation to the next. Oliver Winchester abandoned his carpentry trade and, together with his twin brother, opened a men's clothing store, by some accounts the first in Maryland.[7] Winchester & Company sold suits, shirts, hats, and a variety

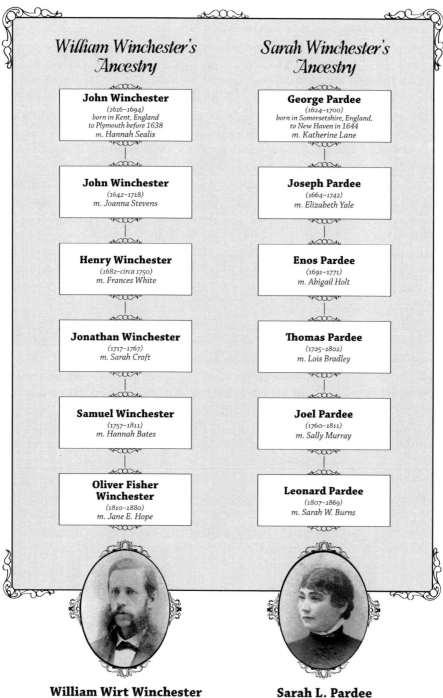

William Winchester's Ancestry

John Winchester
(1616–1694)
born in Kent, England
to Plymouth before 1638
m. Hannah Sealis

John Winchester
(1642–1718)
m. Joanna Stevens

Henry Winchester
(1682–circa 1750)
m. Frances White

Jonathan Winchester
(1717–1767)
m. Sarah Croft

Samuel Winchester
(1757–1811)
m. Hannah Bates

Oliver Fisher Winchester
(1810–1880)
m. Jane E. Hope

Sarah Winchester's Ancestry

George Pardee
(1624–1700)
born in Somersetshire, England,
to New Haven in 1644
m. Katherine Lane

Joseph Pardee
(1664–1742)
m. Elizabeth Yale

Enos Pardee
(1691–1771)
m. Abigail Holt

Thomas Pardee
(1725–1802)
m. Lois Bradley

Joel Pardee
(1760–1811)
m. Sally Murray

Leonard Pardee
(1807–1869)
m. Sarah W. Burns

William Wirt Winchester
(1837–1881)

Sarah L. Pardee
(1839–1922)

of stylish accessories. The Baltimore Street building they rented near the popular Barnum Hotel proved a good venue for brisk business from local merchants and Washington, DC, politicians.

The woman that Oliver chose to marry was likewise accustomed to hard work and meager rations. Jane Hope had been raised by a widow who by the wits of self-education provided for her several children.[8] Jane and Oliver were a good match: they were of similar backgrounds and they each demonstrated strong inclinations to support and care for family members. Oliver not only financed his own family and some of his twin's sons, but also supported his sister Mary Ann Winchester Brett's family, which included several children.[9] Jane also offered a home to her sister and niece, as well as giving care to other sisters and their aging mother.

Oliver and Jane's first child was born in 1835. They named her Ann Rebecca and called her "Annie" for Jane's mother and sister. In 1837, they had a son and named him William Wirt Winchester after one of Oliver's heroes. William Wirt (1772–1834) had been U.S. attorney general under President James Monroe and also a poet of some renown. Many school-children were assigned passages from Wirt's work to recite in school. The most popular were from "The Old Bachelor" and Wirt's opening speech as prosecutor in the famous Aaron Burr trial of 1807. He also authored a biography of Patrick Henry, the first documented attribution of the famous quotation "Give me liberty, or give me death!" Wirt articulated the aspirations of the industrial age. He instructed: "Seize the moment of excited curiosity on any subject to solve your doubts; for if you let it pass, the desire may never return, and you may remain in ignorance."[10] Wirt's sentiments describe the Oliver Winchester that those who worked with him recalled—a person who seized every business opportunity that presented itself. His naming his son for the statesman indicates the level of admiration that Oliver had for Wirt.

Oliver and Jane did not have another surviving infant for six years. In 1843, a son was born, and he was named Oliver. But in the summer of 1845, Ollie became quite ill. He was dead before his second birthday.

The twin brothers Oliver and Samuel worked well together, but by 1845, when they had nine children between them, it was obvious that the clothing store could not adequately support the two families. Oliver pondered how to proceed in the clothing business. Ten years of merchandizing had demonstrated to him that most men's shirts did not fit properly. He experimented with slight variations on the traditional shoulder seam and landed on one particular design that appeared to offer a better fit. Oliver made a carefully proportioned drawing that redesigned the cut of men's shirt collars and shoulders so that the seam from arm to neck would be curved rather than straight, which would alleviate the pull and creases on the neck band. He began making shirts from the new design, received many accolades for it, and sold out as quickly as he could produce shirts.

He documented his design and applied for a patent that read in part, "Be it known that I, O. F. Winchester, of the city of Baltimore and State of Maryland, have invented new and useful Improvements in the Method of Cutting and Fitting Shirts, and that the following is a full, clear, and exact description of the principle or character which distinguishes them from all other things before known."[11] As he waited for the patent registry, he brought his drawings to a New York clothier named John Davies, who had been in business in Manhattan for about twenty years and had garnered a handsome living from his shop. After he saw Oliver's drawings, the two hatched a business plan together. Davies loaned Winchester money to open a shirt factory in New Haven, where a steady supply of garment workers could be found. The two men were convinced that if they applied theories of mass production to shirtmaking, they could make a lot of money. They were right.

After a series of family deaths in 1846, including his brother's wife, Oliver could scarcely have chosen a more inopportune time to leave Baltimore and return to New England, but that is precisely what he did. Oliver's move back to New Haven allowed Samuel to remarry since as sole proprietor of the Baltimore store he had a fighting chance of supporting his large family. Samuel and his new wife went on to have three children, adding to his six.

Buoyed by an infusion of capital from Davies, Winchester went to work. He rented a small house and a shop on State Street, and the first bundle of shirts emerged. A patent for the Winchester shirt was granted in February 1848, and the Winchester & Davies Shirt Manufactory opened later that year. A merchant from that era recalled that "Mr. Winchester was in the habit of buying his cotton cloth by the piece or two, and taking it to his shop on his shoulder or under his arm."[12] At the shop he proceeded by "cutting out shirts," then assembling and stitching the garments himself. Within a short time, he was limiting himself to the cutting, and was hiring out the stitching to women working in their homes, issuing bundles of shirt pieces in lots of twelve. By the time he could afford to purchase cotton yardage in larger quantities, he also began hiring cloth cutters. The fledgling factory showed signs of success.

The Winchesters' fresh start in New Haven was complemented by a new baby when Jane gave birth at age forty. The baby girl was named

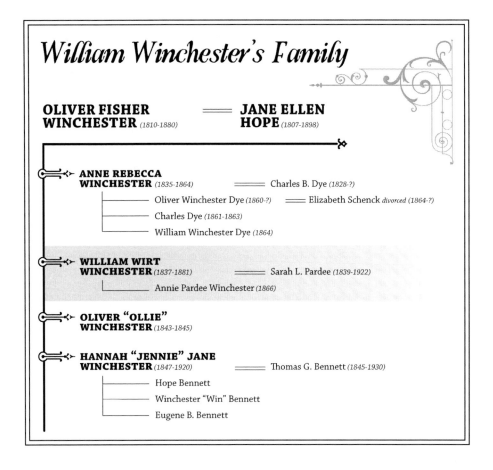

William Winchester's Family

OLIVER FISHER ══ **JANE ELLEN**
WINCHESTER *(1810-1880)* **HOPE** *(1807-1898)*

ANNE REBECCA
WINCHESTER *(1835-1864)* ══ Charles B. Dye *(1828-?)*
      Oliver Winchester Dye *(1860-?)* ══ Elizabeth Schenck *divorced (1864-?)*
      Charles Dye *(1861-1863)*
      William Winchester Dye *(1864)*

WILLIAM WIRT
WINCHESTER *(1837-1881)* ══ Sarah L. Pardee *(1839-1922)*
      Annie Pardee Winchester *(1866)*

OLIVER "OLLIE"
WINCHESTER *(1843-1845)*

HANNAH "JENNIE" JANE
WINCHESTER *(1847-1920)* ══ Thomas G. Bennett *(1845-1930)*
      Hope Bennett
      Winchester "Win" Bennett
      Eugene B. Bennett

Hannah Jane for Oliver's long-lost mother, but they always called her "Jennie."

Oliver moved the business and his home to larger quarters on Court Street. The surrounding neighborhood had been New Haven's economic heart and was a combination of merchant shops, houses, small factories, and commercial enterprises. A livery stood at the head of Court Street, so visitors to banks or the courthouse could valet their rigs. The Exchange Building had offices for attorneys and accountants, and a few millinery shops were interspersed with a tin man, a clothing store, and private residences. By 1850, the Winchesters lived at 57 Court Street, with the adjacent Winchester & Davies Shirt Manufactory at 59 Court Street. The Pardees resided at 65 Court Street, and Leonard's wood and metal shop was just around the corner on Artizan Street (a few years later, Oliver Winchester's venture into the arms business would also begin on Artizan).

New Haven's milieu proved the perfect incubator for the little shirt factory that Oliver Winchester established. Although no record of his net worth appears until later, it is safe to surmise that his overall wealth was not significant, but his enterprise was surviving. By 1856, he was well past survival and on the verge of huge success. Output from the Court Street factory reached 1,200 shirts per day, with 300 employees on the premises. However, women working in their homes were the lifeblood of the business. According to Edward E. Atwater's *History of the Colony of New Haven* (1881), Winchester had 5,000 workers scattered throughout Long Island, western Massachusetts, and Connecticut. This figure may be an exaggeration, but another historian put the number at 3,700.[13] The truth probably lies somewhere between, and it is a formidable statistic. The work-from-home set-up had women stitching together pieces that had been cut at the factory. Samuel C. Winchester & Company in Baltimore, owned by Oliver's brother, sold shirts manufactured at the New Haven factory, as did John Davies' New York store. Both sent sons to work in Oliver's factory to learn New England's garment industry.[14] Winchester's main competition was from Chauncy B. Peck's shirt manufactory on Orange Street. It advertised "drawers, shirts, collars, and bosoms," made to order. Oliver's patented shirt collar quickly outsold Peck's.

Sewing machines had been invented in the 1840s but were not widely used because the brotherhood of tailors objected to them as job stealers, and more significantly, patents on the machines taken out by more than one "inventor" were in dispute until the middle 1850s. Winchester was not fully convinced the newfangled sewing machines would help his business, but he installed a few and put women to work at them. Most of the shirtmakers were American-born white women in their teens or twenties.[15] Stunned by new levels of output, he immediately bought more machines and hired more young women to sew.[16] The entire garment industry was transformed by sewing machines, and Winchester & Davies was on the proverbial cutting edge.

William Winchester prepared for his accession to the management of the shirt company. He worked at the factory and occasionally traveled with his father. He applied for a passport just after his twenty-first birthday in 1858 and ventured to Europe. The auburn-haired young man described as having a sallow complexion may already have been troubled by health problems then. Upon returning aboard the British steam frigate the RM *Niagara* by way of Boston, William focused on increasing production at Winchester & Davies.[17]

The younger Winchester was markedly different from his father.[18] Never described as robust, as his father assuredly was, William had been raised by two parents in a secure, if sometimes crowded, home. He had been able to attend school and travel. As William set out to begin a career, his father's shirt factory provided an incredibly lucrative entrée. The elder Winchester had had none of these opportunities. He wanted his son to have what he had not had. So the young Winchester was given an official position, and it was well known that he and John Davies' son, Cornelius, were poised to take over one of the most profitable clothing mills in all of New England.

Oliver Winchester and John Davies established a firm friendship as they built their successful business partnership. The two invested in other enterprises, and often socialized and traveled together. Each was determined to leave a financial dynasty to his respective son, William W. Winchester and Cornelius Davies. Winchester convinced Davies to leave the selling of shirts to others, liquidate his Manhattan shop, and move to New Haven to concentrate on the manufacture of shirts. The fortune that the two would turn over to their sons was to be made at the factory. By 1860, Davies had relocated his family to New Haven.

The city had become congested with workers and immigrants, and besides the successful shirt factory, other enterprises—manufacturing carriages, guns, corsets, cigars, and clocks—required large numbers of workers. Next to the Winchesters' Court Street house stood a large boarding house occupied by dozens of young Irishwomen who hired out as domestic help and laundresses. The enormity of the Irish potato famine could scarcely be made more obvious with any other records than the lengthy lists of single women living without family far from the land of their births.[19] Most of these women were not skilled enough to work at Winchester & Davies and so were relegated to laundries or hired as chamber maids and domestic servants.

John Davies and Oliver Winchester commissioned the construction of a large new factory nearby, in the same Court Street neighborhood. The five-story brick building was completed and outfitted in 1859. It accommodated 2,000 workers six days per week cutting cloth and operating 500 foot-powered sewing machines. One floor was dedicated as the ironing room, where ironing tables circled a center stove. Ironers had to walk the heavy irons back and forth from stove to table, keeping the irons hot enough to eliminate wrinkles in the stiff cotton. Another floor was designated the sewing room, where three long rows of tables extended the entire length of the building. The center row held the cut garment pieces, and sewers and machines lined the two outside rows. Overseers walked up and down, inspecting progress.[20]

Mass production of clothing was nothing short of astonishing, and Winchester & Davies emerged a vastly successful venture in piece-work and assembly-line clothing. By the end of the decade, the men had invested $400,000 in capital and used 1.5 million yards of cotton cloth, 400,000 yards of linen, 25,000 gross of buttons. The annual output in 1860 was 480,000 shirts. It was a far cry from just ten years earlier, when Oliver had carried a length of cotton to his shop to cut. The net worth of the company was over $1 million.[21] Winchester and Davies reveled in their newfound wealth. The money allowed the partners to dabble in other investments, and Winchester cajoled Davies to gamble on his latest passion, a small gun factory called the Volcanic Repeating Arms Company.

By the beginning of 1860 the Winchester household, like the Pardee one, was more financially secure than it had ever been. Oliver and Jane presided over a household with an estimated value of personal property at $187,000.[22] Daughter Jennie, at age twelve, was attending a local school and given private lessons in French, art, and music. Three of her cousins, all near her age, lived with the family. Sons and daughters of Oliver's twin also called the Court Street house their home from time to time, particularly George Winchester, who boarded with the family for several years while clerking at the shirt factory. Irish servants tended the household, and two lived at the residence. Assured of financial security, both Davies and Winchester bought tracts of land just outside town to build the homes of their dreams.

With William's livelihood firmly established and his education completed, the time was right for marriage. It is not possible to determine precisely how much contact there was between Sarah "Sallie" Pardee and William Winchester in the middle 1850s. How did the son of the shirt manufacturer and the daughter of the finish carpenter carry out a courtship? There is no doubt that by the beginning of the 1860s Sarah and William were keeping company.

It would have been difficult for the Winchesters to object to Sarah if they had had any inclination to. She was the daughter of a successful craftsman and had been afforded an education and music lessons. In her own right, she was bright and striking, if a little shy. And although at the moment the Winchesters had more money, it was she who was the more genteel, she who lived in the better neighborhood, and she who had had a private French tutor and music lessons. She possessed a social dignity and would make a good wife for William. There would be no objections from the Winchesters.

As William Winchester contemplated marriage, his sister, Annie, wed Charles B. Dye, a farmer's son from Broadalbin, New York, who was ordained to the ministry in the Presbyterian Church just before they married in 1859. He was assigned to a church in Tonington, Connecticut. Just how well Dye was accepted into the Winchester family, which was not of the Presbyterian faith, is unknown. He was a pious and strict man, and may only have been tolerated by the streetwise Oliver Winchester. As many as forty years later, family members had never achieved a familiar rapport with the stodgy minister, still referring to him as "Mr. Dye."[23] The addition of grandsons added some warmth to the relationship. A year after the Dyes married, they had a son and named him Oliver "Ollie" Winchester Dye. Another son, named Charles, came a year later.

The looming civil war could not be ignored, and war changes everything. The social and political turmoil that produced the Civil War had been smoldering in New Haven, as it had in the rest of the country, for decades. Even though the abolitionist voice was growing more strident, New Englanders were not uniformly in favor of freedom for slaves, although most Yankees believed in ending the institution of slavery nor did they all object to unequal treatment of blacks, who even in the North were routinely relegated to separate churches and neighborhoods. In March 1860, when Abraham Lincoln campaigned in New Haven, he promised to lead the nation through uncharted and potentially explosive territory. Lincoln predicted—correctly, it turned out—that the path would be fraught with fearsome obstacles.

Politics aside, New Haven had very close economic ties with the South. As a practical matter, most of New Haven's factories depended on the South because it was the largest and most profitable market for carriages, clocks, guns, and clothing. They also depended on the area for raw materials: the cigar companies imported tobacco and the shirt companies, cotton. War with the South meant that the shirts produced at Winchester & Davies and balustrades lathed at Leonard Pardee & Company had a smaller market and difficult-to-get, more expensive raw materials. Despite their financial interests, however, the Pardees and the Winchesters, along with their extended families, supported the Union, the new Republican Party, the cause of abolition, and President Abraham Lincoln.

The war did not dissuade William and Sarah from marrying. They were married on Tuesday, September 30, 1862. The midweek, Civil War wedding was not a particularly lavish affair, and although the registry does not mention the clergyman, it is likely that the wedding was witnessed by the Baptist Reverend Benjamin Hill. The Winchesters were benefactors of the Baptist church, and Hill is clearly listed as presiding at the weddings of Sarah's siblings. The bride and groom were feted by both sets of parents.[24]

At the time of their wedding, William was twenty-five and Sarah twenty-three. A beautifully petite young woman, she wore her dark hair in tight curls about her face. Dark eyebrows highlighted her brown eyes and light complexion. She was an attractive woman of society, marrying a man of her own choosing. Physically, William was her opposite; his lean, five-feet-nine-inch frame, almost a foot taller than his bride's, made her appear tiny. He had blue eyes and reddish hair, with heavy mutton-chop whiskers extending down past his collar. They were a handsome, if incongruous, couple.

Sarah was a very different bride than either of her older sisters. Mary and Nettie had married when they were slightly younger than Sarah. Neither had married a merchant, as Sarah did. Neither had entered a family with overpowering personalities like the senior Winchesters.' Underscoring all these differences, Sarah married in wartime, not in the more carefree and prosperous middle 1850s. William and Sarah's wedding was an isolated happy day as bad news trickled in from battlefields. The Union's ability to win the war looked bleak at that moment, and unbeknownst even to Sarah's family, her brother-in-law, Homer Sprague, had been severely wounded by that time.

Adding to the somewhat unsettled nature of the early days of her marriage, Sarah agreed to live with her in-laws until such time as a house could be built on Prospect Hill, recently purchased by Oliver Winchester. The war ate up building materials, so the construction project was delayed for the duration of the conflict. The newlyweds lived at the Court Street house in a full household, including the elder Winchesters, their daughter Annie Dye's growing family, their daughter Jennie, assorted cousins, and lots of hired help.

Like other Yankee women, Sarah spent the Civil War years making do without items in short supply, sending sewn or knitted clothing to Connecticut troops, and reading battlefield dispatches in the *New York Times* or the *New Haven Palladium*. Just weeks before her wedding, the bloodiest of Civil War battles at Antietam had McClellan's Union forces pushing Lee's Confederates back into Virginia. As 1863 began, President Lincoln issued the Emancipation Proclamation, and within months, Congress passed a conscription law.

Why did some men enlist while others did not? Historical records about individual decisions are sketchy at best. When war broke out, William Winchester was twenty-four years of age and military service was purely voluntary. By the time conscription was instituted in 1863, he was a married man, although marriage was not grounds for exemption. The possible exemptions from conscription were a medical problem, being an only son, or working in an occupation deemed a higher necessity that soldiering. Conceivably, William could have claimed all three. It is likely that he and his father believed keeping the doors open at Winchester & Davies was more useful than fighting. It is also possible that the consumption that would eventually kill him had already taken a toll, making him a poor candidate for military service. And there is no doubt that Jane Winchester would have strenuously objected to having her only son join the army. A substitute could be purchased for $300, and William could easily have afforded that. Any one or some combination of these reasons would explain why William Winchester remained in New Haven throughout the Civil War.

Sarah's brother, Leonard M. Pardee, was among the first volunteers to leave for war. Just a little over a month after Abraham Lincoln was sworn in as the sixteenth president of United States, the long-simmering conflict ignited at Fort Sumter in South Carolina. The first of thousands of battles that would scar the nation over the next five years occurred that April morning. President Lincoln called for an immediate 75,000 volunteers. On April 21, 1861, Leonard left his carriage-trimming tools, barely took time to say good-bye at 10 Brown Street, and enlisted in the Union Army. He was twenty-three. Pardee and his comrades fully expected to be home sleeping in their own beds by the Fourth of July.

In the first week of May, Private Pardee was absorbed into the Second Connecticut Infantry, a regiment eight hundred strong, mustered for three months. The men congregated at Brewster's Park, near the edge of Long Island Sound, and were issued Sharps rifles. For three days a carnival atmosphere prevailed, where shouting and singing and shooting anticipated a quick victory. With his cohorts at the wharf, Pardee boarded the steamer *Cahawba,* and on the tenth of May he was standing in Washington, DC. His regiment marched into Virginia and spent a few weeks drilling and camping in the verdant countryside.

On July 21, 1861, Leonard was one of 60,000 young men from North and South fighting the battle of Bull Run at Manassas, Virginia. He was in the first brigade under Colonel E. D. Keyes, and part of Brigadier General Daniel Tyler's division. Tyler's men forced the Confederates across Stone Bridge and hammered away at their right flank and rear. An account of the performance of the Second Connecticut reported that it was "acquitting itself with great credit, maintaining its regimental formations throughout the action, and demonstrating by its coolness under fire the excellence of its material and the thoroughness of its discipline. Its losses were one killed and fifteen taken prisoners and missing."[25]

But the Union performance, overall, was miserable. The troops did not follow the retreating rebels, who reconnoitered and came back to rout the Yankees. Before the battle was over, 4,700 bodies needed burying. The message that Leonard took away from the battle of Bull Run was the same heard in the White House and in New Haven: this war would not be quickly won. He was mustered out of service on August 7, 1861, having completed his three-month commitment. Most of his regimental comrades reenlisted for three years, but Leonard did not. He returned home to Brown Street, where his parents and younger sisters anxiously awaited news of him. He went back to his carriage-making job, but even that was changed by the war. Carriage works were "now fashioning large bars of iron and heavy oak into ponderous gun-carriages," and had whole rooms with "scores of girls and men working on knapsacks and haversacks."[26]

Sarah's brother-in-law Homer Sprague, Nettie's husband, was the next family member to volunteer for active military service. He enlisted as a captain on December 8, 1861, and was commissioned with Company H of the Thirteenth Connecticut Infantry in February 1862. For the next four years, five months, and eight days, he kept a diary. Its entries were "jotted down at odd moments, in the midst of weary marches, on picket duty, on horseback, in the rain."[27] Homer's notes were the basis for a regimental history published in 1867.

Right from the beginning, Homer's narrative is full of disdain for men like his brother-in-law Leonard (although he did not specifically name Leonard) who entered the war with overconfident bravado and bombast, underestimating the human cost of war. Homer argued that the men who joined after realizing the true nature of the war—the men of his regiment, for example—were the real heroes. They joined "not with hot haste or mad excitement, not with noisy or glittering parade, nor yet with lavish outlay of money did its officers collect a thoughtless or mercenary throng. But uniting ardent zeal with a cool estimate of the dangers and sacrifices, and holding up to view the great issues of Religion, Liberty, Civilization and Union, they made deliberate selection of their men."[28] Homer believed the men mustered at the end of 1861 gave a more calculated personal sacrifice than the early volunteers, who he claimed joined for personal glory and public adulation. Homer was a fiercely caustic critic. Time and again throughout his life he used his pen to sermonize or to skewer those with whom he disagreed.

William Converse, Sarah's other brother-in-law at that time, Mary's husband, did not volunteer. At first glance, he appears a more likely candidate for military service than Homer Sprague. For one, he had no children to support. In addition, he was younger, more athletic, and less scholarly than Homer. It is likely, however, that William was the linchpin of Pardee's wood shop, for, although he had only rudimentary skill as a craftsman, he was a keen businessman and skilled bookkeeper. As Pardee aged and became more infirm, he relied on William to generate income for himself and his wife, their as-yet-unmarried daughters, and William and Mary. In addition, if Pardee's wood shop stayed in business, several craftsmen could keep their jobs.

Naturally, Sarah and William Winchester followed the course of the war and the welfare of those engaged in battle, especially relatives and friends. Before the young Winchesters celebrated their first wedding anniversary, staggering death tolls came in from Pennsylvania's Gettysburg battlefield. In the second half of that grim 1863, William's sister, Annie Dye, was pregnant with her third child. Early in September, two-year-old Charles became deathly ill and died. After the boy's death, Annie Dye's pregnancy progressed only with great difficulty. To the entire family's horror, Annie passed away at the Court Street house the day after giving birth to her third son on January 16, 1864.[29] Baby William, named for William Wirt Winchester, lived for only nineteen days. A despondent Charles Dye grieved the loss of his wife and two small children, as he and little Oliver were all that remained of what had been a cherished family. If Charles was stunned by his wife's death, Jane Winchester was inconsolable at the loss of her daughter.

Annie's death was also a turning point for Sarah and William Winchester. After that date, there was no suggestion that they would establish a home separate from William's parents. When the couple had married during the war, the combined living arrangement had been intended to be temporary. After Annie's death, the house on Prospect Hill was to keep the elder and younger Winchesters together. Perhaps having her son live in her home eased Jane's enormous grief. A long-term shared household, however, diminished any distinctive identity that the younger Winchesters might otherwise have achieved.

⊷ ⊰◆⊱ ⊶

Toward the end of 1865, three years after her wedding, Sarah realized she was pregnant. The news was met enthusiastically by William and by her parents, and the senior Winchesters were overjoyed, since their only living grandchild, Ollie Dye, did not bear the Winchester name. Beginning in May 1866, Sarah quit making social calls and remained at the Court Street house.

In the early hours of June 15, 1866, William sent a servant to summon Dr. Ives, the family's physician. Sending for the doctor may have been intended to bring some comfort, but it also signaled alarm. Dr. Ives had been in attendance at the births of Annie Dye's sons, and had been at her side when she died. That Annie died in the same house under the care of the same doctor could not have been lost on Sarah. Evidently she labored long but had good delivery of a baby girl. The child was not immediately named, and when Dr. Ives listed the birth in the town records, he wrote simply "female child of William and Sarah Winchester."[30] Later, the couple named the baby Annie Pardee Winchester, honoring William's late sister.

Although Sarah was recovering well, the baby had trouble feeding and digesting. A wet-nurse was summoned, but Annie's weight dropped steadily. Any remedy that Sarah tried was not successful, and Dr. Ives determined that the child suffered from marasmus, an acute inability to absorb calories and make protein. In short, she could not digest. The wailing infant could not be soothed and was slowly starving to death. On July 25, barely a month after her birth, Annie Pardee Winchester died, her tiny casket placed at Evergreen Cemetery not far from the gravesite of her aunt Annie and little cousins. Sarah and William were grief-stricken and remained secluded for an extended time. It was almost a year before Sarah ventured anywhere.

As it did to countless other mid-nineteenth-century mothers who lost babies to infant mortality, the loss cut Sarah deeply. Religious beliefs typical of the time asserted that God condemned infants to eternal damnation because they had not grown to be baptized. The concept of infant damnation was anathema to young women coming of age after the Civil War. They sought out an image of God as a loving parent rather than a wrathful prosecutor. The idea of eternal condemnation for innocent infants almost single-handedly doomed American Calvinism.[31] Mothers of lost infants at this period were likely to search for a spiritual connection with the deceased.

Sarah's youngest sister's wedding was set for just two weeks after the death of baby Annie. In light of Sarah's weakened condition, the senior Pardees decided that the wedding should take place in Manhattan rather than New Haven, allowing Sarah and William to decline the invitation and remain in mourning. At nineteen, Estelle married George Gerard, a onetime law student at Yale who had cut short his studies to join the Union Army. During the war, he had served in the Carolinas with distinction. At twenty-six on his wedding day, George was a traveling salesman for the Singer Sewing Machine Company. The Gerards planned to live in New Haven.

Belle married in October of the following year, 1867. Her new husband, Louis Merriman, was a local man who worked in his father's carriage works, Benjamin H. Merriman & Company, on Summer Street. Their wedding was presided over by the aging Baptist minister Benjamin Hill, who had witnessed the marriages of the elder Pardees. New Haven's town records give a reliable statement of Belle's and Louis's ages on their wedding day: Louis was thirty and Belle twenty-four. From then until the day she died, Belle lied about her age, shaving off anywhere from two to fifteen years. When they had their first child two years later, the couple claimed they were still ages thirty and twenty-four, respectively. The reality gap only grew wider with passing time.[32]

A flurry of Pardee grandchildren arrived on the scene in the immediate postwar years, but as Sarah watched her sisters have children, she had no more. Between 1868 and 1870, Estelle and George Gerard had a daughter and a son—Sarah Louise (nicknamed Saidee, distinguishing her from the other Sarahs) and George; shortly thereafter, Belle and Louis also had a daughter and a son. Evidently the Merrimans were undecided about naming their daughter. Town records list her as Maria Isabel, and the family had at least a few relatives also named Maria. Throughout her life, though, she called herself Marion Isabel. To her parents and to her aunt and uncle, Sarah and William Winchester, the little girl was simply "Daisy." Born just three years after Sarah's baby, the little girl spent considerable time with William and Sarah, and Daisy quickly became Sarah's favorite. The Merrimans' son, William Winchester Merriman, arrived next. Nettie and Homer Sprague had their fourth child—Goldwin "Goldie" Smith Sprague, who came in line after their William, Charles, and Antoinette. Children were not forthcoming for Mary and William Converse.

Sarah's father's health was weakening as he saw his youngest daughters married. He suffered terribly with an ailing back, working less and giving more responsibility to his son-in-law William Converse, but since Converse had very little skill as a craftsman, he would not be carrying on the Pardee woodworking factory. And since the younger Leonard showed no interest in the firm, his father, with Converse's help, took steps to dissolve it. They sold the Water Street mill and the adjoining Brown Street house. The entire Wooster Square neighborhood, at one time Pardee's highest aspiration, had become shabby in recent years. Some of the large old classical homes had been turned into boarding houses for immigrants. As Leonard and Sarah Pardee approached old age, they bought a residence on the more fashionable Orange Street, near the corner of Humphrey.

Leonard Pardee died in June of 1869 after a lengthy paralysis from a spinal disease, quite possibly a form of the rheumatoid arthritis that would afflict his daughter Sarah. He was just past sixty years of age. He left an estate of over $70,000 under the care of his widow, who served as executrix.[33]

Six months after he died, his son, Leonard, married Sarah Domkee, establishing an entirely new generation of Leonards and Sarahs. Like all previous Pardee weddings, Leonard's was held before the Baptist preacher Benjamin Hill. The couple settled in Orange, a short distance from New Haven, and remained in that locale throughout their lives. Eventually they had two daughters, Sarah (yet another) Catherine and Louise Beecher. Like his father, Leonard never ventured far from his native town.

The descendants of Sarah and Leonard Pardee scattered across the nation. The band of cousins born between 1856 and 1875 shared the bond of their common Pardee grandparents, but most similarities stopped there. The ten grandchildren (including two Williams and two Sarahs) grew into distinctive individuals, and even though they dispersed from Connecticut to Florida and from Massachusetts to California, each maintained a lifelong relationship with Aunt Sarah Winchester. They came together once again after her death, as her heirs.

Even though Sarah Winchester stayed close to her several nieces and nephews, the loss of her own infant never seemed far from her mind. She took steps to ensure careful maintenance of her daughter's small grave at Evergreen Cemetery and placed the tiny newspaper notice of her death in safekeeping. It is unknown whether Sarah hoped to have more children, but none were forthcoming.[34]

Sarah's marriage was a solid one, built upon her and William's having known each other since childhood. He was about to take over management of a large and successful garment factory just as his father intended. William's attention was divided between growing responsibilities at work and his new wife. Sarah and William Winchester forged a firm alliance. There was no hint that the Winchester & Davies Shirt Manufactory, not to mention William and Sarah's life, was about to be irrevocably altered.

CHAPTER 3

"The Gun That Won the West"

＊─❖❦❖─＊

I N THE MIDDLE 1860S AS WILLIAM WINCHESTER WALKED TO HIS OFFICE
at the shirt factory each morning, he presumed his father's investments in the arms industry were purely the whim of a wealthy
man. About eight years earlier, Oliver Winchester had invested
cash accrued from the Winchester & Davies Shirt Manufactory in a
promising but weak Volcanic Repeating Arms Company, which produced a repeating revolver with "volcanic" firing power that was primarily designed by two of the company's principals, Horace Smith and
Daniel Wesson. The company was mismanaged, and when it went bankrupt, Oliver Winchester, as a board member, was in a position to purchase the firm's machinery, backlog, and patents. The shrewd Winchester
struck a good bargain, and his investment of $40,000 for assets valued at
$57,000 paid off Volcanic's debts. As Smith and Wesson went on to form
their own successful enterprise, Oliver Winchester established the New
Haven Arms Company.

Winchester hired a mechanic from his shirt factory, Benjamin T.
Henry,[1] who proved a remarkable gunsmith. Henry translated the concept of the volcanic revolver to a rifle and succeeded in designing the
first repeating rifle. Its single barrel held multiple rounds of ammunition from a magazine that loaded from the bottom. It could fire off fifteen shots in just over ten seconds.[2] Dubbed the "Henry," it was the first
of its kind and was patented in 1860. Advertisements offered "Henry's
Repeating Rifles" for $42, along with the traditional carbines, muskets,
and shotguns.[3] Oliver Winchester was elated and began calculating how
to increase production.

With the nation teetering on the brink of civil war, Winchester was
aggressively peddling Henry's repeating rifle to military ordnance officials, who were then furnishing soldiers with single-shot carbines.
Winchester believed the repeaters would give an edge to the Union

Army, and he was certain that government contracts would pay off handsomely. Winchester pestered Union military officers to purchase repeating rifles for infantry troops, proposing an initial delivery of 40,000 rifles. One brigadier general was strictly opposed to purchasing anything but standardized weaponry, arguing, "A great evil now especially prevalent in regard to arms for the military service is the vast variety of new inventions, each having, of course, its advocates, insisting on the superiority of his favorite arm over all others and urging its adoption by the Government. . . . we must adhere to the rule of uniformity of arms for all troops." The general advocated "arms for all troops of the same kind." Many officials believed the repeater was experimental and unreliable. And in fact, early models did have serious drawbacks: exposure to mud and rain caused their magazines to rust and their cartridges to jam. Mechanics at the New Haven Arms Company worked feverishly to solve the problems by redesigning the loading system. But officers decided against Henry's repeaters, instead purchasing an estimated 1.5 million muzzle-loading muskets, mostly the single-shot Springfields or Sharps. This line of thinking confounded Winchester, who wondered in a company memo, "Where is the military genius that is to grasp this whole subject?"[4]

The single-shot muskets had their own drawback in that they required a high level of manual dexterity, which was seriously lacking in many new recruits. The muskets also required time, precious seconds and minutes that could cost a man his life. Sarah Winchester's brother-in-law Homer Sprague wrote an account of the performance of Sharps rifles in an 1863 battle at Irish Bend, Louisiana:

> Nothing . . . is more difficult than to load and fire advancing without breaking into hopeless confusion. Here the rigid drilling we had received, and the perfect confidence we had in our success, sustained us, notwithstanding the shower of missiles that drove in our faces. . . . Our five hundred men were in the midst of three thousand rebels. All seemed lost. Suddenly, however, from the gleaming rifles of our advancing line, there poured a steady stream of lead, every man loading and firing three times a minute, and the twenty or thirty shots per second making with the answering fire of the rebel line a prolonged and tremendous roar.[5]

Interestingly, Sprague's detailed journal of more than three years of war service never mentioned a repeater, and he was related by marriage to the repeating-rifle company's owner. Sprague may have agreed with the general who wished to maintain "the rule of uniformity of arms for all troops." But even President Abraham Lincoln, who had test-fired a repeater and was given a Henry as a gift, thought the breech-loaded rifle had the potential to provide victory. Evidently he held little sway on this subject with his generals. Over the course of the war, the government ordered fewer than 2,000 Henry rifles, although it placed orders at Lincoln's command for 37,000 Marsh breech-loading rifles, some single-shot and some repeaters. Individual soldiers invested in Henrys in a greater number than the government, and about 8,300 were purchased privately. Repeaters accounted for less than 1 percent of the rifles in use in the war.[6]

Oliver Winchester's insistence on increasing production in hopes of procuring government contracts poisoned his working relationship with his gunsmith and New Haven plant superintendent, Benjamin T. Henry. The mechanic deeply resented Winchester's aggressive demands, and the association between the men deteriorated further when Winchester engaged Samuel Colt's Patent Fire-Arms Manufacturing Company in Hartford to assemble four hundred new Henry rifles that his own factory could not put out in a timely manner. Winchester appreciated Henry's skill as a gunsmith, but in continued frustration over poor production figures, he privately leased another factory in nearby Bridgeport and hired an additional superintendent to run it.[7] He did not want to send contracts to Colt again.

By the fourth year of the war, it was obvious that the Union Army would not be purchasing rifles from the New Haven Arms Company. Oliver Winchester began looking to foreign governments for more favorable sales. He booked passage on a European tour, ostensibly to console his wife after the deaths of their daughter and grandsons, but in reality to market repeating rifles manufactured by his latest investment, the New Haven Arms Company. His wife would visit the Baden spas while he hosted shooting demonstrations and attended rifle competitions to promote repeating rifles. The plan was agreeable all around, and on New Year's Day, 1865, Oliver and Jane set sail for Naples on a junket to host rifle demonstrations in European capitals. From Italy they would travel to Constantinople, then circle back to Zurich, Paris, and finally London before returning home. If he could bring home contracts, he could ensure the viability and growth of the small company.

For the first time in her life, Sarah Winchester took charge of a household. In Jane Winchester's absence, she was given control of the Court Street house, supervision of its servants, power of the pocketbook, the challenge to maintain an orderly, efficient home, and the freedom to carry out the assignment as she saw fit. For his part, William also had charge of an operation, along with Cornelius Davies: the huge shirt factory. The

Winchester & Davies Shirt Manufactory had officially been turned over to the next generation, into the able hands of William and Cornelius. William's promotion to partner in the shirt company was made official. He and Cornelius planned to work as partners and friends, as had their fathers. Both young men had married, and William's future as a leader in New England's garment industry looked bright as the Civil War waned. Sarah did not need to worry about a livelihood, a home, or being able to afford whatever they needed or wanted on her husband's significant income.

Oliver expected smooth sailing both at sea and at home, but when he completed work in Naples and Constantinople and arrived in Switzerland, he had a game-changing cable waiting for him from his son and John Davies. It briefly stated that Henry had filed papers with the Connecticut State Legislature to reincorporate the arms company as the "Henry Repeating Rifle Company."[8] Henry had overthrown Winchester and taken control of the New Haven Arms Company. Sarah and William's reign was abbreviated when the parents returned to New Haven in haste.

Oliver was beside himself with fury, blindsided by Henry's unexpected maneuver and distressed to have radically underestimated the depth of animosity that Henry bore him. He railed against Henry's disloyal tactics and threatened revenge, but even then, it was clear to Oliver that Henry had the law on his side. In perhaps the greatest misjudgment of his life, Oliver Winchester had signed a power of attorney over to Henry, giving him control of the company while he was in Europe. Almost as angry at himself as at Henry, Winchester vowed he would never again find himself so swindled. Taking a step back and evaluating his choices, he devised a plan. He did not attempt to contest the power of attorney, nor did he file objections to the new company name. Instead, he cabled instructions to William and John to call his personal loans to the arms company. The two immediately ordered the banks to call the loans and pulled Winchester cash from the company.

If Winchester underestimated Henry's animosity, then Henry miscalculated Winchester's business sense. Winchester's survival instincts told him that the lifeblood of any enterprise was cash, and by pulling his out of the company, Henry's scheme would be dead. Back in New Haven, on July 1, 1865, Winchester filed papers of association with the Connecticut State Legislature for the Winchester Repeating Arms Company. His cosignatories were his two most reliable allies: his son, William, and his closest friend and business partner, John Davies. The Winchester Repeating Arms Company was born with plenty of financial backing, and the Henry Repeating Rifle Company was broke. It had nothing to subsist upon. Neither Henry nor the New Haven Arms Company had any financial ties to the Bridgeport factory that was already up and running as the Winchester Repeating Arms Company. Oliver took his time, but the next year he offered to buy the former New Haven Arms and pay its debts. The stockholders feared losing all their investments, so they agreed, ostracizing Benjamin T. Henry.

The ultimate irony of Henry's aborted takeover was that his invention came to be known ubiquitously as the "Winchester." Up to that date, Oliver Winchester had had no inclination to attach his personal name to the Henry, apparently satisfied simply to make money from it. Henry's attempted coup pushed Winchester to establish a separate company under his name. Defeated, Henry went on to live out a rather obscure life in New Haven.

— ▪✦▪ —

What did all this mean to William Winchester? If Sarah wondered, she had her answer within the year. William sold his interest in the Winchester & Davies Shirt Manufactory to Cornelius Davies and became the secretary of the new Winchester Repeating Arms Company. Swept into the corporate structure of the new firearms company, William was caught in the battle between Henry and his father. Had it not been for Henry's defection, William would have remained with the shirt factory. Oliver insisted on a corporate team he could trust. For better or worse, the erstwhile shirtmaker was in the arms business. It was a completely unexpected turn of events, and one that had lifelong implications for William and Sarah Winchester.

The couple's adjustment was exacerbated by the twenty-mile distance between New Haven and Bridgeport. It required William to remain in Bridgeport for days at a time overseeing a growing number of mechanics. Before long the factory had 260 employees, and William's father hired Nelson King as superintendent. The first order of business required alterations to Henry's designs so as to avoid any implication of impropriety or suggestions that Winchester stole the designs. King proved quite talented. He, along with a few others, improved the repeater's design by placing a cartridge-loading port at the center of the frame. As the firm's catalog stated, "Not only can this gun be fired thirty times a minute continuously as a repeater, but it can be used as a single loader . . . retaining the magazine full of cartridges to be used in an emergency, fired . . . at a rate of one hundred twenty shots per minute, or two shots per second loading from the magazines, . . . an effectiveness far beyond that of any other gun."[9] Nelson King, as much as Benjamin T. Henry, is credited with revolutionizing modern weaponry with his alterations to the magazines and lever-action designs.[10] Soon Winchester had an annual output of 12,000 guns.

The Yellow Boy, named for its bright brass—looking receiver, was the first firearm to bear the Winchester name. The firing was the same as the Henry rifle's, but the entirely new magazine could retain cartridges, requiring fewer motions to load and fire. Production of Yellow Boys began in 1866, and over the next thirty years, a total of 170,000 Model 1866 Winchesters were produced.[11] It was reissued one hundred years later as the Centennial Model 1966.

The Winchester Repeating Arms Company was officially incorporated in 1867, and financial records from that date declare a net worth of $450,000, with the value of the Bridgeport plant listed as $150,000. There was a total of about $325,000 in liabilities, including $136,500 owed the stockholders.[12] The company's survival for the next five years while most competitors succumbed to postwar economic doldrums was purely attributable to Oliver Winchester. Yet he was not satisfied to simply survive. He wanted to thrive. He persisted in forging political links to procure government contracts. Winchester won the battle with Henry, but his most frustrating defeat, the inability to convince his own government to purchase rifles, was a war he never quit trying to win. In one particularly transparent attempt in 1866, he agreed to add his name to the Republican ticket to run for the position of Connecticut's lieutenant governor with gubernatorial candidate Joseph R. Hawley. A longtime friend, Hawley had been one of the founders of the Republican Party in Connecticut, and as editor of the Hartford Evening Press, had had a sturdy platform to proclaim the abolitionist viewpoint in the prewar years. During the war, Hawley served as a lieutenant colonel, leading both white and black regiments to success for the Union. Hawley's prewar politics and wartime reputation, coupled with Winchester's recent business victory over Henry, earned them the popular vote in 1866. Winchester's only previous political experience had been as city alderman for New Haven's fourth ward in 1863. His role as lieutenant governor was equally short-lived: he served only one year. Hawley had a much longer political career, so it is ironic that Winchester, not Hawley, was nicknamed "Governor." Like the famous Samuel Colt, who had always been called "the Colonel" despite never having served in the military, Winchester was called "Gov" or "Governor" by everyone who knew him for the rest of his life.

Oliver Winchester emulated the late Samuel Colt in more ways than one. Colt, the so-called P.T. Barnum[13] of the arms industry, had made a fortune after the Texas Rangers and the U.S. government ordered his revolvers. Winchester was convinced government contracts offered the most direct path to a fortune. When Colt died in 1862 at the relatively young age of forty-eight, he was the most renowned weapons manufacturer in the world, possessing a flamboyancy that captured the public imagination as if he too were a circus ringleader. He tinkered and invented, but mostly he sold. He concocted clever marketing schemes such as publishing endorsements of the Colt revolver from the Texas Rangers. He provided user manuals with his guns, an entirely new concept that was very well received by the paying public. A brilliantly successful ploy of his was to hire artisans to engrave presentation pistols for politicians or heads of state. Playing to the substantial egos of those who made the decisions on large arms purchases turned out to pay off handsomely. Colt aggressively sought international markets, often making trips to Europe, Asia, and the Middle East. He did not hesitate to sell weapons to both sides of a conflict, including leading up to the Civil War. He stopped selling to the Confederacy only when war was declared in 1861.

Colt's factory in Hartford exhibited the most efficient processes of industrial America. He was admired at least as much for his streamlining of gun manufacturing as for his sales skills. He built a renowned factory, and as if to challenge Mother Nature, set it on a floodplain. He conquered the elements by building a huge dike to protect it. On a hill just above the factory, Sam Colt and his wife, Elizabeth, built "Armsmear," or "meadow of arms," their personal estate. The palatial mansion stood a shrine to the arms industry that had brought them great wealth.

There are so many parallels between the careers of Samuel Colt and Oliver Winchester that there is little doubt that Winchester imitated Colt. Although Winchester was slightly older and had made his money in the clothing business, both were New Englanders, and they had lived in Baltimore at the same time. Both were challenged by technicians who believed themselves swindled out of an invention.[14] Both men were uncommonly competitive, and favored the selling of products over inventing them. The two men repeatedly tried to convince the U.S. government to invest in large stores of military long arms.[15] As the weapons industry mourned the death of Sam Colt, Oliver Winchester stood poised to fill the void he had left. Winchester, who had had a firsthand look at factory production in the Patent Fire-Arms Manufacturing Company when his own stock had been assembled there, assessed Colt's estate and admired the Colt legacy.

Winchester wanted every bit as much, and he entered the arms arena bent on making at least as much of a statement as Colt. He planned a factory to best Colt's. In 1870 he lobbied a divided board to build a new factory in New Haven on a swath of land below Prospect Hill, where he and his partner Davies had just completed extravagant homes. The board favored the status quo, pointing out the success of the Bridgeport shop in saving Winchester's place in the weapons industry when Henry revolted. But the Bridgeport factory was operating at full capacity and was still inadequate to meet shipping deadlines. The company had a backlog of orders from Mexico, Turkey, France, Siam (Thailand), and the Bavarian countries. The small building had no room to expand. Oliver and William had to convince a board of directors to invest in a new factory, and it took more persuasion than expected. The indomitable Oliver prevailed after ousting two naysayers—who apparently owned the Bridgeport building. The board agreed to pay Winchester $12,000 for land adjoining his home estate on the west side of Prospect Street.

Winchester's imitation of Colt's hillside lookout became a reality. A factory was under construction by the end of 1870, with the board of directors stipulating that the building costs could not exceed $80,000.[16] In six months' time the firm was operating at its new headquarters. The newspaper reported that the new Winchester factory was "mammoth," its centerpiece a brick building with a cupola, and multistoried wings extending in two directions. The main entrance faced the family mansion, just like Colt's, and all the workers knew that Oliver Winchester could stand in his grand parlor and gaze down on the production rooms, their smokestacks billowing testament to the factory's profitability.

Foreign markets for gun and ammunition sales made up most of Winchester's business. The French government purchased thousands of rifles to defend Alsace-Lorraine and Paris during the Franco-Prussian War, although the arms could not save Napoleon III. A number of orders for rifles and pistols were received from South and Central American countries and the Caribbean, including Chile, Peru, and Haiti. The Winchester Repeating Arms Company ran advertisements in the Spanish-language version of the *New York Times* that circulated in Mexico and South America.[17] Contracts that Oliver had procured in Turkey demanded shipment of thousands of rifles, which were due at the same time the company needed to move from Bridgeport to the new factory in New Haven. The transfer was carefully timed so that as a machine finished a task, it was loaded onto a wagon. By the next morning the same machine was set up in New Haven, cranking out parts once again. The Turkish contract for 20,000 rifles valued at more than $550,000 was shipped on time. In the summer of 1871, an additional order for 30,000 rifles and ammunition also came from the Ottoman Empire. These were produced at the New Haven factory in a record six weeks.[18]

Ammunition sales accounted for a substantial portion of the Winchester wealth. The dangerous work of stuffing ammunition packets was carried out by women and girls. They worked in a remote location so as not to threaten gun production, filling casings with explosive powder that often ignited and injured the workers, a brutal proposition.[19] One accident when a cartridge exploded touched off a whole series of explosions, including a box of gun powder. Several girls working in the cartridge room were burned, and a superintendent was seriously hurt by flying debris. Word traveled fast around New Haven and rumors reported several deaths, so the plant was surrounded by an anxious crowd within a short time of the explosion. Miraculously, no one was killed.[20] Within a few years, the Winchester Repeating Arms Company became New Haven's biggest employer, and the new facility was quickly outgrown. The factory's location edging the railroad tracks had enough land to make many additions, and twenty-five years later, in 1895, the Winchester Repeating Arms Company employed 1,500 workers in 400,000 square feet of factory space.

＋＋ ▬◆▬ ＋＋

After the Civil War the military was no longer in the market for long arms, causing an industry-wide drop in gun sales.[21] The completion of the Transcontinental Railroad in 1869, however, opened an entirely new market, an opportunity not lost on Oliver Winchester. He opened an office in San Francisco to manage sales in the West. Early in the 1870s he dispatched William and Sarah to inspect the new outlet in San Francisco and prospects for sales there. They set out from New York to Chicago, and proceeded to Omaha. The Union Pacific's line extended across Nebraska and cut through the southern part of Wyoming to Odgen. The landscape from Utah to the Sierra Nevada offered diverse and completely new vistas to the couple, and they proceeded from Truckee over the mountains and into California's great central valley and Sacramento. From there, they went on to the San Francisco Bay, and ferried to San Francisco. The trip gave them a glimpse of a raw landscape.

Sarah and William had an unusual perspective of the West. They were not settlers or speculators and had none of the anxiety of those who had left everything behind. They were traveling merchants, they had plenty of money, and although accommodations on the journey would have been mostly uncomfortable, it was a temporary inconvenience for them since they would shortly return to the comforts of the East.

In San Francisco, William and Sarah found the Winchester office in a wood-frame waterfront building at 108 Battery Street. It was running a brisk business selling repeating rifles in a city still brandishing the aftereffects of the California Gold Rush. The rough San Francisco crowd—ships' chandlers, importers, and seamen from the world over—made

Front and side views of the Oliver and Jane Winchester home on Prospect Street, New Haven, Connecticut, circa 1869. The elevated view, with Mt. Carmel on the horizon in the background, is probably taken from the cupola of the John M. Davies house, which was constructed on adjacent land at the same time. The inset photograph is of Oliver Fisher Winchester, Sarah Winchester's father-in-law and founder of the Winchester Repeating Arms Company. Courtesy The New Haven Museum & Historical Society.

William Wirt Winchester (1837–1881), Sarah Lockwood Pardee Winchester's husband and second president of the Winchester Repeating Arms Company. Courtesy Buffalo Bill Historical Center, Cody, Wyoming; gift of Olin Corporation, Winchester Arms Collection.

Cover of the *Winchester Record,* a publication of the Winchester Repeating Arms Company on the fiftieth anniversary of Thomas Bennett's association with the company. Bennett married Hannah "Jennie" Winchester in 1872 and was the fourth president of the company after Oliver Winchester, William Winchester, and William Converse. Courtesy Buffalo Bill Historical Center, Cody, Wyoming; gift of Olin Corporation, Winchester Arms Collection, WR.9.10.1920.

Studio portrait of an American Indian man holding a
Winchester Model 1876. Although the Winchester repeater
was dubbed "The Gun That Won the West," implying that it
was solely the weapon of American settlers on the frontier,
Winchesters were often owned and used by American Indians
as well. Courtesy Buffalo Bill Historical Center, Cody, Wyoming;
Vincent Mercaldo Collection, P.71.677.

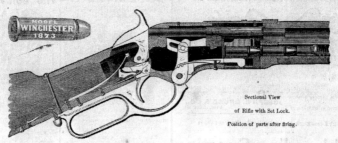

WINCHESTER REPEATING RIFLE

Sectional View
of Rifle with Set Lock.
Position of parts after firing.

The Strength of all its Parts,
The Simplicity of its Construction,
The Rapidity of its Fire,

The impossibility of accidental discharge in loading, commend it to the attention of all who have use for a Rifle for Defense, Hunting, or Target shooting.

For Illustrated Pamphlet and Price List, address

WINCHESTER REPEATING ARMS CO.,

NEW HAVEN, CONN.

Advertisement for the Winchester Model 1873, a lighter and more reliable weapon than the 1866 and an ideal saddle gun for short-range hunting. The frame was constructed of iron rather than the heavier brass, and improvements to its design reduced the risk of accidental firing. Between 1873 and 1924, about 725,000 Model 1873 rifles were manufactured. The gun was made famous by the 1950 Hollywood movie *Winchester '73*, starring Jimmy Stewart. Courtesy Buffalo Bill Historical Center, Cody, Wyoming; gift of Roy Marcot, Tuscon, Arizona, WIN.FORS.1876.11.2.

Handwritten letter from Sarah Winchester to her attorney, Frank Leib, in 1907 expressing "outrage" at the "unwarrantable intrusion" of a developer's laying a sewer to drain in a creek on her houseboat property in Burlingame. The letter acknowledges that Winchester had been ill and had sent her niece, Daisy Marriott, to ask Leib to press charges against the developer. The stationery shows the name of Winchester's San José ranch, Llanada Villa. Courtesy History San José.

that Mr Easton refused to allow Connection
with his sewer - so it is being laid
across my property, to empty into the
creek at a point where it is dry in
the summer! It seems to me an outrage
which should be immediately stopped.
I heard that the ditch for the sewer
was Completed some days since and
that the pipe was on the ground
ready to be laid - Mrs Marriott
was at your office on Saturday to ask
you to take Action in reference to this
matter - but found you were away -
I would see you myself but have
been ill for months and although
much better am still Compelled
to keep very quiet - Hoping you
may be able to protect my property
from this unwarrantable intrusion
Yours very truly - S. L. Winchester

Isabelle "Belle" Merriman, Sarah Winchester's younger
sister, who came to California from New Haven and
lived with her husband and family on a ranch that was
developed into the town of Los Altos and later in Palo
Alto. Photograph from *History of Santa Clara County*,
by Eugene Sawyer (1922).

Formal portrait of Marion "Daisy" Merriman, Sarah
Winchester's niece, with a background of daisies,
taken by photographer Andrew P. Hill circa 1898. Hill
was a well-known landscape artist and photographer
who lost most of his paintings in the 1906
earthquake. Courtesy History San José.

Marion "Daisy" Merriman circa 1900. Daisy lived with
her aunt for fifteen years at Llanada Villa. In this casual
pose, she appears to be standing in a waterless fountain.
Courtesy History San José.

up the ranks of Winchester customers. Fifty dollars bought a repeater, slightly less for a carbine, and for an additional seven dollars, a leather scabbard.[22] Despite its primitive aspect, San Francisco was remarkably similar to New Haven. The foggy, seaside climate was ideal for fishermen, and horse-rail cars along Market Street or schooners at the Vallejo Street wharf matched New Haven's swift current of commerce. The number of Chinese residents was a marked difference from New Haven, but perhaps China could be a new market for Winchester. What San Francisco lacked in aesthetics it began to remedy with city parks and impressive buildings, such as the princely eight-hundred-room Palace Hotel on Market Street, owned by financier William Ralston. That the Winchester company set up shop here demonstrated good business. William Winchester could conclude that his father was not making a mistake in maintaining a visible presence in San Francisco. Company records do not indicate precisely where sales were made, but in 1870, the year after the San Francisco store opened, gun sales for the company as a whole more than doubled.[23]

During that visit to San Francisco, Sarah Winchester sat for her portrait in the photographic studio of Isaiah Taber.[24] The photograph presents the picture of formal propriety: a young Sarah, dressed in a dark silk gown buttoned high to a lacy collar, her hair parted in the center, sits with her gaze focused beyond the camera to some distant and undefined horizon. The image also possesses an undeniable impishness, in the flurry of tight curls circling the small round face and a hint of a smile showing. Taber's photograph captures the enduring enigma that is Sarah Winchester—a curious blend of amusing caricature and refined lady. As Sarah and William were conveyed by carriage from a hotel to the Winchester shop and while they were entertained by wealthy locals, Sarah probably never dreamed that one day she would live there.

⋅━⋅≡✦≡⋅━⋅

Firearms have always played a role in driving America's frontiers. Colonial America, for example, far more than Europe, relied upon and demanded the use of firearms for self-defense, sustenance, and trade.[25] Guns ensured survival, a notion that time and history have never fully dissipated and one that remains a potent theme in American culture. Even Sarah Winchester's immigrant ancestor, George Pardee, was issued a musket with powder and a bandolier so that he could be called upon to defend the village and enforce the law. In the 1640s, each male adult was required to "be compleatly furnished with arms (viz) a muskett, a sworde, bandaleers, a rest, a pound of powder, 20 bullets fitted to their muskett, or 4 pounds of pistoll shott or swan shott at least."[26] A personal arsenal protected the home, supplied a dinner table, and defended the community. Likewise, during the Revolutionary War period after the Boston Tea Party in 1773, the British thought it wise to disarm the colonists. Patriots stockpiled flintlock muskets and rifles, hoarding or stealing gunpowder and amassing stores of bayonets and swords. In early America the right to bear arms and the challenge of democracy were inextricably linked.[27]

As the boundaries of the nation moved ever westward, vanguard explorers and settlers needed reliable weapons. By 1798, the famous inventor of the cotton gin, Eli Whitney, had established the Whitney Arms Company in the town of Hamden, situated at the border of New Haven. Whitney's workers assembled multiple parts into sections, a procedure that differed from systems in England, where workers made or installed a single part. The resulting production effectively outpaced all competitors. During the 1840s, Samuel Colt perfected his revolver and repeating pistol, and some of his earliest designs were manufactured at Whitney's factory. Although Oliver Winchester initially perceived the repeater as a weapon for the battlefield, the Winchester Repeating Arms Company entered the ranks of its predecessors by making weapons as tools of the frontier. After the Winchester was rejected by the U.S. military, it was marketed to go west. "For Indian, Bear, or Buffalo hunting, it is unrivalled," proclaimed an advertisement.[28]

By the time Sarah and William Winchester traveled across the country to San Francisco, the official U.S. policy was to attempt to eliminate the nomadic lifestyle of American Indians and sequester them on reservations. Implementation of the government policies in this area was rife with abuse and fraud. Men appointed as Indian agents routinely hijacked food intended for reservations, reselling it to trading posts, which in turn sold it to starving Indians. Agitation among Indians grew with their hunger, and their leaders knew they would have to resume hunting to keep from starving. They stockpiled weapons, including Winchesters. Over the next few years, as government rations disappeared and more Indians starved, a plan to revolt intensified. According to one diarist, the Lakota Sioux "had been preparing for war by collecting Winchester repeating rifles and plenty of ammunition."[29] They armed themselves by selling mules and horses, hides and blankets. They preferred Henry, Spencer, or Winchester repeaters, but had a cache of old muzzle-loaders, too.

It is estimated that by 1876 "between one-third and one-half of the gathering warriors owned a gun."[30] In the summer of 1876, the Seventh Cavalry of the U.S. Army under the command of General George Custer engaged the Lakota Sioux and Northern Cheyenne Indians in the

Montana territory in what later became known as the Battle of the Little Bighorn. Custer and his troops were defeated, and it was widely reported that the general and his men were armed mostly with single-shot Springfield carbines, while the American Indians carried Spencer and Winchester repeaters.[31] Battles between Indians and white settlers were fast becoming the stuff of mythology. Indians called the Winchester the "spirit gun" because it kept firing.[32] Custer's Last Stand and Indian resistance to white incursion were unlikely but valuable endorsements for the Winchester repeater.

Expansion in the West prompted improvements to the repeater. When critics complained that the rifle lacked the power to take down big game, the company responded by issuing the Model 1876, a rifle with a longer barrel and heavier cartridges, and it sold quickly to anyone heading west as the tool of choice to master the wilderness. The U.S. government provided firearms free of charge to settlers headed to Oregon and California.[33] Cowboys driving herds of Texas cattle north to find grazing land used the repeater on patrol to keep their herds separate from disease-ridden southern longhorn, establishing what they referred to as the "Winchester quarantine." One author insisted that "the Winchester was not an arm of violence. For every outlaw who may have carried a Winchester, there were a thousand men [with Winchesters] who earned their living honestly."[34]

The Winchester repeater was positioned in the vanguard in America's march across the North American continent, as the country lived out its perceived manifest destiny. The repeater emerged as an important symbol of this great westward movement of progress, growth, expansion, and exploitation. The writing of Helen Hunt Jackson during the 1880s in books like *A Century of Dishonor* (1881) and the novel *Ramona* (1884) informed the nation of the horrors that had befallen native peoples, often on the receiving end of gunfire. A driving force of the repeater's popularity was the very real lawlessness of the new communities sprouting in the West. Conventional wisdom asserts that the biggest threats in the open territory were Indians or wild animals. In reality, the most significant danger was from lawlessness. One historian reported that there was "a desperate need to defend oneself against other white settlers who made their living through law breaking and violence."[35]

When a prairie war broke out along the Powder River in Wyoming in 1892 between large-scale cattlemen and individual grangers, the cattlemen imported gunslingers from Texas, among other places, to wipe out the competing small operators. One historian reports that "the cattlemen specifically bought their gunmen new Winchesters; the armed populace that besieged them carried a variety of shoulder arms, among which

Winchester probably predominated."[36] The Powder River conflict under-scored the lawlessness of the West and highlighted the effectiveness and widespread use of the Winchester repeater. The incident was viewed as quite alarming all over the country.

—••— ⊫⬥⊨ —••—

Between the time that William Winchester left the shirt manufac-tory in 1866 and the opening of the new gun factory in 1871, he was employed as the secretary of the Winchester Repeating Arms Company, and his father was president and treasurer. When the new facility opened in New Haven, he was made vice president of the rifle division, a posi-tion in which he excelled. In fact, he designed and patented a reload-ing tool that made the repeater a safer weapon.[37] He never exuded the enthusiasm for the arms industry that his father did, but he followed in his father's footsteps nevertheless. The young Winchester tinkered with gunsmiths and worked with mechanics, displaying some aptitude.

William was succeeded as secretary by Thomas G. Bennett, a recent Yale graduate. Bennett was a large, powerful man with a serious coun-tenance. He was born in New Haven and attended the Collegiate and Commercial Institute, a boys' boarding school near Wooster Square. He joined the Union Army and during the war was attached to the Twenty-eighth and Twenty-ninth Connecticut Volunteers. Wounded in 1864 at the battle of Chaffin's Farm in Virginia, he achieved the rank of captain before being mustered out of the army at the end of 1865. After the war Bennett attended Yale University, earning a bachelor's degree in mechan-ical engineering with the class of 1870. Upon graduation at age twenty-six, he went to work at the new Winchester factory.

Bennett developed more than a passing interest in the Winchesters. In short order he began seriously courting Oliver's younger daughter, Jennie, and they were married on May 9, 1872. One can only speculate about whether marrying the owner's daughter was a wise plan. Bennett's motives were always suspected, and his rise up the Winchester corpo-rate ladder was at a considerably slower pace than he desired.[38] A decade passed before he was promoted from his starting position of secretary.

In sharp contrast to Oliver Winchester, who tended toward exuber-ance, Thomas and Jennie Bennett were proper and formal, characteris-tics that could be off-putting. Very few ever called Bennett by his given name, and his mechanical-engineering education accentuated his atten-tion to precise detail. Notwithstanding the couple's reserved demeanor, they were well matched, and they were often quite generous to rela-tives or good causes. Thomas Bennett was a loyal man who was deeply devoted to the Winchester Repeating Arms Company, and eventually he served as its president for longer than anyone else in its history.

Oliver Winchester traveled often during the 1870s, sometimes accompanied by his wife, Jane, or by William and Sarah, or by his grandson, Ollie Dye. A few months after the Bennett wedding, Winchester sailed for Europe,[39] where he procured more foreign contracts and expanded the company's commitments to supply ammunition in foreign wars. He and his friend John Davies, who had kept the company books, had deep pockets for the arms company. Between 1865 and 1874, Davies had loaned it about $90,000. When Davies died in 1874, it was a terrible personal and professional loss to Winchester. Davies' heirs were anxious to settle his estate, and Winchester loaned the company cash to pay them. Within a short time, Winchester also had news that his twin brother, Samuel, had died, and he began to give serious thought to the future of the Winchester Repeating Arms Company.

Although Winchester was the company's treasurer, he had always relied on Davies' money-management strategies. He knew he needed a new treasurer. He looked past William Winchester and Thomas Bennett, the two most obvious candidates, and focused on an unlikely fellow. Winchester invited William Converse to join the board of directors of the arms company. At first glance, the association between Winchester and Converse seems odd. Converse was not related to Winchester, but was married to Sarah Winchester's sister Mary. Furthermore, Converse had never worked for an arms company, but had managed Leonard Pardee's wood shop and, just lately, a lumber mill in Albany. Winchester hired Converse as treasurer, and it became apparent quite quickly that he favored his input more than that of his son or his son-in-law. The wages he paid spoke volumes. In 1878, Converse was paid a $5,000 annual salary, William was paid $3,500, and Thomas was paid $2,500.[40] Converse came late to the vineyard but was paid the highest wage, causing a certain amount of resentment. Thomas, who held a degree from Yale and had fought in the Civil War, would have expected to be promoted over William Converse, a sparsely educated man who had not served in the war. And although Thomas's position in the company was safe, after eight years he was still its secretary. He had higher aspirations. William Winchester may have resented Converse's presence, but he acquiesced to the desires of his persuasive father. Converse had a knack for making money grow and cultivating good prospects. He was more like his new boss than either William or Thomas.

The collaboration between Thomas Bennett and William Converse was the single most important reason the Winchester Repeating Arms Company survived in the decade after the rapid-fire deaths of the two

Winchester men in 1880 and 1881. While they followed a course set by Oliver Winchester, their cohesive strategies held the company together in a creative way that also allowed it to expand.

Bennett used his position to court John Browning, a talented Mormon gunsmith who agreed to sell his designs exclusively to the Winchester company. When the distinguished Bennett surprised Browning one day by personally appearing in his dusty Utah shop, the gunsmith was so impressed that Bennett had traveled all the way from New Haven to meet him that he remained loyal to Winchester for almost two decades. Browning's design made the Model 1894 "the best-selling Winchester center-fire rifle ever made."[41] Within ten years, the invention of smokeless powder, a radical departure from the black, sooty smoke produced by gunpowder, completely changed the ammunition industry.

Bennett masterminded a compromise with Colt's Patent Fire-Arms Manufacturing Company when he fooled its management into believing that Winchester was about to go to market with a new repeating pistol. He convinced the Colt company that if it eliminated its plans for a repeating rifle, Winchester would not market its (illusory) repeating revolver. The two companies came to an agreement to stay away from each other's market, and Colt stopped making lever-action rifles.[42] Bennett also recruited William Mason, one of Colt's gun designers, who became one of the most significant designers of the nineteenth century. Oliver Winchester would have been proud if he had been alive to see it.

William Converse used Buffalo Bill Cody's endorsement on promotional material. One of the most popular entertainments of the day was the "Wild West" show, and the best such shows were those put on by the archetypal cowboy Cody. The first Buffalo Bill's Wild West opened in 1883, just as Converse and Bennett took over at Winchester. Buffalo Bill, far more actor than cowboy, helped define the identity of the American West. He often flashed his Winchester repeater, informing audiences that for "Indian fighting" the Winchester was "boss." Buffalo Bill's female counterpart, Annie Oakley, or "Little Sure Shot," delighted audiences with her superior marksmanship, and her weapon of choice was likewise often a Winchester. Buffalo Bill and Annie Oakley were happy to endorse the Winchester, and were supplied with a variety of specialty specimens.

Theodore Roosevelt, at least as famous for hunting as for politicking, was a great fan of the Winchester repeater. He authored a book in 1885 entitled *Hunting Trips of a Ranchman,* in which he praised the gun: "The Winchester . . . is by all odds the best weapon I ever had, and I now use it almost exclusively. . . . It is handy to carry, whether on foot or on horseback, and comes up to the shoulder as readily as a shotgun."[43]

Converse used the quotation on advertisements for years. Later, after Roosevelt was elected president and refused to endorse any product, the company had to limit the use of his name to officially approved statements. But it was widely recognized that Roosevelt took several Winchester rifles on his many hunting trips.

── ▰◆▰ ──

Production at the Winchester factory during the 1870s established the company as the most successful American lever-action repeating-rifle company. Among Winchester's competitors was the Spencer Repeating Rifle Company. Its repeating rifle, a different design than the Henry, had been approved by military officials for use during the Civil War, but did not take the place of muzzle-loaded muskets. After the war, with a serious decline in sales, Spencer officials wished to sell the company. It was purchased by a Boston company called the Fogarty Repeating Rifle Company in 1868. The following year a new corporation called the American Repeating Rifle Company was formed to consolidate Spencer and Fogarty. When the corporation went bankrupt in 1869, the Winchester Repeating Arms Company bought it along with its patents, backlog, and machinery. This set the stage for future acquisitions, as the Winchester Repeating Arms Company took over many of its competitors. In 1888, the company bought the Whitney Arms Company in Hamden, and later that year purchased a half interest in E. Remington & Sons of Ilion, New York. The Model 1876 became the favorite of big-game hunters to take down buffalo, elk, and the menacing grizzly. Buffalo Bill Cody, a self-proclaimed Pony Express rider turned Indian slayer, explained, "While in the Black Hills this last summer I crippled a bear, and Mr. Bear made for me, and I am certain had I not been armed with one of your repeating rifles I would now be in the happy hunting grounds. The bear was not thirty feet from me when he charged, but before he could reach me I [put] more lead [in him] than he could comfortably digest."[44]

By 1876, the year of the nation's hundredth birthday, the Winchester repeater was an icon of the experience of the West. The Centennial Exposition held in Philadelphia in 1876 showcased Winchester products. The display of Winchester ammunition caught public attention at the world's fair, and expanding that part of the company proved financially worthwhile.[45] A bronze medal awarded to Winchester at the fair is in the collection of the Cody Firearms Museum in Cody, Wyoming.[46] The medal cannot be taken too seriously, however, since "the judges handed out more than 13,000 identical bronze medals to exhibitors in various categories."[47] The Canadian Mounties adopted the 1876 as their official weapon, and reports of its success in taking down large game under very cold conditions kept it in use there until 1914.[48] The Centennial Model 1876 Winchester never was as popular as the 1873, which continued to outsell the 1876 into the twentieth century.

The Winchester repeater, conceived as a weapon for the battlefield and for Indian suppression and heavily marketed for foreign wars, had been transformed into a hunting and target rifle. What would be its next incarnation? If, as historian Frederick Jackson Turner reported in 1893 at the Chicago International Exposition, the American frontier was closed, how would the nation define itself? Turner asserted that the nation's history and identity were defined by the great frontier, where "a new environment is suddenly entered, freedom of opportunity is opened, the cake of custom is broken, and new activities, new lines of growth, new institutions and new ideals, are brought into existence."[49] Turner's thesis became a paradigm by which the history of the West was measured for the next hundred years.

From the mythology of the old West, the repeater's appearances at the great world's fairs and in Wild West shows brought it swiftly and firmly into the entertainment industry. Celebrities from Buffalo Bill and Annie Oakley to John Wayne and Jimmy Stewart pulled the repeater out of reality and made it an almost charming and sentimental symbol. A wave of nostalgia for the old West settled on popular culture in the years immediately following World War I, and when the Winchester Repeating Arms Company adopted the advertising slogan "The Gun That Won the West" in 1919, it successfully branded its repeating long arm as an icon of the greatest period of geographical expansion in the history of the nation. The Winchester Model 1873 repeater and the Colt "Peacemaker," also of 1873, were perceived to be among the crucial tools needed to survive and thrive in the West. Both the lever-action repeating rifle and the hip-holstered pistol were successfully etched into the national psyche as "the gun that won the West."

The marketing scheme set the tone for books, Hollywood films, and television shows later in the twentieth century. Looking back at the fairly recent history through rose-colored glasses allowed a magnification of the rifle's role as the most important instrument in the exploration and settlement of the West. It subtly legitimized violence on the prairies as an inevitable truth, and borrowed heavily from this branding to reinforce the Winchester as a symbol of the rugged individualism of a pioneering American spirit.

While a changing American identity was hammered out in the West, and as the Winchester repeater came into its own on the frontier and in foreign wars, Sarah and William Winchester mostly watched from the sidelines. But they were attentive students. The two probably had a good understanding of the West, as they had traveled there. And since they had been in Constantinople and European capitals, they had a broader view than most. Yet they were set solidly in the culture of New Haven, adjusting to a newfound association with the arms industry and representatives of the Winchester name. The immediate challenge before Sarah and William was how to live out their shared dreams. A new home, lifestyle, and work beckoned.

CHAPTER 4

The Winchester Fortune

I N THE YEARS IMMEDIATELY FOLLOWING THE CIVIL WAR, SARAH AND William Winchester's living quarters, daily life, and family ties went through a dramatic transformation. They moved to a stunning mansion overlooking New Haven, an enviable home even to other elites. The Court Street house, crammed in among crowded boardinghouses, faded into memory. Sarah's father, the master carpenter and family provider, died, shifting attention to the new generation of babies born to Sarah's sisters and brother. While William and Oliver Winchester devoted themselves to the arms business, Sarah did not sit idle in the regal rooms she shared with her husband. During the years that she lived under Oliver Winchester's roof, Sarah absorbed life lessons in interior design, construction management, real estate investment, and financial strategy. Throughout the rest of her life, whether toiling at house design or hiring household help, she exhibited money-management skills that none of her siblings displayed and a keen attention to the bottom line in the family enterprises. She was an attentive student of both Winchester men.

A fact that is rarely reported is that it was shirts, not guns, that funded the great Winchester home in New Haven and provided the basis for investments in the weapons industry. The success of the Winchester Repeating Arms Company would never have been possible without the strong financial foundation of the Winchester & Davies Shirt Manufactory. Oliver Winchester had become wealthy over a period of about a dozen years between 1847, when he had gone into partnership with John Davies to establish their shirt factory, and 1859, when they had a new and modern factory built on Court Street, just a block from the old one.

The partners proclaimed their respective personal wealth in about 1860, as they approved architectural drawings for side-by-side mansions on land they had purchased along the aptly named Prospect Street. The new road was cut through Sachem's Woods, the onetime estate belonging to early real estate developers James Hillhouse and his son, James A. Hillhouse. Until 1860, this land was too distant from the center of town to justify building residences, but as Irish immigrants inundated the city, wealthier citizens began building in the surrounding countryside. Winchester and Davies were among the first.

The men did not need to look far to find architects. Henry Austin and David R. Brown occupied offices in New Haven at Chapel and State streets. Austin had studied under the renowned Ithiel Town, one of America's first professional architects. Town had designed Center Church and Trinity Church, two of the three churches decorating New Haven's Green. Although never as critically acclaimed as Town, Austin left his own distinctive mark on New Haven. Among his works was the Federal-style First Methodist Church built in 1849, and the Gothic-style New Haven City Hall built on Church Street in 1861. Also commissioned to build a home for the railroad magnate Joseph Sheffield, he designed several homes in the Wooster Square neighborhood as well. The younger David Brown was groomed by Austin, and favored High Victorian Gothic styles, the most popular of the era.

Austin and Brown designed residences for Winchester and Davies overlooking Yale University and the elm-canopied streets of New Haven.[1] The challenge and incredible opportunity facing the architects was that the two houses would not be constrained by any surrounding buildings, but would sit on open land, an expanse influenced only by the natural setting, and indeed, the landscape became a crucial piece of the new design. By 1866, the homes that Oliver Winchester and John Davies had delayed building because of the war were under construction. The beautiful mansions were built in the style of the Second Empire with Italianate elements. Although not identical twins, they had a marked resemblance. Each house was about twenty thousand square feet in size, with two main floors, plus higher rooms for servants' quarters. Their twenty-plus rooms were decorated with "marble floors, elaborate fireplaces and overmantle frames, sculpture niches, plasterwork ceilings and elegant chandeliers."[2] The Winchester house exterior had a four-story campanile and large bay windows that allowed for a light-filled great room. Five massive palladium windows reaching from floor to ceiling lined up across the back of the house, providing a stunning view down the hill to the surrounding landscape. In the front, a circular drive welcomed horse-drawn coaches. Portions of both houses had mansard roofs, and pavilions overlooked the countryside. As the homes materialized on the hillside above town, they exuded an aura of grandeur and elegance. One observer noted, "Mr. Winchester, and his business partner Mr. Davies, have each erected magnificent houses on the high land to the north of Hillhouse avenue; a drive or walk around their home parks is exceedingly pleasing."[3] It was as if the two men had created the very landscape.

The building project proved a training ground for Sarah and William Winchester, who agreed to live in the new home with the senior Winchesters. The young couple knew the house would one day be theirs. The project also offered an engaging distraction from the grief they felt over the loss of their infant daughter in July 1866. The inevitable construction delays sometimes demanded ingenious remedies. One significant difficulty was resolved by the erection of a large windmill on the Winchester homesite. The city waterworks was lower than the new house, so if the occupants expected to have water, it had to be pumped uphill. It was clear to the young Winchesters that if there was a problem, it could be solved. Designs were submitted, alterations made, and new configurations proposed. Oliver had little time to devote to the actual construction of the estate and turned the task over to his son and daughter-in-law.

Sarah and William appeared captivated by the building design, construction planning, and oversight. If William's livelihood had not already been clearly established, it seems likely that he would have chosen this relatively new profession in the field of architecture. Although he relegated his interest in architecture to that of a hobby, his personal aesthetic was refined as he worked on the project. William relied on Sarah's participation, and she paid close attention to the outbuildings and landscaping, as well as to proposals for interior finishes. William commissioned an artist to paint portraits of his parents, and those portraits hung in the house until at least 1900. This first encounter with architecture and interior design became a mutual passion for the younger Winchesters. The construction of the mansion was a shared project, a true partnership, and the time it took was an all-too-brief period of happiness for the couple. Ultimately, Sarah always kept memories of the Prospect Street house close to her heart, and as many as thirty years later, she referred to it with sad fondness as "the house on the hill."[4]

Upon completion in 1868, the Winchester home housed five adult family members—the senior and junior Winchesters and twenty-year-old Jennie, five female Irish domestics, one Irish coachman along with his wife and baby son, and a Scottish gardener. Davies and his wife, Alice, occupied the neighboring home, with their two youngest daughters, Alice and Charlotte. Their son, Cornelius, the remaining principal of the shirt manufacturing business, had married, and he and his wife lived in a separate house on the Davies property. The large Davies house also required considerable upkeep, and its servant staff also outnumbered the family members living there. Four Irishwomen were employed as domestic servants, and two gardeners and a mixed-race coachman also helped maintain the estate. The Davies house has been restored and serves now as the Betts House for Yale University, and the site of the Winchester house is occupied by Yale's Sterling Divinity Quadrangle.[5]

Sarah and William had reaped many benefits from participating in the process of building their new home. Sarah had learned that architectural and interior design was a potent remedy for depression and grief. In the years to come, she would often turn to the curative powers of work to restore physical and emotional well-being. It had been a pleasurable exercise in self-expression for William, whose health had begun a slow but steady decline. Never very robust, he had a chronic cough, and the cold, wet winters were particularly difficult for him. Sarah and William were to enjoy more than a decade together in the lovely home they did so much to design and decorate.

As the Winchester family ascended to Prospect Hill, they were ushered to a higher social and financial standing. The most significant difference between the Winchester wealth in 1860 and that of 1870 was not so much that Oliver's wealth increased, which it did, but that his wife and children possessed wealth of their own. Whichever household member greeted the census taker in 1870 did not hesitate to disclose how much cash each person held. Jane Winchester had $20,000 in her name, while the twenty-two-year-old Jennie had $10,000. William claimed $20,000.[6] As yet, Sarah Winchester claimed no personal wealth whatsoever.

Oliver Winchester rode a new wave to social prominence and power that came purely with wealth in the years after the Civil War. He was an example of a man of the Gilded Age, a term coined by Mark Twain and Charles Dudley Warner's novel of the same name. The story depicted the garish excesses of the day as a backdrop for a decadent high society embroiled in political corruption. Not surprisingly, the satiric tone of Twain and Warner's *Gilded Age* was drowned out by a new American self-image, one that proclaimed wealth as the surest sign of God's favor. The Gilded Age bred a generation who fashioned heavily ornamented homes with the most current accoutrements and amenities.

Previously social rank had come with good birth and inherited wealth. Old money accrued from property rather than product and passed from one generation to the next. Good birth followed by good breeding had always before led to rock solid social status. For generations, students at Yale University were seated according to the social standing of their fathers. The system of inherited influence was shaken to its core by the Industrial Revolution, as inventors and salesmen entered the ranks of the wealthy and took their places on the social scene. Money measured status as never before, and good birth counted for a lot less than it once had. Samuel Colt, Oliver Winchester, and John Davies, among a host of others, created personal mythologies along with their fortunes. None of these men would ever have been seated at the head of the class at Yale; in fact, none would have had the opportunity even to attend Yale.

Although Oliver may have aimed to accumulate the financial stores of the super rich, like William Astor or John D. Rockefeller, the Winchester fortune never approached the vast wealth of these men, but its significance lay in the fact that it was created by a man born penniless, and in only the last thirty years of his life. Winchester fought his way to join the American industrialists accumulating enough wealth and power to hope to transform the nation, or at least its economy, in the years following the Civil War. Colt and Winchester typified the industrialists of their age, men who reported stories of a rough childhood, underscoring personal grit and determination as ingredients of their financial success. They built fame just as surely as they built fortunes. Their wives and children helped to build impressive homes to reflect the sizable egos and bank accounts of these giants of industry and, after they were deceased, monuments to commemorate them. In reality, Sam Colt's most ingenious invention may not have been the revolver, but rather the incredibly efficient process of producing it in huge numbers[7] and the audacious publicity to sell it. Oliver Winchester's claim to fame was not the rifle that bore his name, but a relentless competitive appetite for business success.[8]

Oliver took advantage of the biggest trade show of his day. The Centennial Exposition held in Philadelphia in 1876 to commemorate America's hundredth birthday showcased inventions and arts of thirty-seven participating nations. The fair's buildings and pavilions had been laid out on over 2,700 acres, carefully landscaped and presenting in a precise and orderly way the arts, crafts, and manufactured goods of the world. The Winchester Repeating Arms Company could not have wished for a better coming-out party than the fair in Philadelphia for the new Winchester Model 1876. Many of the guns sported a "Centennial Finish," which was a golden cast created by the use of cyanide staining on the receiver plate. Custom-designed exhibit cases displayed more than two hundred Winchester weapons at the fair.

American promoters of the fair wished to show a nation celebrating its history and its unity, one healed from the divisive wounds of the Civil War. They were only partially successful; several formerly Confederate states did not participate in the fair. Perhaps it had something to do with the fact that the president of the Centennial Commission and Oliver Winchester's old friend and running mate, former governor Joseph Hawley, was still known as a liberal abolitionist.

An original copy of the Declaration of Independence was set as the centerpiece of the fair. It lay encased in glass, its edges slightly crumpled, near the main entrance. But the largest crowds gathered not there, but around the gigantic Corliss Centennial steam engine. History took a backseat to progress and to America's industrial coming of age. Each time the behemoth Corliss was fired up, an awestruck crowd stood gaping as churning and chugging gears engaged huge flywheels powering a new industrial economy. More than ten million people visited the exposition that year.[9] Fairgoers were captivated by American mechanical ingenuity.

The Centennial Exposition marked the unofficial beginning of the Gilded Age. Taking place during the Grant administration, one of the U.S. presidency's most corrupt, the fair presented ostentation as a great symbol of success. Sarah Winchester, her husband, and her in-laws took many cues from the exhibits, implementing them in updates to their home. An early-day home-improvement show, Philadelphia's exposition endorsed personal "expositions" to showcase possessions and collections acquired by new wealth. The fair offers a glimpse at how the newly rich industrialists demonstrated their personal wealth. Artistic works and an amusement boardwalk balanced the manufactured goods on display. Philadelphia's was the first of the great fairs to offer cultural exhibits, and America's centennial celebration there included historical and photographic exhibits.[10] A heightened appreciation for internationalism accompanied the several foreign exhibits.

Oliver Winchester was all of these things—a patriotic American, an internationalist, and a prime example of the Gilded Age. But perhaps owing to his advancing age, in 1877 he had a serious lapse of judgment and was duped in a social scandal that typified the excesses of the time and resounded from New York harbor to Constantinople.

Winchester had maintained connections with the Turkish government beginning in the early 1870s and had established a track record selling arms to it. When William and Sarah traveled to Constantinople on one arms-selling junket, she picked up enough Turkish phrases that people began to claim that she spoke Persian. In 1872, Oliver Winchester met Captain Edinboro Bey in Constantinople, and Bey turned up in New York a few years later as war between the Turks and Russians loomed, apparently under the authority of the Turkish government to negotiate ship leases in order to transport arms and munitions from the Winchester Repeating Arms Company in New Haven to Constantinople.[11] Bey and a small entourage registered at New York's finest, the New York Hotel.

The dashing military officer swept social circles and ingratiated himself into high-society parties and excursions. The *New York Times* noted that "his *distingué* air and generally 'stunning' appearance had its effect on the circles in which he moved."[12] Bey's schedule included an important appointment to visit Oliver Winchester at his home in New Haven, and Winchester loaned him two thousand dollars against promises of gun sales. Several other industrialists and socialites vouched for the surety of the captain's hotel bills, which accumulated at an enormous rate.

After six months of lavish living in New York as hotel bills went unpaid, some began to suspect Bey was a fraud. Just after New Year's in 1878, Bey disappeared owing thousands to two hotels and several generous benefactors. The *New York Times* and other American newspapers elaborated on Bey's con job, embarrassing Winchester and others who had sought business dealings with the fake. The scam was a costly reminder to the Winchesters that the appearance of power and wealth does not always match the reality. William and Sarah must have been surprised that the senior Winchester had let his guard down and lost money to Bey. Oliver Winchester's age was showing.

In 1880, the Winchester Repeating Arms Company had a net worth of just over $3 million and showed a $300,000 profit. That year the company sold 26,500 rifles.[13] Stockholders earned a $10 dividend for each stock. Since its inception in 1866, the arms company had grown 15 percent; since 1869, it had sold some 200,000 rifles.

Arguably, the most difficult year of Sarah Winchester's life began in the spring of 1880, when the three most influential people in her life died within a ten-month period. In May her mother died, in December, her much-admired father-in-law, and finally and worst of all, in March 1881 her beloved William succumbed to tuberculosis. The foundations of her life were gone.

Sarah's mother had lived out most of her widowhood, ever since Leonard Pardee died in 1869, at her Orange Street house, a large and well-appointed home. When her eldest daughter, Mary Converse, moved back to New Haven from New York in about 1876 so her husband, William, could work at the Winchester Repeating Arms Company, she and her husband moved in with Sarah Pardee. The house provided the Converses with a social presence in New Haven befitting an officer in the Winchester Repeating Arms Company. At the same time, Sarah Pardee subdivided a piece of property she owned on nearby Eld Street and provided a house for each of her youngest daughters, Belle and Estelle. It is not clear whether she was concerned about the ability of her sons-in-law to provide or simply wanted the two youngest daughters together. As it turns out, neither made a good marriage, and maybe their mother had understood that. In any case, the two were neighbors and started families at the same time. The ages of their children were almost exactly matched.

Sarah Pardee died at the house on Orange Street on May 11, 1880, four days before her seventy-second birthday. On Friday, May 14, a funeral service was held at Belle's. Friends and relations joined the six Pardee siblings at 2:30 p.m. to mourn her loss. Pardee was buried at Evergreen Cemetery in the Pardee plot, next to her husband, Leonard, and her first-born, Sarah, who had died some forty-five years earlier. Her children paid $510 for a monument for their mother's grave.[14]

Jane Winchester attended Sarah Pardee's funeral, escorted not by her husband, but by her daughter and son-in-law, Jennie and Thomas Bennett. Oliver Winchester had suffered a stroke early in 1880 and had been confined to his bed for months. By summer, he regained the ability to walk with a cane and by sheer will recovered some speech. For most of the summer and fall he was able to be taken about, inquire after business, and do some quiet socializing. But just before Thanksgiving, he took to his bed again and in two weeks faded into a shadow of his former formidable presence. He died on Friday morning, December 10, and the *New Haven Palladium* eulogized, "For thirty years one of our leading manufacturers, he succeeded in developing an industry that has made his name known throughout the length and breadth of the civilized world."[15] The family patriarch and businessman extraordinaire had also been a director of Yale National Bank and the New Haven Water Company, a Republican and contributor to Abraham Lincoln, a councilman from the fourth ward, and lieutenant governor of the state of Connecticut.[16] But all of those accomplishments paled next to what the newspaper termed his "indomitable energy," explaining that "he won his way by energy, perseverance and success."[17]

Oliver Fisher Winchester had been a complex combination of highly laudable attributes—resourcefulness, fortitude, and optimism—mixed with ruthless determination. Abandonment in childhood had undoubtedly left him a driven man. Winchester rifle historian Harold Williamson notes Oliver Winchester's role as a man of his age: "Winchester's career was in the best American tradition. His success was achieved as a business man, and starting with little or no capital he died, leaving a personal fortune amounting to nearly one and a half million dollars."[18] Winchester had made many enemies but also had had extremely close friends. He had political supporters as well as many who wanted to destroy him. His son was nothing like him, but had deep respect for him. Oliver Winchester had built his own mythology right alongside his business enterprises.

There is no indication that Sarah Winchester idolized her father-in-law, but she did exhibit considerable respect and appreciation for him. "Father," as she and William had called him, was a formidable and guiding presence in their lives, and now he was gone. On the Tuesday following Oliver's death, a funeral was held at the Prospect Street house on the hill overlooking the vast Winchester Repeating Arms factory. Carriages came up the circular drive and coachmen delivered their passengers as dignitaries and Winchester employees paid their final respects. The minister from Calvary Baptist was in attendance, but a prominent preacher from Brooklyn issued the thirty-minute sermon. The Reverend Doctor H. M. Gallaher, preacher to the wealthy, had known Oliver, among other industrialists, and he outranked the local clergyman. Other mourners included Cornelius Davies, the son of Oliver's late partner; the Converses; dozens of relatives from Boston, Baltimore, New York, and New Haven; Winchester factory employees; household servants, coachmen, and several groundskeepers. Among the eight pallbearers were men who represented Winchester's interests and preferences—two Yale professors, one in law and the other in astronomy, and Nelson King, the former superintendent of the Winchester factory. The other pallbearers were Edward E. Hall, Jeremiah A. Bishop, S. M. Wier, N. D. Sperry, and Augustus Brown. The arms company closed its doors for the day of the funeral in honor of its founder.

After the service at the house, the carriages proceeded to the Evergreen Cemetery, and the local preacher prayed a brief interment invocation. Oliver Winchester was laid to rest next to his long-deceased infant son, his daughter Annie Dye, and his grandsons. At age seventy-three, Jane grieved the death of her husband of almost half a century. Jennie and Thomas and their children comforted her, but William was inconsolable. The loss of his father was an eventuality that he could not bear. Sarah stayed at his side, but he was devastated. He faced the daunting challenge of managing all the Winchester interests, a serious threat to his already fragile health.

William was well enough on January 25, 1881, to go to Manhattan, where he and Sarah met Estelle and George Gerard to sign papers before a notary for Sarah Pardee's estate.[19] Apparently the Gerards' marriage was in trouble by then, as there is no account of the two of them together after this date; they divorced sometime within the next few years. On February 7, the Winchesters appeared once again before a notary, this time in New Haven. William may have begun to doubt his recovery, for two days later he returned to New York and signed a draft of his will. In the following weeks, William wrote two large bank drafts to Sarah, one on February 17 and one on March 2, totaling $7,500.[20]

On that same March 2, the board of directors of Winchester Repeating Arms met and released William from his role as president, which he had assumed upon his father's death. He knew about this action, and may even have requested it, but it must have been quite alarming for Sarah even though she knew very well that the company needed an active manager and that her husband would never be well enough to fill that role. William Converse was made acting president, switching positions with William, who was named vice president. Once again, Bennett remained as secretary.

The family did not let many people know the extent of William's latest illness, and his condition in the first days of March looked like what he had suffered in other winters. The Visiting Nurse Association of New Haven provided medical help, but William did not rally as he had previously. Sarah waited for his strength to return, but two doctors, named Cheney and Mitchell, were summoned. Each dedicated considerable time at William's bedside, but at 9:30 p.m. March 7, 1881, William Wirt Winchester died at the Prospect Street home from a tubercular condition that had persisted for years. The next day, the newspaper noted that "his death last evening was a surprise to his many friends and acquaintances." It described William as "a companionable gentleman [who] called about him a large circle of warm and appreciative friends who will sincerely mourn his death."[21]

Jane Winchester arranged the memorial service for her son and requested the Baptist minister. Undertakers Robert and John Blair prepared William's remains for burial and built a casket. Once again carriages arrived at the house on the hill, condolences were whispered, and the entourage proceeded to Evergreen Cemetery, where William was buried next to his infant daughter, Annie, who had died fifteen years earlier. Sarah insisted on a cemetery plot and marker distinct from the senior Winchesters'. If the little family had not had its own home in this life, it would for the hereafter. The granite monument marking William's grave is not a traditional headstone like the surround of the Oliver Winchester family, but resembles a boulder from a natural setting. Years later, its polished face was inscribed with William's, Sarah's, and baby Annie's names and death dates.[22] The widow deposited money for the perpetual care of the Evergreen Cemetery graves of William and Annie, but over the years she worried about its condition and sent additional money.[23]

The untimely deaths of Sarah Winchester's mother, father-in-law, and husband, falling one upon another, left her an extraordinarily wealthy woman. It took a few years to determine just how wealthy, and to absorb the concept of the independence and freedom that her money could purchase. When William died, Sarah was just over forty. She had never lived in her own home, and like most other women of the era, had never kept her own finances. She had never personally purchased real estate, and never invested her own money. She simply did not know the facts of her financial situation. The immediate task before Sarah was to step beyond emotion to the practical tasks of settling her husband's estate. She had accompanied William to New York when his will was drawn just a month before his death and was aware that she was an executrix. The will read,

> I William W. Winchester of the city of New Haven, State of Connecticut do make and publish the following as my last will. First, my just debts being first paid I give, devise, and bequeath all the rest and residue of my estate both real and personal & wherever situate, to my beloved wife Sarah L. Winchester in fee simple absolutely & forever. Second, I appoint my said wife Executrix and Thomas G. Bennett and William W. Converse both of New Haven Executors. Hereafter I direct that no bond be required either from said Executrix or from said Executors. In witness whereof I have hereto set my hand and seal at the city of New York this 9th day of February AD 1881.
> William W. Winchester.[24]

Sarah took comfort in the fact that Thomas Bennett and William Converse would offer counsel. She was not sure what William's death meant in financial terms. She knew only that her husband, her friend and helpmate, was gone.

Sarah's mother's estate had not been settled by the time William died in March 1881. In a practice common at the time, creditors and debtors were called forward by a notation in the newspaper and "a notice on the signpost nearest to where the deceased last dwelt."[25] Pardee was owed $1,100 in rents for houses, and her estate was billed for medical care and funeral expenses. Sarah and each of her siblings inherited a one-sixth interest in the real estate and stocks, bonds, and cash in their mother's estate. Her stock portfolio consisted of 224 shares in the Winchester Repeating Arms Company, valued at $22,400 altogether, which were divided among the heirs. Adding in other assets, each of her six adult children received $4,313.48. Sarah Burns Pardee did not die a poor woman. Her son, Leonard M. Pardee, however, was strapped for cash and held two very large mortgages. He immediately signed over his portion of his mother's estate to his sister Sarah in return for ready bank drafts.

Pardee had given homes to Mary, Belle, and Estelle, but she still owned a few other properties, which were sold.[26]

Oliver Winchester's estate was vastly more complex. Oliver named as coexecutors his son, his son-in-law Thomas Bennett, and his trusted employee and Sarah's brother-in-law, William Converse. His will was probated on December 20, 1880, and as was the procedure after Sarah Pardee's death, notice to creditors was posted on a signpost near the Prospect Street house and in the newspaper. Jane was to live out her life in the house on the hill. Horses, carriages, household furnishings, clothing, jewelry, and art were to be distributed among Jane, William, and Jennie. An assortment of promissory notes was collected. A large portion of Oliver's wealth was 4,000 shares of Winchester Repeating Arms Company stock, valued at $400,000. At this juncture, of the 10,000 shares of stock issued from the Winchester Repeating Arms Company, Sarah Winchester owned 777, including those she inherited from her mother. Her sister-in-law, Jennie Bennett, owned 400, and in the wake of Oliver's death, Jane owned 4,440 shares. According to Oliver's will, upon Jane's death her shares would be divided in half and inherited by Jennie Bennett and William Winchester. Since Sarah was William's heir, she would receive his portion when her mother-in-law died.

Various pieces of real estate were to be kept or disposed of at the direction of the executors. A site adjacent to the arms factory was appraised at $50,000. Oliver had also owned a parcel where a school had been built at Shelton and Division streets, which was listed as worth $3,000. The executors sold some real estate and invested as well. The Court Street property, where the shirt factory had been and where the Winchesters had lived for their first dozen years in New Haven, was sold. The proceeds were invested in land that adjoined the current gun factory to allow for future expansion. An assortment of railroad, bank, and utility stocks and bonds left to Jane were worth about $75,000.

Oliver's will established a $50,000 trust to benefit his grandson, Oliver W. Dye. Groomed since boyhood for the arms industry by his powerful grandfather, Ollie would come into the trust when he reached his thirtieth birthday in 1889. But for reasons that are open to speculation, whether he was an alcoholic, a gambler, or a homosexual, he was never accepted by his strictly Presbyterian father nor by his mother's family. He played the part of the recipient of inherited wealth who squandered many chances at an upright life. Sometime during the 1890s he ventured down a traditional path and married Elizabeth H. Schenck in Fulton County, New York. The marriage quickly declined, and the couple were divorced by the turn of the century. All efforts to rescue Ollie eventually failed, and most of the family was embarrassed by the man. Even a bequest from his grandmother, Jane Winchester, did not save Ollie from himself. Sarah Winchester noted ruefully to Jennie Bennett that for Ollie, "money in trust would serve his best interests far better than actual possession of it."[27] Years later a rumor circulated in California that a nephew of Sarah Winchester's came to ask his old aunt for cash and she refused to see him but sent a check to the parlor on a silver tray. If there is any truth to the rumor, this is the young man it would have been—her husband's nephew, Ollie Dye. He disappeared from the family and from history in about 1900.

By and large, Oliver Winchester's estate was put in a trust to benefit his wife for her lifetime, then be divided between Jennie and William or their heirs. It is unlikely that Jane Winchester could have broken it if, for some reason, she did not want to include Sarah. William's portion, then, about $300,000, which amounted to half the probated value of Oliver's will, was inherited by Sarah.

An inventory of William Winchester's estate showed that he owned 521 shares of arms company stock that went directly to Sarah. She also inherited cash and other stocks and bonds, two horses with harness, two chaises, and one coupe. Some household furniture, including the organ she had moved from her mother's house, completed the legacy left her. William's estate was valued at $362,330, in today's dollars about $8 million. Since the amount included the $300,000 worth of stock from his father's will, which would not have gone to him until his mother died, for the time being, until Jane Winchester died, Sarah Winchester in her own right controlled 777 shares of Winchester Repeating Arms Company stock, a value of $77,700.[28] Between 1880 and 1885 she earned an average of $7,900 annually as dividends from the stock in her possession. In today's dollars, it would be about $160,000 per year.

William's executors, Sarah, Thomas Bennett, and William Converse, established a system whereby Sarah's financial dealings were run through the Winchester Repeating Arms Company. If she desired a bank draft, a withdrawal of cash, or the ability to invest, Converse carried out her wishes at the arms company.[29] A year before William died, he had earned $4,500 in salary as vice president of the arms company, and he had been awarded cash bonuses along with stocks, which provided regular cash dividends. Sarah did not have an immediate need for cash. So as Bennett and Converse managed the arms company and administered the estate of Oliver Winchester, they were also called upon to handle Sarah's finances. The two men supervised every detail, and as a result became the most influential financial advisers to three of the wealthiest women in New England: Jane Winchester, Jennie Winchester Bennett, and Sarah Winchester.

When Oliver Winchester died, William automatically took over as president of the Winchester Repeating Arms Company and named William Converse vice president, with Thomas Bennett remaining as secretary. As a son-in-law, Bennett had expected to outrank Converse, so he was dismayed by the new slate of company officers. Although for some months in the final year of his father's life William had asserted authority in company decisions, becoming president brought pressures and demands for which he was ill prepared. Moreover, he was physically weak from an extended case of consumption. After his father's funeral William's health went into a sharp decline and he deteriorated rapidly. He was not up to the challenge of filling his father's shoes. William Winchester died just three months later.

Within weeks of William's death, the board of directors of the Winchester Repeating Arms Company gathered and voted to install Converse as company president and Bennett as treasurer, a source of quiet frustration for Bennett, the only male family member remaining on the company board of directors. Apparently no serious consideration was given to the possibility of Sarah Winchester's taking a management role in the company. Elizabeth Colt, upon the death of her husband in 1862, had remained on the board of directors and sponsored a new factory when the old one burned in 1864. So it was not unprecedented to have a woman or the widow of one of a firm's principals maintain a seat on a board. Neither Sarah nor William had displayed the passion for the arms business that the senior Winchester and the Colts had. Sarah retained a boardroom vote only as a majority stockholder, but took no visible role in company management. Bennett accepted the position of treasurer, but a year later, he was elected vice president.[30]

Converse surprised Bennett and the board by openly seeking Bennett's counsel. Converse appreciated Bennett's talents more than Oliver had, and did not presume that his marriage to Jennie had been a plot to take over the company. Converse and Bennett developed a strong working relationship, in many ways reflecting that of Oliver and William. Converse was the affable salesman and Bennett, the detail-oriented engineer. As Converse focused on the business of Winchester, Bennett set his sights on making the design of Winchester rifles as competitive as possible.

Faced with overwhelming grief, Sarah spent some months at the seashore. By June, she had returned to New Haven and dined with Jane Winchester and Thomas Bennett, as mentioned in a letter from Thomas to his wife, Jennie, who was in Boston with their children, Hope and Win.[31] Later Sarah embarked on a European tour. Although she was listed as a permanent resident of the house on the hill at 423 Prospect Street until the middle 1890s, city directories noted that she "removed to Europe."[32]

Her mother-in-law presumed that when Sarah returned to America, she would carry the Winchester mantle in New Haven society. The terminal illness and death of her sister Mary Converse in 1884 brought her back to New Haven.

⊷ ⚔ ⊶

If ever there was a time when Sarah may have sought out spiritual guidance, it would have been in that tumultuous year that culminated with William's death. Did she consult a medium or employ spiritualist techniques, the planchette (Ouija board), for example, to conjure William's spirit to speak to her? Perhaps he would tell her how to proceed with her life. In the early 1880s, the notion that one might contact the dead was based on the hope that science had bypassed religion and represented a rational way to go beyond death, reaching a higher plain. It was not superstitious, nor did it equate to atheism. Rather, it leaned toward a belief in a more benevolent God than traditional Christian faiths preached about, and a God who was not wrathful. It is entirely possible that Sarah visited a medium or attended a séance. Neither would have made her unusual in any way. Women of her class and race commonly visited mediums and spiritualists in that period.[33] It would have indicated an independent person who was reaching past traditional religion to science to answer age-old questions about death and the hereafter and to commune with a deceased spouse. The thinking went that modern science could bridge the chasm between life and death, and that people could learn to communicate with lost loved ones.

In *Prominent American Ghosts* (1967), Susy Smith names a Boston medium that Sarah Winchester supposedly consulted, Adam Coons. The story and the medium's name have been repeated since then in a variety of articles and brochures. An examination of Boston city directories from that time reveals a list of spiritualists, but none by the name Smith gives. Moreover, scholar Emily Mace searched several years' issues of the *Banner of Light,* the most important spiritualist periodical published in Boston in the late nineteenth century, and reported no listing for a medium of that name.[34]

Sarah took decisive steps to put her business affairs in order. Counsel from Bennett and Converse helped, and she appreciated their input, but slowly she began making her own decisions. She hired Charles Morris of the law firm of Morris & Merwin to draw up her will, which remained in effect at the New Haven law firm until 1909.[35]

If she had wanted to, Sarah could easily have joined William's mother and sister in New Haven society and charity circles, but apparently she was much less like other women of her social class than Jane Winchester and Jennie Bennett were, so she chose not to. Jane and Jennie lived out the roles of wealthy matrons and made significant philanthropic contributions. They oversaw the completion of the Winchester Observatory at Yale University that had been funded by Oliver a decade before. Financial problems at Yale during a widespread economic downturn resulted in the opening of a scaled-down version in 1882. The observatory housed the Yale heliometer, a divided-objective telescope, at the time the only one in America. It measured six inches in diameter, the largest heliometer in the world. A second dome held an eight-inch telescope. The observatory was important to Yale's science department for the next seventy years, but by 1920 it had dropped the "Winchester" in its name, and after that it was known as the Yale Observatory. The building was razed in the 1950s, but the house next door, at 459 Prospect Street, which had been the house for the Yale Observatory officer, still stands.

Jane made other significant contributions to Yale University. She donated $130,000 for the construction of Winchester Hall, which was completed in 1892. Then, in 1895, she and Jennie established a fund at Yale in honor of William Winchester to provide an annual award for graduates who wished to further their study in architecture by traveling abroad. There is no indication of what Sarah thought about this, or whether she was asked to contribute to the fund, but the award highlights William's interest in the field of architecture. The William Wirt Winchester Traveling Fellowship remains a prestigious prize to this day.

If the relationship between Jane Winchester and her daughter-in-law was strained, it was not obvious. Sarah sent lovely gifts to William's mother on birthdays and holidays, and in turn, Jane sent notes of thanks. Sarah always sent two gifts even though her mother-in-law's birthday fell just after Christmas. Among the gifts Sarah sent were a salad spoon and fork of ivory with ebony handles for Christmas and a reading glass with a handle of iridescent pearl for birthday. For Christmas in 1890, Sarah sent her a silver bonbon dish, and for birthday a little silver tea strainer. In 1891, she decided on a silver crumb tray and a bread fork. In 1892, when Jane received a Japanese ivory carving and a cut-glass mucilage bottle with a silver top, she wrote to Sarah that it matched perfectly the silver fittings on a writing desk that Tom Bennett had given her. Each year the gifts that Sarah sent to "little mother" were unique and specially chosen. From 1894 to 1896, she sent her a silver sugar bowl and cream pitcher from India, with native handwork of a jungle motif; a bohemian glass pitcher; a Japanese ivory tray; a silver bedroom candlestick; and a silver bread tray. Of the silver vase she sent in 1897, Sarah later thought, "I should have sent it with a sad heart if I had realized it would be the last."[36]

Jane Winchester lived to be ninety years of age. She drafted a will about six months after her husband died, and it remained intact until her death seventeen years later. Sarah Winchester was not named in the will. Jane left all her personal possessions to her daughter, Jennie Bennett, and left money in trust for a sister and a niece. The inventory of real estate and stocks and bonds on hand at the time of her death in March 1898 belie the simplicity of the will. Jane had been very wealthy, and her daughter now was also very rich. Sarah inherited William's portion of his father's stock in the repeating arms company, as specified in Oliver's will.

Jennie Bennett went on to honor her mother by funding the $95,000 Jane Ellen Hope Building at Yale University designed by architect Leoni Robinson in 1901. As the outpatient department of the hospital, it offered medical care to the poor and became the face of the institution in the community. The dedication plaque described Jane Winchester as a woman "whose life was lived simply and quietly in doing the duty that lay nearest at hand with no thought of self and was filled with kindness and helpfulness to others."[37] It is not clear why Jennie used her mother's family name rather than the Winchester name except to specifically memorialize her mother as distinct from the arms company and her father. Oliver's donations had funded science, engineering, and astronomy facilities. The Jane Ellen Hope building housed the health clinic dispensary, which provided health care to women and indigents. In 1982 the building was completely renovated as teaching facilities for Yale's School of Medicine under the direction of architects Alexander Purves and Allen Dehar.

Sarah Winchester did not make significant philanthropic contributions till twenty years later. After her sister's death brought her home from her travels in Europe, the middle-aged widow had two choices. She could stay in New Haven, live on Prospect Hill with her aging mother-in-law, and do charity work. Or, she could leave the city of her birth, strike out on her own, and build a new life. She opted for the latter. She had all that money could buy, including freedom, and clearly she did not want to remain in New Haven at the house on the hill socializing with Jennie Bennett and her mother-in-law in a looming shared widowhood. She began to make plans. Less than one year after Mary Converse's death, Sarah Winchester left New Haven for California.

CHAPTER 5

A California Dream

S ARAH WINCHESTER HAD THE MONEY TO DO WHAT SHE PLEASED AND GO where she wanted. She could have occupied the finest house in New York or an isolated villa in Italy, so one wonders what possessed her to choose the mostly unknown California. She had traveled extensively with William, and in the years since his death had been in Europe again. In fact the New Haven public believed that she was living in Europe.[1] Why, then, California?

Although Europe gave her distance from New Haven and all its burdensome memories, her well-established American roots would not be easily displaced. Neither did she harbor a desire to cut ties with family. But every turn in New Haven must have summoned phantoms from a sad past. Even New York was too close, with its inevitable social demands and business commitments. California, on the other hand, was as far as she could venture without leaving the country. It offered what historian Kevin Starr codified in his book *Americans and the California Dream, 1850-1915* a new way to interpret life and a new vantage point from which to review the past. The allure of a Spanish heritage, Gold Rush legends, and an agreeable climate made it a place where a life could be remade and health improved. The soil was so amenable that even one of limited experience could cajole it into bountiful production. She could invest her most personal hopes in the Golden State.

California's vast geography of valley and mountain, seaside and desert, stretching from the 42nd parallel south to Mexico, had been claimed by Spain in the eighteenth century just as serious foment for American Revolution was beginning in New England. With a string of twenty-one missions hugging the coastline from south to north, Franciscan missionaries introduced European culture, language, domestic and farming arts, plants and animals (along with disease and discrimination), forever changing the landscape and the people. In the beginning of the nineteenth century, Spain lost influence in its distant colonies and they fell away like seeds scattering from a flower in decline. Mexico declared independence from Spain in 1821, and California was part of Mexico until the Mexican War of 1846. As that war ended in 1848 with the U.S. gaining California and a huge portion of the Southwest, nuggets of gold had been found at John Sutter's mill in Coloma, setting off the largest gold rush the world had ever seen. In 1850, California was admitted to the Union as the thirty-first state—a free state—breaking the exceedingly volatile deadlock between slave and free states and pushing the nation toward Civil War.

Thirty years later, during the 1880s, when Sarah Winchester was considering moving there, California was undergoing a vast reorganization in virtually all aspects. Enormous cattle-grazing ranchos dating from the Mexican era were whittled down, divided and subdivided into vineyards and fruit orchards. Railroads were constructed, new banks found investors, and the state's politicians realigned themselves to reflect changing demographics. Chambers of commerce and business interests initiated marketing campaigns to lure citizens from the East. Prospective settlers, people like Sarah Winchester, saw promotional pamphlets and read testimonials about an idyllic California.

The most widely read was Charles Nordhoff's *California for Health, Pleasure, and Residence: A Book for Travelers and Settlers* (1872), a railroad promotional piece designed, among other things, to dispel lingering fears about the lawlessness of Gold Rush California. He suggested, as any good railway promoter would, that Americans should relocate within their own country instead of venturing to Europe or Asia. New rails allowed settlers to return to the East within a week if obligations arose. One could more easily maintain family ties in the United States than from abroad.

Nordhoff was among the first to formulate the perception of California as a tourist destination. He resolutely proclaimed, "certainly in no part of the continent is pleasure-traveling so exquisite and unalloyed a pleasure as in California. Not only are the sights grand, wonderful, and surprising in the highest degree, but the climate is exhilarating and favorable to an active life."[2] Other persuasive claims emphasized California's most popular selling point, its mild weather. "There is not a better, more salubrious, tonic and health-giving climate on the Pacific Coast than in Santa Clara Valley. The mean temperature is about 70 degrees in the Summer and 55 degrees in the Winter."[3] For anyone who had ever suffered a nor'easter, this was profoundly tempting. At just past forty years of age, Sarah Winchester was beginning to feel the effects of rheumatoid arthritis, a malady that dogged her remaining forty years. Warmer temperatures could go some way toward alleviating her painful discomfort. Her doctor suggested that her health would improve if she lived in a drier and warmer environment.[4]

One particularly intriguing essay was written by a fellow Connecticut native, the controversial Reverend Henry Ward Beecher:

> The fame of your valley has come over the plains and mountains and assailed our ears until, with the description of the scenery, of mountains, of mines, of trees, of shrubs, of farms, gardens and harvests, of people and prospects, I will not say that we were wearied, but will say that we were somewhat stunned, and it gave the belief that if nothing else excelled in California, the art of exaggeration was rife, and yet, having come as an arrow through the air, and without time to fill my mind what I saw upon the surface, teaches me a lesson of the estimation of the truth, and I will say with her of old, "The half has not been told me." This goodly land which, farthest from the East, seems to have been the last work that God had in hand, and he furnished it to suit the home of man the best.[5]

Beecher's comments underscore the impression that westward expansion and manifest destiny were the work of divine will, and those who complied would be duly favored. The last work that God had in hand, indeed. This line of thought placed Winchester safely under the guiding star of a predestined national identity.

Winchester had read accounts of the wonders of California. Ultimately, though, her decision to move across the country was not based solely on promotional pieces. She had fond memories of San Francisco from the early 1870s, when she and her husband examined the West Coast outlet of the Winchester Repeating Arms Company. In California she could continue to seek the financial counsel of William Converse and Thomas Bennett in New Haven, and she was quite sure they still wished to court her powerful boardroom vote. She relied on arms company bookkeepers, and since William's death, all her financial affairs, including banking and real estate transactions, were funneled through them. Could she blend into the landscape in the open territory of the West? Perhaps she was so caught up in her own plans that it never occurred to her that her name, wealth, and social standing would draw even more attention in California than they had in New Haven. She either radically underestimated "Winchester" name recognition or presumed that Californians would not be particularly interested.

Winchester plotted her escape and imagined a self-contained enclave where she had only to rely upon her intellect and bank book to retreat from the outside world. The availability of land in California played very well into her quasi-utopian dream, and it appeared there was no end to hundred-acre parcels available for purchase, and by her standards, for relatively little money. She would buy rich land ripe for whatever hard work and good weather could generate. Despite the fact that she continued to wear black mourning dresses and hats, the whole concept offered an unexpectedly positive outlook for a widow entering middle age.

Even after adding up all the benefits of California, however, Winchester would have needed more than sunshine and a change of scenery. She would have gone to California, just as thousands of others did and continue to today, to escape a troubled past and to find health and happiness. She would no longer be hemmed in by social demands and the expectations of New Haven society, nor haunted by reminders of grief and loss at every turn. She hoped that California still held the magic of the Gold Rush, with treasure to be found just below the surface. She was seeking her own gold, staking her new homestead, knowing very well her inheritance would go a long way toward purchasing the life she wanted. California it would be.

Winchester shared her idea with her sisters and invited them to join her. Belle Merriman and Estelle Gerard needed little coaxing. Buried in the fallout of a broken marriage and possibly an alcohol addiction, Estelle wished to start a new life. She hoped California would provide prosperity and happiness for her children, Saidee and George. Belle may have had to convince her husband, Louis, who was the oldest of the little entourage at just over fifty. Starting over for him could be problematic. Their almost grown children, Daisy and Willie, offered no resistance. With Sarah footing the bill, the choice seemed clear.

The three Pardee sisters found an additional and irresistible motivation. Their older sister, Nettie Sprague, was also moving there. Nettie's husband, Homer Sprague, had accepted the presidency of a small academy for young ladies near San Francisco. All four remaining sisters would be together, then, leaving behind only a brother. Perhaps this prospect was the most tantalizing for Winchester. Beginning in the summer of 1885, one by one, family by family, the Spragues, the Gerards, the Merrimans, and Sarah Winchester boarded trains bound for the West Coast, each stepping toward his or her own as-yet-unrealized California dream.

⊷—⧉⊹⧈—⊶

Mills College was the unwitting linchpin in Sarah Winchester's decision to move to California. When officials at the tiny college in Oakland hired Professor Homer Sprague, they hoped he would bring excellence, distinction, and fund-raising skills to the young woman's institution. They were in for a big disappointment.

Like Sarah's, Homer and Nettie's desire to leave New England was precipitated by a death in the family. When Sarah and Nettie's eldest sister, Mary Converse, died of cancer in October 1884 after a brief few months' illness, Nettie was devastated. Mary's death had been sad for Sarah, but for Nettie, it was a life-altering event. Mary had been Nettie's constant companion, and the two were very much like twins. On and off over the years since their combined wedding day, the two sisters had shared a household. When Homer had gone off to war, Nettie and the children were taken in to Mary's home. When the Converses returned to New Haven after a few years in New York, they stayed with the Spragues.

Homer Sprague knew Mary's death was taking a terrible toll on Nettie. As he cast about for a way to assuage her grief, he secured an invitation to serve as president of a small college for young women in California. Perhaps a move to a new land with a good climate would be just the thing for Nettie. And it appeared that the younger Pardee sisters would also be nearby. So, in the summer of 1885, less than a year after Mary's death, the Spragues sold their Boston home and its contents. Two of their sons, one a lawyer and one a merchant, remained in Boston. A daughter had married a New York clergyman and resided there. Only one child, William, who was studying medicine, joined them in California. The Spragues established themselves at Mills College, in the Oakland hills overlooking San Francisco Bay. Homer's new position, the stunning landscape, and California life appeared the perfect curative for Nettie's grief at the loss of her sister.

When Homer was hired, Mills was undergoing a restorative of its own. The widowed Susan Mills owned the seminary for young women outright, but had initiated a process to turn the institution over to a board of trustees so that it would survive her death. The school had been the lifelong work of both her and her late husband, and she took every precaution to ensure its viability into the future. In her zealous optimism she recruited Sprague sight unseen, based on his reputation and his several publications, from Boston.

When the Spragues arrived on September 30, 1885, they were greeted with exuberant fanfare and escorted to their new quarters at the school. An official presidential inauguration was held in October, and the school put on a real California welcome. Mills College could not have been more enthusiastic and laudatory to Professor Sprague and his wife. A boisterous parade followed the swearing-in to welcome the new and much-anticipated educator from the East. Everyone associated with Mills, from the students to Susan Mills, believed Sprague would bring a brand of legitimacy that the school had yet to enjoy.[6]

Rather than making him feel important, the hoopla had the opposite effect on Sprague. He was appalled and embarrassed by the public spectacle, and he complained about the "Barnum-like show business," and the "the pomp and parade and 'booming' with which my arrival here was heralded." Although his first impression of California and of Mills was not positive, he set to work at once getting to know the students, the faculty, the curriculum, and Susan Mills. He hoped to make a name for himself by modeling Mills on Wellesley, the highly acclaimed women's academy in Massachusetts. To that end, he taught classes in Greek, Latin, and English from two to five hours per day, and each week he delivered school-wide lectures. Sprague's assertion that "show business" was a mainstay of California life proved quite prophetic, but he was never able to appreciate the casual atmosphere of everyday life in the West.[7]

The chemistry between Homer Sprague and Susan Mills was explosive from the very beginning. Sprague wanted exclusive authority over behavior and curriculum. Mills was reluctant to give up her influence. Sprague vociferously objected to the expensive fashionable dress of some of the young ladies, believing it distracted from more serious academic and moral endeavors. He wished to instill "the virtues that ennoble womanhood."[8] When he declared that for an upcoming school event the students were required to dress conservatively, the young ladies appealed to Mills. The aging matriarch sided with the girls, acquiescing to their requests. The girls wore expensive social attire, entirely inappropriate in Professor Sprague's mind. He was shocked and publicly humiliated that Mills had overruled him. He was also irritated by what he perceived as exceedingly slow academic progress. Students were assigned essays to be read at a public event, but he thought the results were so poor that it would be an academic embarrassment to have them read publicly. He ordered the papers corrected, but was horrified to learn than some of the faculty were themselves incapable of making corrections.

Sarah Winchester arrived in California in time to spend the winter of 1885–1886 with the Spragues. It was immediately apparent that Mills College was not a good fit for Homer, and that Nettie missed her three adult children and increasing number of grandchildren in the East. Not only had she lost a sister, but she had also left behind three of her children. Nettie was not as well-traveled as Sarah, and both the Spragues appeared uncomfortable away from their native New England. Despite her sister's unhappiness, Sarah clung to hopes for California. She, for one, was relieved to be away from the house on the hill and New Haven, especially during winter.

By the spring of 1886 it was clear that the Spragues' tenure at Mills College was an unmitigated disaster. In April, Sprague came down with an illness serious enough to keep him in bed for a few weeks. And although some students gave him an engraved gold-handled walking stick at the end of the term, the fact remained that he was not very well liked. The board of trustees asked for his resignation. Sprague refused, reminding the board that he had been hired by Mills and was obviously working for her, not a board of trustees. He was indignant because he felt he had uprooted his wife and sold his New England home under false pretenses. He accused Mills and the board of not disclosing pertinent facts about the school. The board declared his position vacant without his resignation, and by the end of 1886 he was without a job.[9]

Homer Sprague retaliated with his best weapon. He published an essay in booklet form entitled *To My Friends,* which detailed meetings, letters, and memos between himself and the Mills College Board of Trustees. It was a brutal and scathing boardroom exposé that accused the board and Mills of lying to him to lure him into the presidency. He claimed that he was never told that Mills owned the school and property personally, and was leasing it to the board. He believed this financial setup to be an anomaly in academia that bordered on the unethical. In his most caustic accusation, he stated that "calling an inferior school a college does not make it such."[10]

Mills was terribly embarrassed and shocked that Sprague actually published his accusations. She felt she had to defend her board of trustees if for no other reason than to appease benefactors. She counter-published her *Rebuttal of Homer Sprague's "To My Friends,"* claiming that Sprague had had all the pertinent facts before he came and had known very well the financial and administrative structure of the school. Mills found Sprague to be a self-righteous and arrogant man whom she was pleased to be rid of.

Sarah Winchester had known Homer Sprague for thirty years and had repeatedly seen him refuse to compromise rigid morals or controversial progressive ideals. He could not bring himself to converse with or tolerate anyone who offered a dissenting opinion. He had been run out of town as president of the Connecticut State Normal School because he had made so many enemies as he advocated for a free public-school system. He had been fired from a Massachusetts school for abolitionist speeches. The stiff-necked Homer Sprague could not look past political or moral disagreement to get work done. His claims about Mills may have been true and the college's academic standards low, but the underlying problem may have been that neither he nor Nettie could acclimate to casual California.

Sprague found a new position in an outpost even more remote than the California coast. He became the president of the four-year-old University of North Dakota. His tenure there lasted only a couple of years, and "the severity of the winter climate and the health of his family caused Mr. Sprague to remove again to California in 1891."[11] By 1900, Nettie finally got her wish and the Spragues returned to New York to live near their married daughter. Homer retired from teaching but was in great demand on the lecture circuit. He found more success as an independent scholar than as part of any institution. Ultimately, Homer Sprague authored scores of articles and thirty books or pamphlets, most of which were essays on Shakespeare's plays. Apparently he worked better alone.

Despite the upset in the Sprague household and the likelihood that Nettie would not remain in California, Sarah was determined to stay, so she began scouting for a place to call her own. She began by asking advice of Edward "Ned" Rambo, the San Francisco agent for the Winchester Repeating Arms Company.[12] He had been hired out of Chicago to operate San Francisco's sales office, the major Winchester outlet in the West. Without hesitation Rambo insisted that Sarah go to see the Santa Clara Valley, thirty miles south of San Francisco. Rambo told Winchester that the charming valley had become his "new haven," and he believed she would like it as well. Her aching joints reminded her that she did not want to live in foggy and damp San Francisco, and she agreed to accompany him on a tour. Ned Rambo proved a valuable guide as she said good-bye to the Spragues and boldly embraced California.

In the spring of 1886, with Ned Rambo as her escort, Sarah Winchester toured the valley by carriage. Rambo, his wife, Mary, and baby son had been in San Francisco since 1883. Under Rambo's direction, the Winchester sales office took a decided turn upscale. He abandoned the deteriorating Battery Street location and opened a new office on Market Street, the city's main commercial thoroughfare, just a block from the exclusive Palace Hotel. Rambo's gun and ammunition sales stood out as a significant entry on the arms company's account ledgers. He rented a flat for his family, but neither he nor his wife was particularly fond of city life. It was not long before he discovered the Santa Clara Valley, and was so enamored of it that he purchased thirty acres there.

When Sarah Winchester first laid eyes on what today is the Silicon Valley she was enthralled. In the middle 1880s the Santa Clara Valley was an expanse of cattle-grazing land. The pastoral scene, so simple and quiet, lay far from industry's hum and crowded streets. Lying at the southwest edge of San Francisco Bay, thirty miles south of San Francisco and twenty miles east of the Pacific, the valley reminded her of the Llanada Alavesa, an open plain at the base of the Pyrenees in the Basque country that she and her husband had seen ten years before on a trip to Switzerland. She remembered a wide-open valley dotted with cultivated land and decorated with large, old estates and rural villages. The California valley she saw on tour with Rambo bore a striking resemblance to that European valley, and at once she felt a strong desire to stay there.

About forty miles long and averaging thirty miles wide, the Santa Clara Valley is surrounded by undulating foothills framing it in bright grass, green in winter and soft golden brown in summer. Although the valley is not very far from San Francisco, its climate is dramatically different. When the San Francisco peninsula is blanketed in coastal fog, temperatures can reach a high of only about sixty degrees in summer, while the valley is fog-free and can be as much as thirty degrees warmer. This fact alone was enough to entice the arthritic Winchester.

It so happened that when Rambo showed Winchester his property, he also took her to see a ranch for sale a short distance away. A forty-five-acre place owned by John Hamm, the ranch was quiet, warm, and isolated. The property formed a reverse L shape, stretching south down the Santa Clara—Los Gatos Road from Stevens Creek Road, with the lower portion containing the bulk of the acreage. At one time, the Hamm property had been part of the 270-acre Hargis wheat ranch, but portions had been sold for smaller fruit farms. This property had an eight-room farmhouse that appeared to be smack-dab in the middle of the sprawling valley, hills rising in the distance in every direction. The springtime view presented at this site was irresistible.

By New Haven's standards, the Hamm house was very small. Winchester knew the modest house could be enlarged, but she worried that the farm did not have enough land. Seeing the vast landscape assuaged her doubts, and she calculated that in the future she could buy adjoining properties. She went ahead with the purchase, paying Hamm $12,570 for the house and forty-five acres. She christened her new home "Llanada Villa," reminiscent of the Llanada Alavesa.

Rambo understood and perhaps explained to Winchester that the valley was on the verge of a major transformation the likes of which had not been seen since the Spaniards first arrived in 1769. By the time Rambo and Winchester toured the valley, grazing and grain growing had depleted the soil. But the temperate weather and alluvial soil deposited over thousands of years by flooding creeks and rivulets made ideal conditions for successful fruit farming. Rambo had planted an orchard on his modest thirty acres, and he encouraged Winchester to do likewise. Far surpassing his optimistic predictions, the following year, 1887, a quarter of a million fruit trees were planted on what had been wheatfields in the

Santa Clara Valley.[13] Millions more were planted in the following decade. Sarah Winchester and Ned Rambo were among the earliest settlers coming to the valley to grow fruit.

Over the next thirty years Winchester's house was variously linked with three distinct communities—San José, Santa Clara, and Campbell. Letters addressed to Winchester to any of these towns would find their way to the widow. Moreover, the post offices, school districts, and other official boundaries shifted as the population grew, so her home was listed, at one time or another, in each town. The Winchester place sat equidistant, approximately two to three miles from each.

The largest town in the valley was San José, the self-proclaimed "Garden City," an old pueblo dating from 1777 and California's first secular settlement. Fifty miles south of San Francisco, it still had features of its Spanish and Mexican heritage. In the 1880s just as Winchester was making her purchase, the old St. Joseph's Catholic Church sat on one side of what had been a large and extremely dusty colonial plaza. Adjacent to it teetered a dilapidated Chinatown, although in a fit of anti-Chinese sentiment in 1887 someone torched it, forcing the Chinese to move to the edges of the city limits. Two years later, the oversized and garish (even in its day) Gothic-Victorian City Hall was built across from the former Chinatown. The Spanish ancestry of the town of about 15,000 people faded as the plaza was reduced in size into a Victorian oval and landscaped with palms and statuary, green grass and cobbled walkways, completing a metamorphosis from pueblo plaza to Main Street district.

San José had educational institutions, although none as revered as New Haven's Yale. California's State Normal School (today's San José State University) was located in town, and Stanford University was on the drawing board at the north end of the valley. Two religious institutions were also located nearby, the Catholic Santa Clara College (eventually Santa Clara University) for young men and the Methodist College of the Pacific (later removed to Stockton as University of the Pacific). A variety of secondary schools made high school education widely available.

The ostentatious Victorian Vendome Hotel was built on twelve acres on the north edge of downtown, a dozen three- and four-story office buildings housed commercial enterprises, and Santa Clara County and Agnew hospitals cared for the sick and the insane, respectively. An amazing and world-renowned observatory was completed in 1888 atop the 4,000-foot Mount Hamilton to the east. Lick Observatory was named for James Lick, an eccentric who had made a fortune in real estate during the Gold Rush. Like Oliver Winchester's namesake observatory at Yale, this West Coast location facilitated important advances in the study of astronomy. Lick Observatory has outlived Yale's, which was razed in

1956, and remains a scientific resource right down to today. When Sarah Winchester stood on the front porch of her new house and looked to the east, she could see the glistening white speck of Lick Observatory on the mountaintop in the distance.

The oddest feature of San José was also the one of which its residents were proudest: a 207-foot-tall tower looming over a main intersection in town. The Electric Light Tower at Santa Clara and Market streets was lit for the first time on December 13, 1881, making San José the first city in California to use electric lights.[14] The magnificent symbol of inventiveness and progress was lost on Sarah Winchester, who could have bought any house in town. She preferred to be away from the spotlight, social demands, and urban life, even if it meant not having electricity. She wanted a farm.

In 1887, San José was 7.5 miles square and boasted concrete sidewalks and several lines of horse cars. The towns of San José and Santa Clara were connected by The Alameda, a willow-lined road built by American Indians at the behest of the Franciscan Friars during the Spanish colonial period. The mission in Santa Clara was one of California's chain of twenty-one and was that town's most distinctive feature. The mission grounds had been transformed by Jesuit priests into a school for young men, and Santa Clara College had opened as the first college in California in 1851. Santa Clara also had an old plaza, but on a smaller scale than San José's, and its small commercial district flanked a main street with a stagecoach stop and an assortment of merchants, including a notary public whom Winchester often hired to witness official documents. Pacific Manufacturing Lumber Company stood on the outskirts of town, and supplied Winchester's prodigious appetite for lumber.

Campbell lay south of Santa Clara, on the road to Los Gatos. In other words, one would pass Winchester's place making the trip from Santa Clara to Campbell. It was named for the farmer upon whose land the tiny town sprouted in the middle 1880s. Campbell was not an old pueblo like Santa Clara or San José. Instead, Campbell grew in importance as the fruit-canning industry took hold in the valley. If a gardener or orchard worker at the Winchester place needed the odd farm implement or gardening supplies, he would head to Campbell. The Campbell School District served the Winchester property, and children of her employees attended Meridian School just down the road.

Winchester's Llanada Villa was situated outside of the towns on a country lane called the Santa Clara—Los Gatos Road. Precisely what its name implied, it led from the town of Santa Clara south past Campbell to Los Gatos and then on over the Santa Cruz Mountains. In the twentieth century, after the death of Sarah Winchester, the road was renamed

Winchester Road, and later Winchester Boulevard. Her property line commenced at Stevens Creek Road, which had been named for Elisha Stephens, a grizzled frontiersman who led the first wagon train over the Sierra Nevada in 1844, predating the more infamous Donner Expedition by two years. Official records misspelled Stephens's name, accounting for the difference in spelling between the road and the man.

The 43,000 people living in the valley when Winchester arrived were a microcosm of California's population. The majority had not been born in the state, but were displaced Southerners or had come from the East. Northern Europeans, mostly from Ireland, Germany, Scandinavia, France, and Britain made up the second-highest ranking. The county had a significant Chinese population of about 4,000, mostly working in fields or as household servants. Descendants of Spaniards and Mexicans of old California were dwindling, and there were very few American Indians and even fewer black people. Japanese laborers had yet to arrive.

Sarah Winchester staffed her house and farm with these valley people. Her first hire was Ned Rambo. He continued to operate the Winchester office in San Francisco, but also took over management of her farm as foreman. For several months a year, the Rambos lived at their farmhouse a half mile away. Winchester retained her New Haven reinsman, Frank Carroll, an Irishman. She set his family up in a house on the ranch. Over the years other employees were American, Danish, Italian, Irish, Chinese, and Japanese.

<hr />

Sarah Winchester's plan to gather her brood of relatives under one roof proved better in theory than in practice. Each sister had family complications, and after Homer Sprague's debacle at Mills College, it was evident that attempts to keep the sisters together were untenable. After Sprague accepted the presidency of the University of North Dakota, Sarah could rescue Nettie only for a few weeks each year. When Nettie visited, she came alone. After a three-year stint in the frigid, arid North Dakota, the Spragues returned to California and lived in Berkeley, where Homer started a successful lecture bureau. By the turn of the century, they had relocated to New York City.

Sarah's sisters Belle and Estelle, with their respective families, arrived late in 1887. Estelle had recently been divorced, so she came with just her nearly grown children, Saidee and George. The remote Llanada Villa could not have been in sharper contrast to the bustle of New Haven, and the isolation of Sarah's new home shocked her family members. The men in the family—Louis Merriman and his son, Willie, and young George ᵣerard—wanted work, but not farm work. They were city men. It would be highly unlikely for them to find a livelihood out in the middle of the valley. Adding to their discomfort with the situation, the farmhouse was undergoing a massive remodel. Although plans were in place to accommodate all, the sisters concluded that each family should have its own living quarters until construction was complete. It was probably decided that there would be positive aspects of having a bit of distance and independence from the wealthy Sarah, too. Within months of their arrival, by the spring of 1888, Sarah's sisters and their families were ensconced elsewhere.

Still smarting from her divorce, Estelle had accepted Sarah's offer of a refuge to start a new life. Her son and daughter, at ages seventeen and nineteen, did not seem reluctant to put three thousand miles between themselves and their father. Estelle claimed that her children needed the social and business opportunities of the city, but in reality living at the ranch would have been very restrictive for Estelle herself. The fact that Sarah's house was incomplete gave Estelle a good excuse to move to San Francisco, where the climate and activity level were more in keeping with her familiar New Haven. With Sarah's financial support, the Gerards moved into a San Francisco row house at 504 Buchanan. About a year later, when it had become clear that Sarah's house would not be finished anytime soon, the Gerards moved to more permanent quarters at 524 Turk Street.

Estelle told new acquaintances in California that she was a widow. In truth, her ex-husband remained in New Haven, owned his own business, and lived a long life.[15] Estelle did not work, but lived on the monthly support payment of $150 provided by her sister. She visited the Winchester ranch often, boarding the San José—bound train in the city. Frank Carroll, in a top hat, met her at the station and drove her the short distance to Llanada Villa in a carriage. By 1893, after six years in California, the youngest Pardee sister, at age forty-eight, began to show signs of illness. Toward the end of the year her health took a decided turn for the worse. Fearing the damp San Francisco climate was compromising her weakening condition, George and Saidee took their mother to Aunt Sarah's ranch. They hoped the warmer, drier weather in the valley would heal her and that Sarah could coax her back to health.

Winchester called in her personal physician, Euthanasia Meade, M.D., a New Yorker who had earned her medical degree at the University of Pennsylvania, had practiced during the Civil War, and had relocated to San José. One of a handful of woman physicians practicing in California, Meade had launched the Woman's Medical Club of the Pacific and had impeccable credentials, although a more disheartening name for a physician is hard to imagine.[16] Meade's home office was located in down-town San José, but she made calls at the Winchester place to tend Sarah Winchester's worsening rheumatoid arthritis. When Sarah sent a message asking her to come to the ranch to examine Estelle, she complied.

Despite her sister's vigilance and Dr. Meade's treatment, after several weeks at Llanada Villa, Estelle succumbed on January 8, 1894.[17] Her life had been somewhat difficult since she wed at age twenty, and California had not been the curative she needed. The official death record made out by Meade listed the cause of death as cirrhosis, a liver disease often caused by alcohol abuse. Although it is impossible to prove, circumstantial evidence points to an addiction of some sort. That her son was a pharmacist only makes this possibility more intriguing. A newspaper death notice, however, stated that Estelle died of consumption, a malady that was easier to explain than cirrhosis of the liver. In California, Estelle had successfully hidden her divorce, and now her cause of death was also concealed.

All too familiar with the loss of loved ones, Sarah Winchester arranged a funeral for her youngest sister. The three remaining sisters lent emotional support to Saidee and George as well as to each other. Estelle's body was cremated at Cypress Lawn Cemetery near San Francisco—among the earliest cremations in California. The practice had very recently been implemented, and the cemetery had just added a large and elaborate crematorium, styled like an ancient Greek temple. Estelle's ashes were inurned in a niche purchased by Sarah.

Adults by now, Estelle's children chose to remain in the San Francisco Bay Area. In the following years, each married. Like their parents, each also divorced. Taking a more modern tack, though, neither was secretive about it, and both eventually remarried. George opened his own pharmacy, which he maintained for more than twenty-five years. Saidee became a popular published poet, and magazines like *Sunset* and *Overland Monthly* ran her pieces. She was an ardent animal-rights activist and published anti-vivisectionist editorials. Both George and Saidee had cordial relations with Winchester and kept in touch with her throughout the years.

Of all Sarah's relationships with her siblings, the most combustible and the most dear to her was the one she had with Belle. Sarah and Belle were two sides of a coin, the one retiring and ruminative, the other expressive and fiercely opinionated. Belle tried Sarah's patience but also boosted her spirits. She was smart and assertive and bumbling and creative. Belle embraced California—its landscape and freedom and mythology—more than any of the Pardees, including Sarah. Belle had her own reasons for leaving New Haven. Her husband, Louis, had been under the thumb of his father and the carriage business, and she hoped that a new start would make him happy. When he arrived in California, he was fifty-two years old, hardly an age where one could start over then. But that is what Belle hoped. Their children, Marion "Daisy," close to twenty, and Willie, a bit younger, were almost the same ages as their Gerard cousins.

Belle and Louis quickly came to the conclusion that living with Sarah was not their best option and were ebullient when she invested in more land. In the spring of 1888, less than six months after the Merrimans arrived from New Haven, Winchester paid $10,000 gold coin for a home for the family on about twenty-five acres bordering "the county road leading to Mountain View,"[18] an old stagecoach stop and watering hole between San Francisco and San José. During the 1880s, the tiny hamlet of about three hundred grew steadily, and in the year 1887, at the height of the county's population boom and the year before Winchester bought a house for the Merrimans, the town doubled in size. On one summer day, realtors logged sales of a whopping twenty-six town lots, one ten-acre tract, and one five-acre parcel. "The town is alive with excitement," one newspaper writer bubbled, "and many strangers are coming in."[19] Winchester and her sister were among the strangers.

Sarah and Belle set to work immediately renovating the newly pur-chased house for Belle's family. The house dated from at least the mid-dle 1860s, but there is evidence that there was a dwelling on the site a full twenty years earlier, so it may have been forty years old when they bought it. The sisters embellished and added to the old redwood-frame structure. It grew from four rooms to twelve, and took on the look of the Victorian era, which both women favored. They added a porch with a low overhang, hemmed in by carefully milled spindles painted bright white, harkening to the craftsmanship of their father's shop. The sisters chose mismatched windows, giving the house an asymmetrical look, the latest fad in architecture. On one exterior wall, the sisters placed a circular window, paned with four glass pieces. Another outside wall had a gothic window, one that looks remarkably similar to one that had been on the house that Sarah was remodeling for herself.[20] In an odd combination, the windows bejeweled the house with distinctive elegance. Both women were pleased with the outcome, and the home became a treasured refuge for Belle. She named the ranch "El Sueño," or, as the sisters interpreted it, "the daydream." The old farmhouse survives to this day, the oldest inhab-ited residence in Los Altos, California, valued in 2005 at about $3 million.

Sarah Winchester and Belle Merriman were not motivated to buy the twenty-five-acre parcel simply by the house. The sisters planned to set up a horse-breeding business at El Sueño. Of the several horse ranches in the area, most were geared to racehorses. The women decided the market was better for large carriage horses, and since Merriman relatives in New Haven sold carriages, they hoped to partner for a good supply of fancy carriage horses. To carry out the plan, Winchester decided to purchase 140 acres adjacent to Belle and Louis Merriman's house near Mountain View.

Winchester returned to New Haven in the spring of 1888 to take care of some financial business, but instructed Belle and Ned Rambo to bring the transaction to fruition. On an April morning, Belle Merriman drove Ned Rambo out Stevens Creek Road and over the hill to look at the ranch. Rambo reported, "Mrs. Merriman kindly drove me over" to see the ranch. Then he asserted, "I am much impressed that Mrs. Merriman is on the right track and can make a success of raising coach or large carriage horses." After seeing the property with Belle, Rambo penned a lengthy letter to William Converse, who was president of the Winchester Repeating Arms Company and since the death of William Winchester had given Sarah financial counsel. "They [Sarah and Belle] have their hearts set on this scheme [to raise horses] . . . and I believe it is a fair business experiment." He discounted the risks of the enterprise. "I take little stock in a new railroad being built, or such an influx of residents on account of the University [Stanford]."[21] Time proved Rambo wrong on each of his assumptions: the railroad *was* built, a significant number of new residents *did* arrive, and Belle Merriman was *not* successful with her horse-breeding farm. At the time, though, Rambo's advice seemed sound, and he received a prompt reply from Converse indicating that Sarah Winchester wanted to go ahead with the purchase. She made arrangements to transfer cash to the Winchester Repeating Arms Company in New Haven, and Rambo was instructed to draw on the money in San Francisco to make the purchase as her agent.

Winchester expected that the acreage would be hers by the time she returned from New Haven in June. But Rambo telegraphed a message that the "title may have a flaw." The seller was an elderly widow, but despite Winchester's $25,000 cash payment, clear title could not be established within the requisite thirty days. A Judge Laine was demanding to know by what authority the original title on the land had been issued. California land transactions during the 1880s were fraught with complications because during the 1850s so many squatters had simply taken land from rancheros. For succeeding generations, proving title was extremely difficult. Rambo thought it was a case of the judge's splitting legal hairs and sarcastically noted, "I should think he would be an expensive lawyer."[22]

The real estate transaction pitched Winchester headlong into California's complicated land history. Originally the acreage had been part of Rancho

San Antonio, a 4,500-acre estate granted by Governor Juan Alvarado of Mexico to a person named Mesa in 1839. Mesa occupied the rancho and built a modest adobe on the banks of Adobe Creek (the remains of that residence became the Merrimans' new home). The widow who owned the land in 1888, named Diel, was willing and anxious to sell to Winchester for $175 per acre; she asked only that Winchester retain her son as a ranch hand.[23] But a portion of the Diel land had been transferred twenty years earlier under questionable authority. It was Winchester's bad luck to have to foot the bill to get the discrepancy straightened out.

Judge Laine was Winchester's first encounter with the legal profession in California, and therefore he had a good chance to snag her as a client. From her vantage point while visiting New Haven, however, Laine's fees seemed astronomical; she agreed with Rambo on this. She cautioned Rambo to do as much as possible of the work himself since Laine charged so much. Winchester arrived back in the valley the first week of June 1888, and still the transaction was not complete. A meeting had been set up "for all the parties involved," and finally, on Friday, June 8, 1888, the real estate deal was sealed, mainly due to the efforts of Samuel Franklin "Frank" Leib, Laine's younger partner, who appeared more adept in title verification than Laine, and who handily facilitated the meeting and documents.

Winchester had no way of knowing, but her trip to the East that spring would turn out to be the last time she would see William Converse. The following year, his throat was consumed by a cancerous growth, and the fifty-five-year-old president of the Winchester Repeating Arms Company died. Thomas Bennett became president of the company. Converse's death and the new roots Winchester was setting down in California compelled a new financial-management strategy for her. She opted to manage her own money, but for legal advice, she hired Frank Leib. Not only was she impressed by Leib's ability to settle the land dispute, she knew that he had other important clients. He had just been invited to serve on Stanford University's first board of trustees.

Winchester's decision to settle in the Santa Clara Valley happened to coincide with the announcement that Senator Leland Stanford and his wife, Jane, would endow a new university with $20 million in honor of their late son. Stanford had been a railroad magnate and governor of California before becoming a U.S. senator. His latest passion was his horse-breeding farm at the northern end of Santa Clara County. His stock farm set a new trend. Many of San Francisco's wealthy citizens bought land on the San Francisco peninsula and invested in racehorses, emulating or competing with the senator. He carried out experiments with bloodlines and training methods, and his horses earned nineteen world records. He even built a museum that proudly displayed skeletal remains of some of his best horses, documenting physical evidence correlating to his breeding theories. His farm's layout was an elaborate affair, a central quadrangle enclosed by ever-larger quadrangles. It boarded over six hundred horses, making it one of the largest enterprises of its kind in the world. Outbuildings dotted the surroundings; they were a blacksmith's shop, a feed mill, and modest housing units for scores of workers. The Red Barn at the core of the farm still stands on the Stanford University campus, and it is designated a National Historical Landmark.[24]

Leland Stanford had been content to spend his remaining days enjoying racehorses. His plans changed radically, however, when his only son died while on a European tour in 1884. The Stanfords, in stunned mourning, cast about to find meaning in their boy's death. While still in Europe, they visited a spiritual medium, hoping to conjure the spirit of the boy at a séance. This kind of reaction to grief was not considered antireligious or even superstitious. It was a sign of faith that the boy's spirit lived in the next world and an indication of the enormous love the parents felt that they would go to great lengths to communicate with him. At first, no one criticized their patronage of a spiritual medium. Within a short time of young Stanford's death, his parents decided to transform their California horse ranch into a college as a memorial to him. Some questioned the wisdom of the idea, believing California could not support a major university. The couple sought advice from educators in the East, and carefully planned the memorial school.

In the nine years between the deaths of the junior and senior Stanfords, public opinion shifted to a far more judgmental stance on spiritualism. It had been generally acknowledged that the new university was founded just after the Stanfords had visited a spiritual medium. Leland Stanford felt compelled to place in the official record of the school that spiritualism played no role in its establishment. Furthermore, he claimed he had written and signed directives to establish the school before he had visited the psychic. He went on that the séance the couple had attended came to nothing and that he believed the medium was a fraud.[25] Nevertheless, as Jane Stanford stood with tears streaming down her face as the cornerstone was laid in 1887 on what would have been the young Stanford's nineteenth birthday, one could only surmise if her thoughts were more spiritual or material.

Just one year after the cornerstone was laid at Stanford, Sarah Winchester purchased the Merriman house just a few miles to the south. It would have been impossible to live anywhere in the vicinity of Stanford University and not be influenced by it—by its size, its goals, its reason for existence being the death of a youth personifying all the hopes and dreams of her powerful parents. Winchester could relate to the couple's grief and their attempts to keep their son's face in their sights. She understood that perhaps Jane Stanford felt her son was somehow kept alive in the new school. Winchester was also intrigued by the idea of creating a memorial to a loved one, but as yet had not determined how to go about making a fitting tribute to William. She studied the scope and design of the new campus.

Construction at the Stanford campus proceeded at a swift clip. The famous landscape architect Frederick Law Olmstead, who designed Central Park in New York, laid out a plan. Low, mission-style buildings designed by Charles A. Coolidge anticipated and underscored the Mission Revival period in California architecture, a style that emerged as typically Californian. "The primarily single-story buildings' relative simplicity and sparseness; their long, continuous arcades; their deep window reveals; and their red-tile roofs evoked the 'Spanishness' of mission architecture."[26] From the very start, Stanford was a trendsetter.

Stanford's opening-day ceremonies, held on October 1, 1891, in the shadow of a hundred-foot-high Memorial Arch, drew thousands, undoubtedly including the Merrimans. A special train brought San Franciscans, and hundreds came on horseback and by carriage. Setting a university in what was still considered the wilds of California was an experiment with little precedent. Leland Stanford recruited prominent businessmen and potential benefactors to his board of trustees. One of that select group was Winchester's attorney, Frank Leib.

Leland Stanford died less than two years later, and his death, coupled with a general financial crisis across the nation, appeared to doom the fledgling college. The Stanford fortune was tied up in probate courts for more than five years, and the estate was finally settled by the U.S. Supreme Court. Jane Stanford used personal bank accounts to keep the school open, though barely. Her most trusted adviser was Frank Leib. She came to rely on his advice and goodwill, and several statements in her letters reflect a tone of sincere appreciation, such as, "I feel very grateful to you dear friend and I shall ever feel in the future that I have one friend who will not fail me in time of need—God bless you."[27] She was not the only one who believed Frank Leib was a godsend to Stanford University. Years later, in the 1920s, the school's president, Ray Lyman Wilbur, credited Leib with holding together the finances of the infant college, ensuring its financial viability. He asserted that Leib was substantially responsible for successfully managing the Stanford fortune after the death of Senator Leland Stanford, and that "Mrs. Stanford believed in him [Leib] and followed his advice implicitly. . . . For this reason more than any other, perhaps, the Stanford fortune was kept together and made the foundation for a great educational institution."[28]

Frank Leib made a comfortable living from demanding and brilliant, albeit eccentric, women. When Sarah Winchester met Leib in 1888, he was forty years of age to her forty-nine and, hailing from rural Ohio, had been in California about twenty years. He was a handsome man, trim and silver-haired, sporting a substantial, down-turned mustache. The detail-oriented Leib found a lucrative niche in California's legal community because he had the ability to untangle complicated land-title disputes lingering from the Gold Rush, when American settlers and squatters had streamed into the Golden State. Leib was almost always successful at convincing courts to follow his logic in determining ownership. For a time he partnered with his next-door neighbor, Delphin Delmas, who subsequently moved to New York and successfully defended Harry K. Thaw, who was charged in the notorious murder of New York architect Stanford White. By 1880, Leib was in business for himself and endeared himself to Senator Leland Stanford when he facilitated the purchase of "the Farm." It is no wonder that Stanford invited him onto the school's new board of trustees, and no wonder that Winchester later hired him, after he solved the problems she ran into while purchasing the Diel property. It was a decision she never regretted.

The quintessential professional, Leib was urbane, supremely competent, and utterly discreet. Over a period of thirty years, Leib and Winchester corresponded on at least a monthly basis and often more regularly. The letters they exchanged demonstrate the widow's true beliefs and desires more than any other source.[29] They allow us to hear Winchester's opinion directly, unfiltered by the press or by legends. Leib and Winchester found in each other intellectual equals. His advice to Winchester's legal questions was always followed with "I will proceed however you direct me to do so." Leib sent letters to whichever of her homes she was currently occupying, often suggesting, "We will meet, either at my house or at yours, and go over the whole matter."[30]

The meticulous Leib set high ethical standards and possessed great forbearance. The latter characteristic became crucial as his career progressed. It could have been the result of being the youngest of a dozen children, or the fact that he ran off to join the Union Army at age sixteen when his mother died, but for whatever reason, Leib was exceedingly patient and displayed an enormous capacity to keep company with exacting and demanding individuals. The first case in point was Leib's own wife. Lida Leib was a Southern lady who never came to grips with the fall of the Confederacy, since her family's money ran out after the Civil War. She went to San José as a nanny, as it turns out, for the children of one of Leib's legal associates. The auburn-haired girl made an impression on Frank, and in 1874, the two returned to Lida's Kentucky home for their wedding. Lida was never happy about leaving Kentucky, and she returned for extended visits throughout her life.

The Leibs purchased a large frame house on four acres on The Alameda, recently San José's most prestigious street. Lida and Frank established a home with (eventually) five children, Frank's successful career, and a fortune, dubbing it "Leibheim," their personalized German *haus* (although their German antecedents were vague at best; the entire family pronounced the name "leeb" rather than the German "libe"). The Leibs added stables and a magnificent garden with a large arbor and shaded trellis draped in wisteria, grapevines, and climbing roses. They improved a carriage house that today is the only bit of Leibheim that survives; it is listed on the National Register of Historic Places.[31]

Southern charm and beauty notwithstanding, Lida Leib's sentiments did not always match her behavior. While she insisted that she loved having her extended family in her San José home, when sisters arrived with husbands or children in tow, Lida had difficulty with the disruption. Frank often found alternative arrangements for the family members. When a sister and brother-in-law moved to San José, for some reason Lida insisted that her sister home-school her children. "Aunt Lida thought and said that my mother should not send us to school at all," her niece recalled. "But . . . this was one of the times when she held out against Aunt Lida." The niece was enrolled in school.[32]

Lida Leib was not the only strong-willed woman in Frank's life. Jane Stanford, his most important client, had alienated some faculty members and administrators at the new school. When the senator died and Jane Stanford hired Leib as her personal attorney, he had to bridge the growing chasm between the school's president, David Starr Jordan, and the widow. Her focus was on infrastructure, but Jordan needed more resources for academics. The formidable widow Stanford was considered downright irritating by many. She limited the number of women allowed to attend Stanford to a precise 500. When President Jordan equivocated and thought the figure could be adjusted as necessary, she fired back, "I mean literally *never* in the future of the history of Leland Stanford Junior University can the number of female students at any one time exceed 500." Her directive was later adjusted in both 1933 and 1973 so that gender would not be a factor in admission.[33] Frank's presence on the university's board of trustees provided a comfort level to the battling principals. Ultimately Jane Stanford entrusted Leib with the management of millions of dollars in real estate, stocks, and bonds.

When Frank's daughter Elna married in 1901, Jane Stanford sent the bride a stunning sterling silver tea service. In her thank-you note, the young woman wrote, "The silver is perfectly exquisite, and handsome beyond compare, and the tender thought which prompted the gift will make it always my most cherished possession." She added that she was sure Mrs. Stanford would enjoy meeting her new husband because "he is the sort of man you would approve."[34] Elna had married astronomer William H. Wright, and the couple lived high atop Mount Hamilton, two thousand feet above the valley floor at the renowned Lick Observatory, to this day visible from the Winchester house doorstep.

Like many Santa Clara Valley merchants and professionals, Frank Leib carried on a side business in fruit orcharding. As "the prune capital of the world," the valley made it possible for a fair income to be earned from growing, drying, and shipping fruit, and the valley's economy relied on it. Initially Leib invested in a Cupertino orchard, paying close attention to production. He studied fruit growing as diligently as he mastered land law, and before long was quite knowledgeable in growing, harvesting, and drying techniques, purchasing his own Anderson Prune Dipper, a contraption to sulphurize the fruit for preserving.[35] Later, he partnered in the Imperial Prune Orchard, a two-hundred-acre spread in the Berryessa district. Eventually he was invested in almost one thousand acres of fruit orchards.

One of Frank Leib's closest personal friends was California's quirky and unaccountably popular horticulturalist Luther Burbank. The academic community was not so enamored of Burbank, but the public lauded him and sought him out as he experimented in plant hybridization and capitalized on Charles Darwin's theories. Burbank was not like his careful lawyer friend, and did not bother to document his findings or adhere to traditional scientific method. Leib and Burbank were an unlikely pair— the precise attorney and the haphazard farmer—but their friendship lasted for decades. Leib visited Burbank at his Santa Rosa experimental farm whenever he needed to get away on vacation. Sometimes Burbank would send an invitation, and on one occasion he sent a telegram that ordered: "Come." After one visit when Leib's car broke down at Burbank's farm, Burbank chided him to get "a good automobile!"[36] Within a short time, Leib was cruising the mostly unpaved streets of the valley in a Mitchell C4 Runabout, purchased for $1,072. Frank Leib's esteem for Luther Burbank, the self-proclaimed "infidel,"[37] offers another example of his ability to enjoy relationships with eccentric or peculiar people.

Although Leib worked out of his San José office in the town's first "skyscraper," the First National Bank building, he had a reputation throughout Northern California. In 1903 he was appointed by Governor George Pardee (who was not related to the Connecticut Pardees) to the bench of the Santa Clara County Superior Court to finish the term of a retired judge. He declined to remain on the bench after the expiration of the term, but for the rest of his life was referred to as "the Judge" by all who knew him.

In a great stroke of luck, Sarah Winchester came upon Frank Leib, and the two carried on business for more than a quarter century. She benefited from his extensive knowledge of California history and law, and he earned enormous fees. Occasionally he had to justify his bill, and just as infrequently she had to admit that her inclination in a legal issue was misguided. If she wanted the best that money could buy, she got it in Leib. She possessed the intellect and instinct to invest wisely, but Leib's expertise and legal advice kept the money growing. The two partnered as architects of her personal investment strategy, a complicated business plan, and eventually, her bequests.

CHAPTER 6

Labyrinth

S ARAH WINCHESTER'S SAN JOSÉ HOUSE HAS OLD BONES, EVEN OLDER THAN
its current owners claim.[1] A full ten years before she purchased it
in 1886, a two-story wood-frame farmhouse sat tucked in a small
grove fronting the Santa Clara—Los Gatos Road. Although it is not
possible to prove beyond a doubt that the early structure was still standing and therefore the one she bought, it is certain that it occupied the
same site. Accounts of her moving into the neighborhood assert that she
added to an existing house, lending credence to the assumption that at
least portions of today's mystery house date from the early 1870s or earlier. By some estimates, the farmhouse was enlarged to twenty-six rooms
within the first six months.[2] The how and why of Sarah Winchester's
house-building has been the stuff of conjecture since she began. What
motivated the seemingly interminable project, which in reality ended in
1906, and how was it accomplished?

From early childhood, Sarah Winchester had been surrounded by
woodworkers and milling operations. She replicated this familiar and
comfortable backdrop at her new home. Typical of members of the upper
class during the Gilded Age, Winchester displayed personal tastes and
experimented in interior and exterior design in a large and over-orna-
mented home and outdoor space. An English observer at the Columbian
Exposition held in Chicago in 1893 noted that the fair looked like "the
contents of a great dry good store mixed up with the contents of muse-
ums."[3] Winchester's home, as well as many others,' could have been
described with the same words. She borrowed heavily from the fairs.
One example came in the form of a beautiful statue of Hebe, the Greek
goddess of youth, a grapevine garland in her hair, and a goblet extended
in her right hand. It stood sentry at the California viticulture exhibit in
Chicago, where shelves displayed pyramids of wine bottles produced
from West Coast vineyards.[4] Winchester commissioned a statue of Hebe

for her San José home, and the goddess stood in front of the house for decades until the elements took their toll on it. The statue was restored in 2004 and stands once again at the Winchester house.

Many parts of the Columbian Exposition were dismantled and shipped to the California Mid-winter International Exposition held in San Francisco's Golden Gate Park in 1894. Some things from that fair also appeared at Llanada Villa. Winchester installed a version of Strawberry Hill, a hill on the west end of the San Francisco fairgrounds for picnics and taking tea. By having the same name, the little hillock on her ranch conjured the fun at the fair. She enjoyed sharing tea and picnics provided by her Chinese cook with her sisters and her niece. The fair's Japanese Village, in later years the Golden Gate Park's famous tea garden, inspired Asian gardening themes. Winchester's property grew "lush with acres of blooming flower-beds bordered with rare dwarf boxwood and shaded by imported ornamental trees and shrubs." A greenhouse that was a miniature of the horticultural building found at the fair was divided equally between space for birds and a hothouse for orchids. Some have estimated that she had over 110 countries represented in the villa gardens.[5]

The widow reflected an architectural awakening across the country and in San José during the 1880s and 1890s. For the first time, several professionally trained architects were working in the valley. At the beginning of 1892, the *San Jose Mercury Herald* ran a special edition entitled "Architecture and Architects," maintaining that "in the history of the development of all towns of note there comes a time when the village builder is replaced by the professional architect, and San Jose is no exception."[6] Winchester hired at least two local professionals. Joseph McKee helped with the initial remodel, charging about $6,000, and Jacob Lenzen designed a stable. Neither man would have been up to the standards of New Haven's award-winning architects, who had designed a number of classic buildings as well as the Winchester mansion there. It is unclear whether Winchester was dissatisfied with their work or simply preferred to do her own design work. As a woman, she had never expected to enter an institution of higher learning to master engineering and design skills. She was a self-taught architect. She superintended construction projects at the San José house and sought out the expertise of hired carpenters.

Winchester drew up plans, instructed builders, studied manuals, subscribed to journals including the *Architectural Record,*[7] and did her own rough drafting and design. If the result did not measure up to her expectations, she had it torn down and rebuilt or discontinued, only to resume a completely different and previously abandoned project. Additions to the house regenerated at spots where a previous extension had been severed. She did not work with a full set of architectural drawings, but sketched plans space by space, whim by whim. The result was a maze of halls and rooms and foyers and parlors, connected by doors and windows and porches and verandas.

The cinder-block-and-brick foundation was extended and a large basement dug to support the mushrooming house. Winchester designed the second floor as a collection of sleeping apartments with adjoining sitting or sewing rooms. Hallways on the second and third floors were lined with built-in drawers for linens and bedding. Some were made with California redwood, but Winchester did not like the look of it and she had it finished to appear as if it were hardwood. In some rooms she had her carpenters hang Lincrusta, an invention of the late nineteenth century of embossed wall coverings that created a faux leather or metal appearance. Lincrusta can still be found in several rooms in the house, and leftover rolls of the expensive wall covering have also survived in storage rooms. The ceilings were decorated with stencils, moldings, and faux finishes of great variety. Dozens of countries were represented in the adornments in the house—German chandeliers, Austrian art glass, English wall coverings, Asian furnishings, and French paintings.

Winchester described her house to her sister-in-law back east as "rambling." That was a bit of an understatement. Victorian homes had many more rooms than houses of other styles before or since. Winchester adopted this cluttered style with abandon, room by room, leading on and on to even more rooms. The emerging labyrinth of rooms and halls and foyers and passages rambled along a path that captivated her creative attention.

Attempting to keep the big house warm in winter was one of her greatest challenges. She hired a San Francisco furnace expert "to see if he could help me out in getting the house comfortably heated for next winter," but the interview left her exhausted. She noted that it "used me up completely for a day or so."[8] Many features of Winchester's house that today seem remarkable or odd were mainstream in her day. She had an "enunciator" installed; this was a rudimentary intercom system, which was used to beckon house servants. These systems allowed communication across the distance of rooms and stairs and were common in the large homes of the wealthy in the nineteenth century.

The house's interior showpiece was then and still is its ballroom. Not a particularly large room, it consists of an astonishing catalog of woods, skillfully carved and placed in dozens of herringbone or diamond patterns, cut and pieced together by expert craftsmen. Winchester ordered specialty woods through the Pacific Manufacturing Lumber Company, a Santa Clara lumber mill whose company ledgers list many of her purchases. The floor is laid in an intricate parquet pattern of teak, maple, ash, mahogany, oak, and rosewood. The walls and ceiling are exquisitely decorated with expertly carved moldings and trims. A resident of New Haven who visited the Winchester house in 2009 remarked that she and her husband agreed the woodwork was "so New Haven."[9] It reminded them of a turn-of-the-twentieth-century home where they had lived.

The ballroom's basic brick fireplace, one that could have been found in any farmhouse, is topped with a carved mantle in stunning polished hardwood. It is flanked by two art-glass windows, each designed around a Shakespearean quotation. One is from *Richard II,* where the king, confined to a solitary cell, grieves the sudden and dramatic loss of what his life had been. "These same thoughts people this little world," it declares. Desperate thoughts are his only companions as he contemplates his fate. Was Winchester's world also dominated by troubling ruminations? A second window bears an inscription from the somewhat more lighthearted *Troilus and Cressida.* It directs, "Wide unclasp the tables of their thoughts," as if Winchester were leaving clues to her burdensome thoughts. Sarah's theme appears to be Richard's and Troilus's theme: a consuming personal grief where consolation is elusive and countless thoughts cannot be quieted.

The transfigured house was bejeweled with an enormous collection of some of the best art glass of the period, crafted by Louis Comfort Tiffany of New York and other glassmakers, from California and Europe. At the end of the nineteenth century, art-glass windows appeared in expensive homes as well as more modest middle-class houses. Even the Sears, Roebuck and Company catalog advised that "art glass doors and windows add tone and refinement to the home," explaining that "the richest effects by the natural light passing through these beautiful color panes, give a soft and mellow glow which adds to the comfort and coziness of the home." Sears's windows were available for $1.85 per square foot for common designs, and upwards of $5.00 per foot for specialty ones. The mail-order store's catalog indicates the widespread popularity of the style, but Winchester's were a far cry from the standard-issue Sears versions. Tiffany produced the Rolls-Royce of art-glass windows.

Winchester submitted design requests to Tiffany and others. The double front doors at Llanada Villa featured glass in four panels, two squares and two rectangles, with a beautifully intricate transom. Windows on the house's upper levels presented spider-web tracery, a particularly popular motif.[10] Two detailed daisy window panels look out over the front of the villa. These, together with the daisy-decor bedroom, were designed as living quarters for Winchester's niece, Daisy Merriman. Many of the decorative windows that Winchester purchased were installed, but an astounding number of them were never used and remain neatly stacked in a storage room at the Winchester house. These specimens are so spectacular that they alone are worth a visit to the house.

Sarah Winchester's labyrinth soothed her need to work and to think. Walking its twists and turns allowed her to conjure new plans, more diversions, and the unexpected decoration. Throughout the 1890s, she persistently added to her house. Each morning the fifty-something Winchester rose and walked her way to work, superintending the construction project. She found great solace in the enterprise.

In 1896, construction at Llanada Villa took on a new dimension. Until that year, no area of the house was over two stories. Winchester began to experiment with higher structures, and a third and fourth story with slightly different ornamentation were added to several sections of the house. In one area she built a Tudor-crenellated tower dressed with shingles, giving a castle-like look to the façade. The third floor was living quarters for a potential of six or seven resident servants. She had a dozen more rooms built above existing ones, creating a third, fourth, and in some cases a fifth story. The house's crowning glory, a seven-story tower, was designed and masterminded by Winchester. Evidently it required several modifications before it matched her vision, and the *San Jose News* claimed in 1897 that "the main cupola was pulled down and rebuilt sixteen times before it was satisfactory and it is now allowed to stand." The tower offered an eastern view to the bay, and on a clear day, one could see almost to Stanford University to the north.

Winchester's manor was Victorian, which by definition defies precise parameters. Primarily Queen Anne in architectural style, it showed Eastlake and Stick elements, although a glimmer of Gothic and a taste of Romanesque appear now and then. It is asymmetrical, another typically Victorian feature and not surprising since it was constructed and altered over a twenty-year period. Nevertheless, the façade has a pleasing aspect, with finial-crowned gables; conical-topped towers, or "witches' caps," which had became quite popular during the 1880s; fish scale—patterned shingle work; and a dozen or more skylighted cupolas. The original exterior was painted blue.

As her architectural experimentation became larger in scale, an amazing infrastructure bloomed at Llanada Villa. The Prospect Street house in New Haven had required creative solutions for utilities, so Winchester was prepared for challenges at her farm in San José. Winchester wished to utilize electricity, so she had a generator built to power water pumps and electrify her home. She installed gaslight chandeliers with electrical switches. A carbide gas-production system was piped throughout her home, with electrical starters to light the lamps. She paid particular attention to quality plumbing systems, perhaps recalling her early childhood at the City Bathing House in New Haven. She told her sister-in-law, Jennie Bennett, "I have also been looking closely into the matter of sanitary plumbing and find that my system has serious defects. I have from time to time rectified some glaring deficiencies, but have decided that nothing but a radical change can make my plumbing beyond reproach."[11] Small water closets adjoined bathing rooms. She purchased two cast-iron bathtubs and new porcelain sinks, requesting that her tile setter decorate them with imported tiles. The shower stall in one of the bathrooms, typical of the 1890s, appears primitive today but was state-of-the-art when installed. A solarium for a dense indoor garden used an unusual and forward-thinking irrigation system: after plants were watered, the excess fell to the slightly slanted floor, where it ran down and was captured under trap doors and piped to outdoor flower boxes. At the time, valley water tables were high, and water conservation was not an issue. Today's drought-ridden Californians could take a cue from Winchester's attempt to recapture and reuse water. Soon she had a wider array and more efficient utilities than many California towns.

Like anyone undertaking a house remodel, Winchester encountered delays and aggravation. In a letter to a New Haven relative, she explained, "I have such dreadful luck with plaster. I have tried different plasterers, having, after my first experience, the work done by the day, but with not much better results. They excuse the defects in all sorts of ways, an occasional earthquake serving them well."[12] Winchester's letters reveal frustration at delays and inevitable interruptions from weather or other, more pressing jobs:

> For one reason or another since I started in to make alterations in my house I have not been able to get anything like settled. It would make a long story to tell all about it. In the first place it is infinitely more difficult to get work done than it would be in New Haven. I am constantly having to make *upheaval* for some reason. For instance, my upper hall which leads to the sleeping apartment was rendered so unexpectedly dark by a little addition that after a number of people had missed their footing on the stairs I decided that safety demanded something to be done so, over a year ago, I took out a wall and put in a skylight; then I had to have plastering done and as that could not well be done in the heat which succeeded, I had to wait for cooler weather; then I became rather worn and tired out and dismissed all the workmen to take such rest as I might through the winter. This spring I recalled the carpenters, hoping to get my hall finished up; then came the necessity for an irrigating plant and this required much work from the carpenters so that they could not get at the hall; then came the need for other outside work which must

be done before the fall rain should interfere. . . . rain revealed to my
dismay, leaks in the new skylight . . . and so it goes.[13]

She was annoyed with the slow progress of construction, but it is also clear
that she routinely dismissed workers for months at a time "to take such rest
as I might." This flies in the face of claims by today's Mystery House proprietors that work at the ranch was ceaseless for thirty-eight years.

Sarah Winchester's attention to the perpetual construction of her
home strikes our twenty-first-century ears as odd. Was she alone in this
endeavor, or were there others undertaking similar projects? In fact,
other women were creating houses that were on the same scale and
with very similar oddities. Elizabeth Colt, in Hartford, had invested years
and hundreds of thousands of dollars on what one historian called her
"rambling, asymmetrical pile of smooth-faced brownstone." An 1887
report in the *San Francisco Chronicle* described new dwellings such
as the Haas-Lilienthal house on Franklin Street as "houses of chaste and
rigid outline, and all angles and florid garniture, houses eccentric and
scrappy as a crazy quilt, apparently pieced together from the leavings
of other houses."[14] If the houses appeared like "crazy quilts" when they
were built, one can imagine that as time went by and styles changed,
they might seem even more unusual.

Winchester was certainly not exceptional in constructing a home of
great complexity. Nor was her desire to shelter relatives unique. Her
attorney's wife, Lida Leib, possessed similar proclivities. Lida attempted
to assuage her perpetual homesickness by inviting relatives for extended
stays at Leibheim, some of whom ended up moving to their own homes
near her. She maintained that she wished, just as Winchester did, "to have
as many of her family gathered together as possible." One of her nieces
noted that "something new had always been done to further beautify,
enlarge or redecorate the house or the garden or both." The house grew,
with the addition of first one wing and then another. When the Delmas
family next door vacated to move to the East, the Leibs purchased their
home. At first, the extra house was used to accommodate overflow
guests, especially Lida's Kentucky kin. But in 1899, as Lida planned her
twenty-fifth wedding anniversary celebration, she instructed carpenters
to build a wing that stretched from one house to the other. Another
niece recalled, "There were already two substantial houses, known as
the house and the other house. The other house and its large garden
had been added . . . when they bought it from Mr. Delphin Delmas."[15]
The new wing reached from *the* house to the other house. The first floor
of the new wing was paneled in polished redwood as a large dining
hall for anniversary guests. The second floor contained several sleeping

apartments. Constructing oversized and cumbersome houses was quite common at that time, in and of itself not a mark of eccentricity for Leib or for Winchester.

Leib's relatives spent summers at Leibheim, and one of the visiting children exclaimed at the "grapes hanging in big purple and white bunches from an arbor! Real ones! Figs, purple and white, thick on trees that had enormous leaves . . . a glossy-leaved magnolia tree had its own beautiful flower as large as a dinner plate." Leib wrote back home about "the pleasure of having so many family members under her two roofs."[16]

For both Lida Leib and Sarah Winchester, reality did not match the ideal when it came to having relatives stay for very long. Lida was a difficult person, and her sisters found relationships with her more congenial when they were not all living in the same house. After a week or two under Lida's "two roofs," her sisters asked Frank to help them find their own homes in San José. All of these tendencies—homesickness for a faraway locale, propensity to invite family members, and routinely making commodious room additions—echo a lifestyle not specific to one person or another, one that Sarah Winchester also adopted.

Frank Leib was very familiar with this outlook. It would never have struck him as odd that Winchester was adding rooms and wings to her already-large house. His own home was often under construction and being quite elaborately, although not always tastefully, remodeled. Transplanted from another part of the country, his wife chose to spend her time and his money remodeling and relandscaping.

Another wealthy woman living a few miles south of Llanada Villa, Mary Hayes Chynoweth, also built an usually large home. She had been widowed in Wisconsin, and she and her two grown sons settled in the Santa Clara Valley in 1887, the year after Sarah Winchester had. She and her sons hired architect George Page to design a home for them. In 1889, when she was sixty-five, the widow married Thomas Chynoweth, a sickly man who was a family friend and twenty-one years her junior. The Hayes mansion (sometimes called the Hayes-Chynoweth mansion) was designed as three houses in one, where private family quarters for each of Chynoweth's two sons with their respective families were separated by her central rooms. The relatives could live together but maintain some level of privacy. A newspaper noted that the Hayes house was "palatial" and was constructed as a "triple residence." It turned out a 22,000-square-foot, fifty-room house, with entries, halls, baths, and basements.[17] The mansion, finished in 1891, was influenced by a variety of architectural trends, favoring the Queen Anne style. Turrets, towers, and gables rested on fancy spindles and variegated sidings. The Hayes

Mansion, the Haas-Lilienthal House, the Leib Carriage House, and the Winchester House are all listed on the National Register of Historic Places. The Carriage House is private offices, but the others are now open to the public.[18]

While the Hayes house was designed and built in just about two years, from 1889 to 1891, Winchester kept building, and so did neighborhood speculation about why the construction continued. The local newspaper seemed unable to restrict its commentary, noting, "As fast as the additions are constructed and the rooms finished on the interior in the rarest kind of wood—and they are all made with the very latest and most modern accessories—they are furnished with the utmost elegance, and then closed, perhaps not to be again used or opened, or if at all, very little."[19] Why would anyone go to so much effort and expense and then not use the space? The Winchester mansion stood as an insight into the complexity of Sarah Winchester's personality. In many ways, it was similar in scope to other homes of the time. But the fact that she personally worked on it and that apparently it never reached completion reflect an interior life and surging intellect without precise objectives. Emotional switchbacks are hidden by a formidable façade, and its creative decoration remained unusually private. One discerning foreign visitor to the Columbian Exposition in Chicago believed the fair's outward beauty masked a striking interior muddle.[20] His commentary suggested that while America put out for the world to see a beautiful and orderly exterior, inside it was confused and in disarray, conflicted by class struggle and disparity between poor and rich. Did Sarah Winchester's house also reflect interior conflicts? Do the Shakespearean quotes embedded in the windows hint at a woman in captivity, like King Richard? The house demonstrated her place at the table of the rich, but she was not inclined to share the inside. Her mammoth house on the open landscape of the valley floor was a statement of some kind, and a steady stream of Sunday drivers passed Llanada Villa as out-of-town guests were treated to the spectacle out on the dusty country road. Sarah Winchester's house served as a tourist attraction long before its doors were officially opened for a fee.

→→ ⬥ ←←

The simple farm and house that Sarah Winchester purchased upon her arrival in California in 1886 sat transfigured into a castle and parkland, a fortress fit for a royal, by 1900. Proprietors of the Winchester Mystery House claim it cost $5.5 million to build, but do not give a source for this figure. The property was virtually self-sustaining, with the fruit ranch, vegetable patch, and elaborate personal garden. So far, she had lived in relative isolation, like Shakespeare's King Richard II, and although her servants were loyal, few could be called friends. Precisely who was to populate this carefully crafted stage? Even though none of her three sisters lived with her at Llanada Villa, the widow kept construction crews busy making more and more additions. Only Daisy Merriman lived with her and her servants. She put into action lessons she learned at her father's workbench and took cues from her Winchester in-laws who had lavished their newfound wealth on the Prospect Street estate in New Haven. Perhaps the question of being finished or finding uses for the rooms never occurred to Winchester, who found great satisfaction in working, most often alone, to bring beauty to her surroundings. A lone newspaper reporter suggested, rather realistically, that the house "is merely a workshop and the structure itself is a collection of notes taken by a woman of great wealth while educating herself in the architecture of several countries."[21]

Taking her elaborate plans into consideration, and even a country work ethic and any number of delays, it still is difficult to justify the fact that the house was not complete to her satisfaction twelve years after occupancy. Letters to Jennie Bennett hint that perhaps she kept building not to *accommodate* more houseguests, but to *avoid* having them. She was not anxious to have visitors. "Although I am sufficiently settled to allow a *small* family to live quite comfortably, I am not so situated yet, as to feel that I can make invited guests as comfortable as to justify me in giving pressing invitations."[22] What must her sister-in-law have thought, that after twelve years, the California home was still not ready for visitors? In her next letter, Winchester responds to Jennie's question as to what time of year is best for a visit to California. "I think eastern people must receive the pleasantest impression and receive the most comfort in making the trip to California in April, May or June. The flowers are at their best, the heavy rains are generally over and the dust of the dry summer has not become as unpleasant as later." But she demurred, "I hope some day to get so situated that I shall feel that it would not be an imposition on my friends to invite them to visit me."[23] This was no invitation. Building activities did not stave off death, as some newspapers had begun to suggest was her intention, but they did discourage out-of-town company.

—— ✥ ——

Winchester's relatively modest farm of 45 acres increased in size in proportion to the burgeoning house. She systematically bought out many

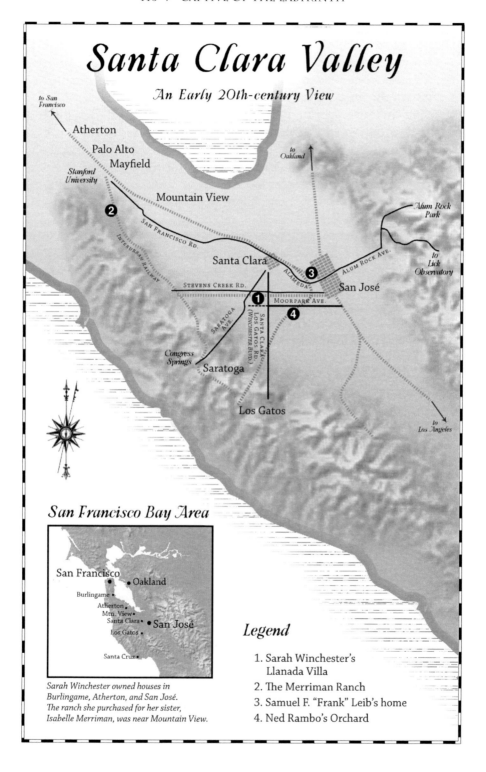

Santa Clara Valley

An Early 20th-century View

to San Francisco

Atherton

Palo Alto

Mayfield

Stanford University

Mountain View

to Oakland

❷

SAN FRANCISCO RD.

INTERURBAN RAILWAY

Alum Rock Park

Santa Clara

ALAMEDA

❸

ALUM ROCK AVE.

to Lick Observatory

STEVENS CREEK RD.

San José

❶ MOORPARK AVE.

SARATOGA AVE.

SANTA CLARA–LOS GATOS RD. (WINCHESTER BLVD.)

❹

Congress Springs

Saratoga

Los Gatos

to Los Angeles

San Francisco Bay Area

San Francisco

• Oakland

Burlingame •

Atherton •

Mtn. View •

Santa Clara • • San José

Los Gatos •

Santa Cruz •

Sarah Winchester owned houses in Burlingame, Atherton, and San José. The ranch she purchased for her sister, Isabelle Merriman, was near Mountain View.

Legend

1. Sarah Winchester's Llanada Villa
2. The Merriman Ranch
3. Samuel F. "Frank" Leib's home
4. Ned Rambo's Orchard

neighbors along both sides of Santa Clara—Los Gatos Road, eventually expanding her personal duchy to almost 160 acres. The extent of her ranch reached from today's Stevens Creek Boulevard south to Moorpark Avenue and from Redwood Avenue on the east almost to Maplewood Avenue on the west.[24]

In 1891, Winchester purchased 24 acres across the road from Elizabeth and Robert Taft. In 1895, she bought the first of several pieces from the Laederiches, who owned the entire 160 acres at what today is Stevens Creek and Winchester boulevards (most recently occupied by the Santana Row retail shopping development). John and Luisa Laederich had come from France and purchased the huge tract in the early 1860s. After John Laederich died in 1874, Luisa Laederich managed the property and cared for the couple's eight children. By the time Winchester came on the scene, Laederich was ready to divide the ranch and sell part of it, and when Winchester called on her, she made a big impression on the Laederich children. They were amazed that Winchester was driven about by a top-hatted coachman, and they gaped at her regal entry to the barnyard. Having one's own driver was an extravagance available only in fairy tales, and as the Laederiches marveled at the sparkling Victoria coach, Winchester wrote a check to their mother.

After Luisa Laederich died, Winchester wished to buy the balance of the family's farm, but disagreements arose among the children as to the disposition of the property. In 1896, Winchester purchased another sixteen acres of it. At the same time, she bought almost nine acres from Sophie and Arthur Pierson for $7,500 in gold coin. A few years later she was able to buy an additional sixteen acres from Laederich heirs, and the following year, bought thirteen more for $5,000. This time a court-appointed referee was required because of disputes between the heirs.

The original entry to Winchester's ranch faced, as it does today, east toward Santa Clara—Los Gatos Road (today's Winchester Boulevard) and the Laederich farm. After she consolidated the former Hamm land with Laederich and Pierson land, Winchester designed a grand south-facing entrance to her villa. She was pleased when the workers built "a very solid road bed ... and it is now all finished except the top dressing of fine gravel on about sixty feet."[25] She had hedges planted along both sides of the new entrance road, and she declared, the shrubs have "now about three years growth and [have] attained a good height." Then she discovered that the county intended to extend Moorpark Avenue through the Santa Clara—Los Gatos Road, taking a portion of the southern part of her land and her new road. Objecting vociferously, Winchester wrote Leib, "If my land is taken all the labor and expense of making a considerable part of this road would be lost," not to mention the ability to have a private grand south entrance.[26]

She was not the only one objecting to the county's plan to extend Moorpark Avenue. Some neighbors attempted to dissuade the county surveyor from approving the road because of the impact it would have on their farms. Winchester wrote to Leib about a woman who had called at her house. "I have learned that Miss Orkney owns property in this neighborhood and she must be cognizant of plans of which I had not heard previously. Such a road would be very undesirable for me."[27] Orkney invited Winchester to join her in filing an objection with the county. Winchester signed the petition, and when the county surveyor held a meeting of all concerned, it was held at the western terminus of Moorpark Avenue—in other words, at the edge of Llanada Villa. In the end, the county board of supervisors approved extending Moorpark Avenue and in the process saved themselves a fair amount of money. Winchester had already built and paid for sixty feet of road, which became the county's extension of Moorpark Avenue.

Reluctantly, she scrapped plans for the grand southern entrance to Llanada Villa and instead had stone pillars and a heavy iron gate installed at the original driveway. Yucca palms stood sentry. A water wagon routinely passed along, spraying to keep the dirt down on the isolated, rural road that gave no hint of becoming anything more. No one could have foreseen that sixty years later the eight-lane Interstate Highway 280 would rip through the southern edge of her property, surely dooming any entrance she may have constructed there.

<hr />

On two pivotal occasions, Sarah Winchester had an opportunity to generate a certain level of public admiration, but instead she sealed her fate to be permanently regarded as a crank. The opportunities she passed up were hosting two U.S. presidents. Up until 1901, when President William McKinley visited the Santa Clara Valley, few presidents had been there—although Ulysses S. Grant stopped once and Benjamin Harrison taught at Stanford University for a few years. McKinley had won by a wide margin in Santa Clara County, and thousands there anxiously awaited his arrival in May 1901. A committee of dignitaries was arranging accommodations for the president, and as one of the wealthiest people in the valley and owner of one of the largest homes, and because of her well-known name, it would have been natural for Winchester to act as hostess. Besides, there was a connection between McKinley and the Winchesters—the president had known of Sarah's husband and had recommended that his name be included on the "Honor Roll" on a memorial to the Historic Families of America in the nation's capital. A letter among her papers states that "the name of Mr. [William] Winchester was suggested by President McKinley to receive this distinction and honor in connection with this National Memorial here in Washington."[28] Despite the apparent goodwill between McKinley and Winchester, she did not extend an invitation to him.

The McKinley presidential tour was documented by a French journalist who was accompanying the president to report to the European press. The official string of coaches wended its way through the valley to view the orchards, vineyards, and commercial districts. The little parade drove right by the Winchester place, without stopping, but the Frenchman was stunned by the size and style of the estate. The "country palace," he declared, was "the finest piece of real estate in the valley." He went on, "The passage leading to this princely habitation is bordered on both sides with a luxuriance of flowers and through a vista of trees and climbing vines, a glimpse is obtained of the villa. The surrounding park is beautiful[,] the useful being added to the ornamental in the shape of a finely cultivated orchard." When the journalist discovered the owner was a woman, he asked, "A lady? How delightful! Is she amiable, intellectual, accomplished, handsome?"[29] Alas, he never got an answer to his query. He did not meet Winchester, but continued with the presidential tour to Saint James Park, where McKinley was enthusiastically greeted and gave a rousing speech. Just a few months later, upon his return to the East, McKinley was assassinated in Buffalo, New York. San José liked him so well that it held a fund-raising campaign to finance a McKinley memorial. It stands to this day at Saint James Park, the same place he delivered a speech on that visit.

Sarah Winchester had yet another opportunity to host the country's chief executive, in May 1903, when President Theodore Roosevelt made his first trip to California. Roosevelt was escorted through Yosemite by naturalist John Muir, and in the Santa Clara Valley was greeted by many dignitaries who once again thought a match-up between the president, the gun-lover Roosevelt, and one of the heirs to the Winchester fortune, Sarah Winchester, was a natural. A longstanding legend has it that when President Roosevelt attempted to visit Sarah Winchester he was met with a locked gate, but the incident did not really happen that way.

President Roosevelt was no more interested in meeting the widow Winchester than she was in meeting him. Before Theodore Roosevelt became president, he had enthusiastically endorsed the Winchester rifle. But since his inauguration, he had refused to allow the Winchester Repeating Arms Company to use his name in advertising.[30] He had a firm conviction and one he had made official that while serving as president he would not endorse any product. The only time the Winchester Repeating Arms Company could legitimately use Roosevelt's name for marketing the Winchester rifle was if and when he commented publicly on the gun. His stopping at Winchester's home surely would have been used by the company to promote rifle sales. For the duration of his presidency, even though he owned and had huge respect for Winchester weapons, Roosevelt did not lend his name to the rifle's promotion.

So on the afternoon of May 11, 1903, when President Roosevelt's carriage along with a parade of local dignitaries and hangers-on drove past Winchester's huge home on the road from Santa Clara to Campbell, people were lining that road to catch a glimpse of the larger-than-life man. One young person, Ralph Rambo, the nephew of Winchester's former foreman, was standing directly across the street from the Winchester place that day. Rambo was unequivocal when he recalled, "the [president's] carriage did not stop," so the story about Roosevelt's being met with a locked gate was clearly someone's exaggeration.[31]

Another reason Roosevelt did not want to stop at the Winchester house that day was that he was not feeling well. By the time he arrived at Campbell he had lost his voice, and he managed only a few remarks: "It is a great pleasure to take part in planting this tree in the presence of the children of Campbell County," he managed to croak. "I do not know of anything that bids better for our material well-being than the tree culture." No doubt someone informed him that there was no Campbell County in California. That night, the Roosevelt train car was pulled onto a siding nearby where the president spent the night, a short two miles from the Winchester place. She could have offered hospitality, but did not. The following day the president went to Stanford University, where he received a warm and enthusiastic welcome.

Sarah Winchester could have gone a long way toward mending fences and placating an inquisitive press by welcoming either McKinley or Roosevelt. She did not, and was judged a lackluster citizen for ignoring such high-powered visitors. Of course there could be another explanation for her choice to avoid the two presidents: perhaps she was a Democrat.

At that time the Santa Clara Valley was mostly Republican, and in turn-of-the-century elections, Republican candidates won by wide margins. California women were not entitled to vote until 1912, but even then, Winchester never registered. Her sister Belle and nieces Daisy and Saidee were registered Democrats (until World War I) and passionately supported progressive causes. They were inspired by the lofty speeches of William Jennings Bryan, the three-time presidential candidate who criticized imperialism, big banking, and railroad monopolies, and who favored Prohibition. Winchester expressed sad regret on America's war with Spain after the sinking of the *Maine* in Havana Harbor in 1898, commenting in a letter to Jennie Bennett, "War is now a sad reality, although it seems more remote from me than from my eastern friends. I hope none of the experiences which seem to be a possibility will come to them."[32] The war was not quite as remote as she expected since young men in Daisy's circle of friends were dispatched out of San Francisco to the Philippine Islands.

Although Winchester was typically uninvolved in politics, she did have something to say to one political candidate, who was running for county assessor in 1902. D. F. McGraw, who was endorsed by the *San Jose Mercury* and its owners, the Hayes brothers, made a costly error when he named Winchester in campaign speeches. He told audiences that he should be elected county assessor because the incumbent gave political favors to the wealthy, specifically to Winchester. He claimed her extensive property was assessed at a measly $640.[33] The truth of the matter was that that figure reflected only the assessment of one of her properties, and that her total assessment was over $80,000. Regardless of the facts, the candidate's public accusations enraged Winchester, and she sent him a letter that got published in another newspaper. "Sir, I have something more to say in reference to the wholly unjustifiable statements regarding my affairs, which you admit having made in your 'talks to the people.'" She pointed out that she was the only private citizen that he chose to malign because "you felt that as a woman—whatever affront you might offer—if I was entitled to vote I could withhold from you." She went on, as the headline stated, to "strongly rebuke" the fellow for lying to the public: "You should have acquired this information before dragging my name into a political campaign in order to help you out in your craving for office." The candidate probably had seen newspaper stories about the reclusive widow Winchester and never dreamed she would comment. She surprised everyone with articulate and justifiable indignation. "I have been surprised and gratified at receiving many assurances that your action has lost you many votes."[34] McGraw did not win his bid to become county assessor.

—◄►—

Few nineteenth-century American women have come down in history as parodied and as fractured as Sarah Winchester. A woman of many paradoxes, the wealthy Winchester worked. She did not enjoy leisure, the most prized goal of her class, gender, and social standing. She preferred work, and she spent her California days and her money building and rebuilding her large, rambling house, working as superintendent of the construction project, a decidedly unfeminine occupation, directing architectural and landscape design, tradesmen, and experimental utility installations. The work improved her emotional and physical health. In another time and place perhaps she would have pursued academic degrees in design or architecture, or at least a contractor's license.

In the rural and provincial Santa Clara Valley, Winchester was one of only a handful of extremely wealthy individuals. And although others built large, unwieldy homes, few carried as recognizable a name or so substantial an inheritance. The public linked Winchester to the large advertisements that the Winchester company ran in weekly newspapers across the country—ads that propelled the Winchester Model 1896 to outsell any other rifle in the world. Sarah underestimated the celebrity that accompanied her name and her money. She did not want public attention, yet she caused quite a stir by building a maze of a house out on a quiet country road. She wanted to work in peace, plodding along in a labyrinth of her own making, perhaps reflective of an equally complex interior life. Despite her best efforts, Sarah Winchester could not maintain the privacy she desired. Neighbors who wished to know her or have access to her were rebuffed. To the local people, she was an enigma. They did not know what to make of her. Eventually, they just made fun.

CHAPTER 7

Daydream or Nightmare

⊷ ⧻ ⊶

A CROSS THE VALLEY AT THE MERRIMANS' RANCH, BELLE HAD FOUND HOME. California in all its golden glory lay before her on the edge of the undulating hills at the pastoral *El Sueño*. She grew more than a dozen varieties of flowers, and lived on a generous monthly check provided by her wealthy sister. Belle kept a menagerie along with livestock and fine carriage horses. Chickens, goats, sheep, and ducks darted about, while deer, foxes, rabbits, and squirrels made constant if shy appearances. Once Belle was badly bitten by a dog, and a newspaper reported, "Mrs. Merriman almost lost her nose a few days since." A vicious dog on the ranch attacked her and badly bit her through the nose. The animal was immediately shot.[1] There is no indication of who came to Belle's rescue, but the incident did not dampen her commitment to animal rights. Ranch life released pent-up passions and provided a platform from which she could engage in physical work and audition her assorted notions about kindness to animals. While Sarah Winchester poured her heart and soul into designing and rebuilding a huge house, Belle spent herself at the ranch. She loved the ranch and its lifestyle. It suited her perfectly. Not so her daughter.

Daisy Merriman, in 1890, when she was about twenty-one, went to live with her aunt Sarah near San José. Her exact motivations are unclear. Perhaps she wished to be close to a town, whereas the Merriman ranch was much further out in the countryside. Subsequent events, however, indicate that at some level Daisy was in conflict with her father. There is no evidence that she had contact with him, including when she held her wedding, after moving in with Sarah Winchester.

Daisy's brother, Willie, younger by three years, remained at *El Sueño* with his parents and developed a business as a teamster. He hauled crops and goods in a sturdy wagon with well-bred horses for customers, his parents, and his aunt in San José. His name appears in ranch records at Llanada

Villa as either coming or going with a wagon or cart.[2] He weathered family conflict and economic hard times and built a life for himself.

Their father, Louis Merriman, went into the grape-growing business. He was in the perfect neighborhood. The vicinity of Mountain View was the heart of grape-and-wine production in the Santa Clara Valley. In 1892 the *San Jose Mercury* noted that "no section of the county has a more enviable reputation of the product of its vineyards than has Mountain View."[3] Eighteen wineries and distilleries were listed in local directories. Wines produced by these wineries were good enough to be awarded gold medals at the Chicago World's Fair in 1893. Santa Clara County's viticulture display was adjacent to the state's.[4] Perhaps Louis could produce an award winner, too.

But just as local wines began to command a profit, grapevines across the county were infected by the root louse phylloxera. The infestation was widespread and destroyed countless vines throughout the countryside, along with the business prospects of winemakers. Only growers who had other significant sources of income survived the three-year attack. Nothing Louis could have done would have saved his vines, and unlike neighbors who also farmed fruit orchards, he had no backup plan. Belle prevailed upon Sarah to finance a garden-supply shop on Mountain View's main street for Louis to operate. It opened sometime in 1894, and Belle created a little flower shop there. She sold arrangements of flowers she had grown at *El Sueño*.

Coincidentally, at the same time that acres and acres succumbed to phylloxera, the national banking system suffered a failure of its own. In 1893 gold reserves fell precipitously, over six hundred banks failed, and the stock market collapsed. Sarah Winchester's finances took a hit as profits at the Winchester Repeating Arms Company dropped in 1893 and did not recover until 1898.[5] Besides missing a portion of the dividends she had come to expect, Winchester lost money she had invested in the stock market, and railroad stocks she owned were suddenly worthless as the companies went broke. Perhaps the change in her finances made her draw a hard line when it came to supporting the Merrimans. Winchester was not in serious financial trouble, and her conservative attitude toward investments withstood the depression.

The downturn in the economy on the heels of the loss of the vineyard proved disastrous for Louis and Belle. In April of 1896, the *San Jose Daily Mercury* ran a notice that Louis had filed for insolvency. "He claims he has no real or personal property, other than wearing apparel of value of $100 which is exempt by law." Among his creditors were other Mountain View shopkeepers, such as Seligman Weilheimer, the proprietor of a general merchandise store, who was demanding $437, and Jacob Mockbee, the blacksmith, whom he owed $175. Belle's floral shop also failed. "Mrs. B. Merriman filed a petition of insolvency. She is a florist in Mountain View and she alleges that a general business depression and bad debts were causes of her failure."[6]

Of course, the other merchants knew very well that the Merrimans were the sister and brother-in-law of the Winchester rifle heiress, the wealthiest woman in the valley. They begrudged the nonpayment of debts, and some took legal action. Contractor J. F. Parkinson sued Sarah Winchester for $300 for lumber he had sold to Louis, claiming that Louis "was acting as Mrs. Winchester's agent."[7] The court sided with Winchester. Even two years later the lawsuits continued, and V. P. Cuvillier claimed $1,602 was owed him for labor. Again, Winchester prevailed, and the Merriman insolvency proceedings absorbed the debts. Suppliers went unpaid and workers did not receive compensation. Case after case reported in the press caused considerable ill will toward the wealthy widow. *El Sueño* was protected because Sarah Winchester's name was on the deed, but her refusal to pay Merriman debts further poisoned her position in the community. When she refused to bear responsibility for her sister and brother-in-law's debts, she demonstrated a realistic and shrewd money-management style. It may have distressed Belle or frustrated Louis, and it certainly angered their creditors. Sarah Winchester navigated the turbulent financial times effectively. She emerged from the depression relatively unscathed, and in 1898 profits showed up on the arms company's ledgers once again. That same year, her mother-in-law, Jane Hope Winchester, died, giving Sarah another huge infusion of capital.

Life in California, although beautiful, was not as idyllic as Belle had hoped, and the streets of Mountain View, at least, were not paved with gold. At sixty-three, Louis was unhealthy. His unsuccessful forays into viticulture and business could be seen as part of life in the Santa Clara Valley at the turn of the twentieth century. He could not be blamed for failed vineyards over the entire valley. With characteristic optimism, Belle lived as if none of these challenges existed. She still had the ranch, and at every opportunity, entertained family and guests at the old house that she and her sister remodeled.

The *Los Altos Star* vividly described one dinner party held at Belle's. The article "A Mid-Winter Feast at Los Altos" detailed the elaborate meal for twenty-two guests and noted that "every course and item was indigenous to the ranch." The decorations were carefully set with "some sort of flower whose poetic meaning represented the first name or profession of one of the guests, and each guest was expected to find his or her place at table by symbolic flower." Sweet Williams graced the spot reserved for Belle's son, Willie. Of course daisies were set for Daisy. For herself, Belle put out bluebells, and at the place set for a local pastor lay "breath of heaven." Bachelor buttons were reserved for an unnamed bachelor, a certain Miss Kitty had a pussy willow, and a retired army colonel found a sword plant at his place.[8] There is no record of whether Sarah Winchester attended, but most of her family members would have scouted the table to find the place setting with their apropos flower.

The evening's menu was planned for royalty, beginning with either turtle or oxtail soup, followed by frogs' legs and trout with watercress. An array of roasted poultry and wildfowl was laid out, including duck, goose, chicken, turkey, pheasant, and pigeon pie. Braised rabbit, venison, beef, sweetbreads, and liver, all products of *El Sueño,* were served by a hired crew of workers. Vegetable dishes of potatoes and peas and salads of cucumbers and lettuces set off the home-bottled clarets, sauternes, and Rieslings. Finally, for dessert, the guests were presented with loganberry pie, currants, blackberries, persimmons, and pomegranates. Music added to the festivities, and the evening was fondly remembered by Belle's guests.

— ◄►◄►►— —

Daisy Merriman managed to establish a life separate from the financial problems besetting her parents by living with her unusual aunt at Llanada Villa. Neither as outgoing as her mother nor as reclusive as her aunt, Daisy walked the middle ground of the Pardee women. While she lived with her aunt, the two supported charitable and social causes. Both served on the finance committee to support a local celebration of California's fiftieth birthday in 1900. The San José Jubilee Committee invited Jessie Benton Frémont, widow of John Charles Frémont, the famous general and explorer known as "the Pathfinder," as a special guest. Sarah and Daisy were paying members of Associated Charities and the local chapter of the Red Cross. Early in 1901, Sarah Winchester was sent a note of thanks from the membership of the Red Cross for a thirty-dollar check.[9] When aunt and niece went visiting, the newspaper often reported their whereabouts: "Mrs. Winchester and Miss Daisy Merriman are in San Francisco for a few days," noted one report in 1901.[10] They were reported as having been seen at the Del Monte Hotel in Monterey and at Santa Cruz on other occasions.

The apparent affectionate bond between the two was echoed in a strong working relationship. Daisy was Sarah's administrative assistant, and she efficiently carried out much of her aunt's business correspondence and banking. Frank Leib's letters make several references to documents that had been couriered by Daisy, or information that had been communicated from her. Despite Daisy's capability and Sarah's unrestrained approval, the niece was not motivated or inspired by work like her aunt and mother. She wanted a traditional life with a husband and children.[11] By 1899, when she turned thirty, most of her peers had already married and begun families. Daisy claimed she was twenty-five, and grew younger than her younger brother.

While living with her aunt, Daisy also formed her own friendships. Among Daisy's friends were Grace Adel, who was younger than Daisy by about ten years, and her brother, Jesse, who had served in the California National Guard in Manila during the Spanish-American War in 1898. Jesse enjoyed a reputation as a ladies' man and only reluctantly considered marriage. A note on the society page of the *San Jose Evening News* one day mentioned that "Miss Daisy Merriman has returned from Alcatraz where she has been visiting friends."[12] At that time, Alcatraz was the staging area for soldiers returning from the Philippines.

A story about Daisy and Jesse splashed across the society pages in the *San Francisco Examiner* and the *San Jose Mercury* in 1901 proved embarrassing for both Daisy and her aunt. A large photograph of Daisy accompanied the article informing the public that Daisy was to be married to Jesse Adel. The impending marriage of one of the wealthiest socialites of the era (notwithstanding the wealth was Sarah Winchester's and not Daisy's) made big news. But Jesse Adel was already engaged to another young woman, Katherine Cain. In fact, they had already procured a wedding license. Did Jesse circulate a story about intending to marry Daisy, or did it originate from someone else as a practical joke? The erstwhile groom asserted, "Some of those who pretend to be my friends have been nagging me to marry Miss Merriman. As my affairs are none of their business I secured the license to marry Miss Cain to stop their tongues and throw them off the track." The story left the door open. Whom would he marry? Jesse elaborated in a rather impolitic tone to assert that he could be happy with either young woman. The newspaper reporter who wrote the story found him quite vain and asserted, "He assumes the air of a conquering hero who has only to raise his finger and all or any of the girls of San Jose will come running to his feet."[13]

The woman engaged to Jesse was tall and blonde, the complete opposite of the dark-haired Daisy. A rivalry erupted after Katherine discovered that a book Jesse had given her had been a gift to him from Daisy. Determined to return the book, Katherine went to see Jesse and found Daisy at his house. In a fury, she threw the book at Daisy. "I did not throw it," she claimed later. "I just laid it on the table." She insisted, "Jesse likes me better than he does her." Within a day of the report, Jesse and Katherine were reported married, with no further mention of Daisy.[14] Jesse's sister, Grace, despite her brother's scandalous behavior, remained a faithful friend to Daisy for many years.

Two years later, in 1903, Daisy's wedding plans were for real. She had been keeping company with a young San Francisco man, Frederick Marriott III, who, like Jesse Adel, had served in the U.S. Army in the Spanish-American War. He had the same name as his father and grandfather, often causing confusion. The grandfather had been a forty-niner and one of San Francisco's pioneer newspapermen as the proprietor of the *San Francisco News Letter;* he died in 1884. The son, Frederick Marriott Jr., took over editorship of the *News Letter,* had a passionate interest in experimentation with airplanes, and became known as "the flying editor." He went through a messy public divorce in 1892 and later remarried. Frederick A. Marriott III was a tall, sandy-haired fellow, with blue eyes and a sturdy physique; he was five years younger than Daisy. He worked for the *Wasp,* a political-satire newspaper that was the first color, comic-style paper. Eventually the *Wasp* and the *News Letter* merged, becoming the *San Francisco News Letter Wasp.* After military duty, Fred reluctantly returned to work for his father's paper. His true interests were in the military and the emerging automobile industry.

In the months leading up to Daisy's wedding, Sarah Winchester preferred to be nearer San Francisco to attend events held in honor of the bride and to make wedding plans. She leased an expensive home in San Mateo belonging to Mr. and Mrs. P. M. Roedel, who were visiting Honolulu for six months.[15] From the vantage point of the Roedel house, Winchester prepared for the wedding and surveyed real estate investment opportunities in San Mateo County.

Daisy wed in July of 1903 in a small but elegant affair, one befitting San Francisco society. Winchester hosted and paid for the wedding held at the exclusive Palace Hotel on San Francisco's Market Street; the hotel dated from the early 1870s, when Winchester had first visited San Francisco. The latest renovations had enclosed the carriage court as a stunning pavilion; it was the perfect venue for Daisy's wedding. At thirty-four, Daisy was well past the usual age for marriage, but like her mother, she skimmed years from her actual age. Not only did she claim she was younger than her years, she also pretended to be younger than her new husband. The Reverend Robert C. Foute, rector of Grace Church, officiated at the Episcopalian service. The *San Francisco Chronicle*'s notice of the wedding was far more subdued than the half page that had run about Jesse Adel and Daisy in the *San Francisco Examiner* two years earlier. The short article on the Merriman-Marriott wedding misstates some facts, asserting that Daisy was Sarah Winchester's adopted daughter:

> Fred Marriott, Jr. and Miss Marion I. Merriman of San Jose were married in this city July 3 at 2 o'clock at the Palace Hotel. The groom is the son of Fred Marriott, proprietor of the *San Francisco News Letter.*

The bride is the adopted daughter of Mrs. S. L. Winchester, one of the most prominent and wealthy women of San Jose. For some time Mr. Marriott was associated with his father on the *News Letter,* but finally engaged in commercial business. Their wedding trip is to Santa Barbara. They will live in San Francisco.[16]

Belle and Louis Merriman were notably absent from their own daughter's wedding. It is unknown whether they took offense at the assumption that Daisy was Sarah's adopted daughter. Perhaps the financial woes of the Merrimans did not give Daisy the social status that Aunt Sarah could provide. A few months after the wedding, however, Daisy visited her mother. The *Mountain View Register* reported that "Mrs. F. A. Marriott of San Francisco is a guest of her mother, Mrs. L. A. Merriman."[17] As usual with things related to Daisy, there was no mention of Louis Merriman.

In a strange set of circumstances, Rev. Foute, the presiding vicar, died shortly after the ceremony but before he signed Fred and Daisy's marriage certificate. When Fred Marriott submitted the certificate several weeks later to San Francisco County for an official stamp, the county recorder rejected the document as incomplete. It was duly recorded only after the San Francisco district attorney issued a statement that there was no legal reason to reject the document despite the missing signature because the ceremony had been duly witnessed by the many guests.[18] It was an inauspicious beginning to the marriage of Daisy Merriman and Fred Marriott, and unfortunately, prophetic.

Daisy's marriage was a big adjustment for Sarah Winchester. Before the wedding she had spent considerable time examining real estate in San Mateo County, hoping to live closer to the newlyweds, who intended to reside in San Francisco. She commissioned Daisy to look for a suitable place, and her niece zeroed in on Atherton, an aristocratic enclave halfway between San Francisco and San José.[19] It had been the beautiful estate of the late Faxon Dean Atherton, a New Englander who had made a fortune shipping goods in and out of Chile during the 1830s and 1840s. He had married a Chilean woman, Dominga de Goñi, settled in California, and had seven children. Well established by the time of the California Gold Rush, Atherton was perfectly poised to make another fortune. In 1860, he purchased over six hundred acres on the San Francisco peninsula that he named "Valparaiso Park" in a nod to his wife's heritage and the source of his great wealth.[20] By the time Winchester bought a portion of the old Atherton estate in October 1903, it offered residents the mystique of old Spanish California with all the social amenities of contemporary society. The woods at Atherton provided a private, healthy respite from a crowded San Francisco and its social demands. Those residing in the neighborhood were the exclusively wealthy of the era.

Just three months after her wedding, Daisy found a house for sale built by a local speculator named Frank Moulton on almost six acres just south of El Camino Real at Atherton Avenue. When Daisy took her aunt to see it, Winchester promptly bought "the Moulton Place at Fair Oaks" for $32,000. Moulton's daughter recalled that when Winchester stopped to see the house, "she took out a checkbook, and bought it." From that time, Winchester could be reached by telephone at "Menlo 291." The Moultons seemed only too happy to sell to Winchester.[21] This purchase began a property-buying spree in Atherton that lasted a decade, eventually including forty-five acres there.

In December 1903, just two months after purchasing the Moulton house, Winchester purchased the house next door to it, "the Britten place," which was set on four acres fronting El Camino Real, and invited Daisy and Fred Marriott to live there. Between 1903 and 1912, Winchester bought more properties in the immediate vicinity, repeating the pattern she set in San José, buying out all surrounding properties as they came available. The largest was a thirty-acre parcel slated to be a subdivision that came on the market in 1905. She purchased the entire tract for $55,000, effectively eliminating the subdivision and ensuring privacy at her home.

Several wealthy San Franciscans built large homes in the Atherton district. The most ostentatious was Linden Towers, built by the James Flood family. The Flood fortune came out of Nevada's Comstock Lode, and Linden Towers emerged "a 43-room mass of turrets, cupolas and gables, capped by a striking 150-foot tower." If the Flood family suffered from bad taste, the press hinted, it was probably due to its recent arrival from Ireland and lack of blue-blood pedigree. The press used many of the same adjectives attributed to Winchester's San José house, but also dubbed Linden Towers a "beautiful atrocity" that resembled a wedding cake designed by a "mad confectioner."[22] Yet discussion of Winchester's home carried an underlying hostility missing from descriptions of the Flood house. Both may have deserved architectural critique, but the Floods were not labeled superstitious nor presumed to be burdened by guilt or afraid of death. Their money came from silver, not guns.

The same architect for Linden Towers designed a home for Maria O'Brien Coleman, the sister of a silver baron who had inherited his estate of $4 million.[23] A marriage of Italianate and gingerbread styles, the mansion had finely crafted wood floors, marble sinks, and crystal chandeliers. The home was intended for Coleman's son as a wedding gift, but was never occupied after the young man's wife died under suspicious circumstances. The elaborate and beautiful Coleman house stood vacant all the while Winchester lived in Atherton.

The Marriotts had not found living in San Francisco agreeable, but Atherton did not work for them, either. The Britten place on the San Francisco Road was too far from Palo Alto's train station, and since Fred had gone back to work for his father's *News Letter,* he required rail transport to San Francisco every day. The following year, Winchester purchased the Marriotts a home on Waverley Street, just a few blocks from the Palo Alto station. This new house may have been a compromise, allowing Daisy to live near her aunt, but Fred still felt it was too far from his office in San Francisco's Halleck Building, so he kept a room during the week in a hotel in the city, a practice he maintained for decades.

The Waverley Street home satisfied Daisy, but it did not generate social life befitting the upper class. Daisy and Fred wished to receive invitations to social events each season and mingle with San Francisco's elite. Winchester hoped the purchase of a summer home near Burlingame would encourage the most exclusive invitations and put Daisy in a position to be in demand to attend private parties. In February 1904, when Winchester was back in San José, the new Mrs. Marriott came to spend a few days with Aunt Sarah. Shortly after that visit, Winchester purchased a large tract of land just north of Coyote Point on San Francisco Bay near the hamlet of Burlingame.

During the last half of the nineteenth century, the San Francisco Peninsula lay in a panorama dotted by country estates of wealthy city dwellers escaping the relentless summer fog. Nabobs like "Billy" Ralston, William Sharon, Faxon Dean Atherton, and the Crockers built manors and estates, eventually as far flung as Jane and Leland Stanford's farm at Palo Alto. That the Winchester rifle heiress aligned herself with the elite is no surprise. She became quite enamored with the rocky beach and eucalyptus-groved landscape at the site of the land she purchased at Coyote Point, which in ancient times had been an Indian village. Abundant oyster beds echoed back to the Milford home of Winchester's mother. Sarah named the site "The Pasture." Most recently the site had been a portion of the San Mateo Stock Farm, a world-renowned horse-breeding establishment along the lines of Leland Stanford's stock farm near Palo Alto.

The other half of the San Mateo Stock Farm was purchased by Francis and Harriet Pullman Carolan, a young couple of wealth inherited from George Pullman, the "Palace Car Prince" and creator of the Pullman railcar. Harriet had been provided the best that money could buy in her youth, including attending Miss Brown's finishing school in New York and enjoying a six-month tour of Europe. The tall, dark-haired Harriet had been born the same year as Daisy. Francis Carolan was the eldest son of Irish immigrants, ordinarily a strike against someone, but his father was a very successful hardware merchant in San Francisco. Francis was educated at Cornell University and was a member of the exclusive Bohemian Club. He was also an impeccable dresser, had a charming personality, and loved a life of money. He drew about him a fraternity of friends who were hard players and drinkers—cards, the horses, and sports of all sorts. Francis did not intend to work as hard as his father had, instead marrying an heiress, which allowed him the life of a gentleman of leisure. When golf was introduced at the turn of the twentieth century, Francis Carolan was among its newest aficionados and invested heavily in the latest pastime, cofounding the exclusive Burlingame Country Club, an institution that survives to this day.

The Carolans named the retreat they purchased next to Winchester's land "Crossways Farm," thinking of it as an annex to their nearby home called "Crossways." Francis built a regulation-size polo field, complete with extensive pony stables, trainers' quarters, and grooming stalls. He also put in a tennis court, and a large barn accommodated his extensive collection of coaches. Crossways Farm was Francis's personal playground, where polo players from many parts of the world congregated. And to satisfy Harriet's penchant for extravagance, the couple contracted with Willis Polk, an up-and-coming San Francisco architect, to design a polo-viewing stand and pavilion for entertaining. The pavilion turned out to be an architectural gem designed in a French neoclassical style that made it look like a small version of a French chateau. The roof was built as a viewing platform for polo matches. Harriet could not have cared less for sport, but she loved lavishing expensive art and décor on her estate, and the polo pavilion broadened her design venue. The couple's closest friends were Charles and Ella Hobart Baldwin, who were of about the same age and inherited wealth. Ella's father was Walter S. Hobart, a silver baron in the Comstock Lode in Nevada's silver mines. The two couples socialized often or went sporting.[24]

If Winchester wished to insert Daisy and Fred Marriott into the social milieu, they were in the right neighborhood. Crossways Farm parties and sporting contests were detailed in the press every season. Winchester and the Carolans shared a driveway, and the two must have offered a striking contrast. By 1907 many wealthy citizens had purchased automobiles, and Carolan guests roared up their driveway in the latest models, undoubtedly snickering at Winchester's regal yet old-fashioned entry by liveried coachman. Frank Carroll's top hat and Sarah's distinctive veil and other mourning clothes were far out of fashion by that time. Trappings of the Victorian age had died with the queen in 1901, but Winchester blithely carried on for Victoria in regal style and conservative temperament. She took little notice that a new and modern century had dawned.

When Winchester bought the Burlingame land, she was not interested in procuring invitations to the polo field or Crossways Farm for herself. She wished to place Daisy and Fred Marriott in an appropriate social landscape, knowing her niece's parents were useless to provide any kind of legitimacy for her. Daisy and Fred would spend summers and other extended stays with Aunt Sarah and then return to their Waverley Street home. Rather than building a traditional home, she decided to go with a new trend and buy a houseboat, commissioning the construction of the craft from a boat dealer in Marin County, Crowley & Pederson Harbor Boats & Barges, of Sausalito. According to the *San Mateo Times,* "Mrs. S. L. Winchester purchased an ark in Belvedere recently, which she caused to be towed over to her waterfront at Burlingame and anchored there. She then fitted it up handsomely and now, with Mr. Fred Marriott and wife, who is Mrs. Winchester's niece, she is using it for summer quarters. The novel experience is said to be very delightful."[25] Winchester was not alone in this unusual desire. At the turn of the twentieth century, more than sixty houseboats, or "arks," as they were commonly known, floated in the area of Belvedere and Sausalito across the Golden Gate in San Francisco Bay.

Winchester's "ark" was a fine specimen, and estimates of its size range from about 375 square feet to 2,400.[26] The larger estimate probably includes a spacious deck on all sides. The boat's layout was not disputed, and was reported to have three bedrooms clustered in the center with a very small bath. A kitchen looked out over the bow and a living room was placed aft. The craft was covered with a hip roof, and it had an observation deck. When the boat was underway, two lifeboats were tied to davits at the bow, and one aft. When it was docked it crouched behind a dense grove of eucalyptus trees, shielded from passersby on Oak Grove Avenue and a rail stop. As many as forty trains per day, including the Sunset Limited, sped by going to or from San Francisco.[27]

Winchester left most of the landscape in its natural condition, improving only the driveway and immediate surrounding of the boat. She had a curved Japanese moon bridge installed, something like one she had seen at the California Mid-winter International Exposition held in San Francisco in 1894, and placed it over a creek bed that ran between the railroad tracks and the craft. The bridge allowed for the ebb and flow of tides and kept passengers high and dry if they came by train. The path from the bridge led directly to the living room. Occasionally the Marriotts or Winchester entertained guests at the houseboat. The Reighley family of Burlingame came out to the ark to enjoy a bay excursion. One guest recalled that the interior was decorated with "dark wood, very lavish," and that an elaborate wood carving hanging over Winchester's bed was a likeness of her late husband, William Wirt Winchester.[28] Fred Marriott invited business associates to the boat, and Winchester invited her Episcopal pastor, the Reverend William Brewer, from St. Paul's Episcopal Church in Burlingame. Winchester and Brewer found common interests. He was a bibliophile with a particular interest in collecting examples of bookplates. Winchester's namesake Lockwood Sanford had specialized in bookplate design, and Brewer was keen to hear anything Winchester could share about Sanford's designs and methods. Eventually, Brewer collected over 7,000 bookplates, and he gave lectures on the topic (in 2003, his bookplate collection came up for auction). Winchester and Brewer developed a warm acquaintance, and she contributed money to both a school in San Mateo where Brewer had previously been rector and the new Saint Paul's. He found a benefactor in Winchester, but the two had more than a financial connection; Brewer officiated at funerals and weddings for Winchester's relatives. Ultimately, he would also officiate at her funeral.

<hr />

In the summer of 1905, Winchester spent the month of July on the houseboat, but it was a working vacation. During that sojourn she began proceedings to purchase an additional fifty acres adjacent to the houseboat's mooring site, as well as spending considerable time trying to solve a more perplexing problem pertaining to litigation about *El Sueño*. Belle Merriman informed Winchester that the Southern Pacific Railroad planned to bisect the ranch near Mountain View. One particular leg of track was slated to run from the village of Saratoga north to Palo Alto and Stanford, a plan that would cut through the Merriman ranch. In the Santa Clara Valley, the local Interurban Electric Railway shared tracks with Southern Pacific. The small railway ran forty-four trains per day to the railroad giant's two, and Southern Pacific management was distressed to be edged out of a profitable local market. In an aggressive business arrangement it acquired the Interurban and ousted the smaller company's management in favor of its own man, Oliver A. Hale. He happened to be the managing partner of Hale's Department Store, one of the longest-lived retail department-store chains in California. Hale and his brothers owned clothing stores in Salinas, Sacramento, San Francisco, and Stockton. Despite his affable, rotund appearance, the bespectacled and mustachioed Hale was one of the most powerful men in Santa Clara County, with influence extending throughout the state.

Hale exhibited a voracious appetite for acquiring rights-of-way through valley ranches for the rail line. He did not *ask* landowners in the path of the track for permission to take the railroad through their land, but instructed surveyors to establish the most cost-effective route and then *announced* the result. He was quick to label any naysayers as anti-progress.

The Palo Alto line was to snake north from Stevens Creek, curling around El Monte Canyon toward Palo Alto. Hale boasted in a newspaper interview that rights-of-way had been obtained, neglecting to mention that he had not acquired the necessary easement through the Merriman ranch.

Sarah Winchester wanted to know why she had not been contacted by the Interurban to discuss the proposition. She wrote of her concerns to her attorney Frank Leib, saying, "All I know of the route as surveyed has come to me through 'hearsay.' It would seem that as the owner of the land, I should have had submitted to me a map . . ."[29] The proposed line would cut a wide swath, separating the Merriman house from the fields, and the grazing land from the water supply at Adobe Creek. The railroad plans worried Winchester because they would render the ranch useless for farming. She explained her position to Leib: "There are only two fields on the ranch—one of forty acres and one of a hundred acres. And I am told that the [rail]road was laid out to traverse the entire length of the larger or hundred acre field. This field has been used largely for pasturing cattle and horses. The animals have been able to get water from the creek which runs along the boundary on one side. The railroad I am told would cut off the larger portion of the field to that stock."[30] The Merrimans would not be able to keep livestock on the hundred acres if the railroad went through.

Winchester was extremely distressed to think that her sister's living situation would be disrupted. "I could bring myself to consider the subject in merely its financial aspect, except that the place in its *present entirety* is the much loved home of Mrs. Merriman which it must cease to be if this road should be carried through it as proposed." As the Interurban Railroad persisted in its intention to take her land, Winchester grew more frustrated and angry. She was surprised by her own rage, but felt justified in her indignation. "This is certain—that the more I think on the distressing question the more intense is my feeling of opposition and indignation. So that although naturally a very peace loving person, I feel myself getting so belligerent that I am strongly disposed to let this aggressive corporation *fight* for what it can get. If I could *know* that by taking this course I could *compel* a change of route—I would be willing to part with considerable money and maintain my rights instead of accepting any amount of 'damages' for an injury that 'mere money' cannot compensate."[31]

Did Sarah Winchester seriously expect the railroad to change its plans? Railroads all over the country wielded enormous power at that time, and in almost every case of conflict, the rails won out over locals. Complicating her position, moreover, was the fact that Leib served on the board of the railroad, knew its plans and projects intimately, and was quite friendly with Oliver Hale. But Winchester must have had faith in

Leib, and she also believed that the railroad company would listen to reason. It was beyond her imagination that a perfectly good livestock farm would be ruined, and she thought she could convince the surveyors to reroute the line to skirt the edge of the ranch so that the cows and horses could water at Adobe Creek.

Hale looked at Winchester in very simple terms. In his mind, she was an obstructionist. He dealt with her by ignoring her. In truth, she was not simply anti-progress, as he believed, but could be reasonable in certain cases. In 1898, for example, when the Mountain View Road District board petitioned the Santa Clara County Board of Supervisors to establish a public road along the northwest edge of *El Sueño,* she fully cooperated and appeared in person to sign documents.[32] County supervisors approved the plan, and Edith Avenue became a forty-foot-wide public road with land taken from the ranch. The new road did not appreciably damage the function of the ranch. The railway project was an altogether different story. Hale told Leib the path was set, and Winchester had no power to change it.

A rumor circulated that Merriman and Winchester were so angry that they "went out every night for two years, pulling up survey stakes that the company had put down."[33] There is no doubt that the sisters were angry, but Winchester did not live at *El Sueño,* as her sister did, and would not have been there "every night for two years." A restraining order filed against Louis and Belle Merriman by the San José Los Gatos Interurban Railway Company indicates the real culprits. It demanded that the Merrimans desist "from pulling up the stakes set by its engineers or in any way interfering with the preliminary survey of a proposed electric railroad."[34]

Ultimately, the Interurban Railway, owned and managed by Southern Pacific, won the right-of-way through *El Sueño.* It procured first 3.38 acres, then another 1.62 acres. The total purchase does not sound like much as compared to the full 140-acre ranch, but it accounted for an eighty-foot strip running through the land and cutting off the creek from the grazing pasture. The land could never sustain livestock again because any animals there would be unable to get to the water at Adobe Creek.

In the end, when Winchester paid a $500 attorney fee, she resentfully wrote to Leib, sending a check "in payment of your services in connection with the Railroad invasion of my property in Mountain View. I would have been willing to pay ten times the amount if it could have been *prevented,* but I know that it was impossible to do that." Her letter has a sarcastic tone, implying she was not completely convinced, as she states she was, that Leib had done everything he could to save *El Sueño.* Adding insult to injury, the following year Winchester received a bill from the county tax collector for the land she had been forced to sell. "I suppose Mr. Hale failed to have the deed recorded," she wrote bitterly. "Consequently the tax collector cannot change the charge."[35] She forwarded the bill to Leib.

Hale could be charming, but he failed to appease Winchester. When he needed to finish business with the widow, he chose to write to Frank Leib instead. "If it should appear to you that the enclosed letter is not couched in sufficiently diplomatic terms, kindly revise same, and I will dictate a letter embodying your amended views."[36] Winchester's anger would not be easily dissolved by charm or "diplomatic terms." Within two years, the Interurban Electric Railroad was renamed Peninsular Railroad Company, and it bought more acreage from *El Sueño* and other ranches and built electric tracks parallel to its steam-engine tracks. Today's Foothill Expressway runs along the same swath of land, slicing the one-time *El Sueño,* and remains a significant barrier between the town of Los Altos (the former pasture) and the old Merriman house.

The strip of land sold to the railroad company in 1905, but the transfer was not recorded until two years later. At that time, the remaining part of *El Sueño* was sold. One hundred acres went to the railroad company, which in turn sold it to the Altos Land Company. The real estate representative, Walter A. Clark, purchased a remaining sixty-six acres from Winchester.[37] The following year, in 1908, the Merriman house sold to the Chandler School, a girls' institution. The Altos Land Company, represented by Clark, plotted out an entirely new town, resulting in Los Altos. He laid out streets and divided the land into small residential and commercial lots. Today Los Altos is an upscale community in the Silicon Valley with a median home price of $1.1 million.[38]

None of the unfortunate events they had lived through in California—phylloxera, bankruptcy, or family feuds—could have prepared the Merrimans and Winchester for the loss of their much-loved *El Sueño*. In the summer of 1907, Oliver Hale died unexpectedly of a ruptured appendix. A memorial was attended by upwards of two thousand mourners, and dozens of newspaper column inches were devoted to tributes to Hale. Presumably, neither Winchester nor the Merrimans attended the service, but Winchester took no comfort in his demise. *El Sueño* was gone and had been carved up against her wishes. She believed she had been swindled by the Southern Pacific Railroad, she was laughed at by the neighbors, and she was even ridiculed in the newspaper. She summed up her feelings in a note to Frank Leib: "I will sorrowfully accept it [$30,000 for *El Sueño*], claim no more 'damages' and consider one more distressing episode added to the list of harrowing experiences which I have met with since coming to California."[39]

CHAPTER 8

Guns, Guilt, and Ghosts

The First Commentaries on
Sarah Winchester's Odd House

—◄◆►—

EWSPAPERS BEGAN PRINTING COMMENTARIES ON SARAH WINCHESTER'S unwieldy and unaccountably unfinished mansion in 1895, after about eight years of construction at Llanada Villa. The articles speculated on Winchester's behavior and her motives for building, and subsequent articles built on the first, often repeating whole paragraphs word for word. Inevitably they would add a new twist. Looking at these articles from an era known for yellow journalism, we should not be surprised that the truth was stretched to entertain at least as much as to inform. The articles ran as news stories, when really they were serial editorials. From the earliest articles until about 1911, the press assigned a succession of motivations to Sarah Winchester. First and foremost, papers identified her as superstitious. Added to that, in order, were claims that she was a snob, she was afraid of death, she felt guilty over deaths caused by Winchester guns, she was a spiritualist, and, following the 1906 earthquake, she was mad. Angry ghosts and associations with the occult appeared in articles about Winchester after the earthquake—relatively late in the complex story line.

The local newspaper, the *San Jose Mercury and Herald* with the *Evening News,* was owned by the Hayes brothers, sons of Mary Hayes Chynoweth. Chynoweth, like Winchester, built an overly ornate Victorian home in a rural valley. Chynoweth was a public figure in the community, presiding over religious services in a chapel of her own design, and she fully embraced spiritualist beliefs. An unpleasant word about Chynoweth would never have appeared in the Hayes-owned newspaper, of course. But Winchester was sharply different from Chynoweth in two ways that sealed her fate to be reported on as a fanatic: she was supremely private, rarely mingling socially, and her fortune came from the firearms industry. There is no evidence that anyone at the newspaper ever considered that Sarah Winchester's compromised physical appearance and abilities might have caused her to remain in isolation. In all likelihood, neither Chynoweth nor Winchester would have made value judgments on a person's preference for privacy or gun ownership. But the press did.

In 1895, Sarah Winchester's house was described as dreamlike: "The first view of the house fills one with surprise. You mechanically rub your eyes to assure yourself that the number of turrets is not an illusion, because they are so fantastic and dreamlike. As you approach nearer, others and many others are still revealed in a bewildering spectacle. How is it possible to build on an already apparently finished house and preserve its artistic appearance through so many changes, is a query that no one can answer, but the fact remains that it continues to be done."[1] The homeowner declined to be interviewed, so, lacking any logical explanation for the excessive number of turrets, spires, and chimneys, the press and the neighbors began formulating theories. One local reporter embellished the speculations into an entertaining story. Like the house, that first article generated countless additions.

The dominant theme permeating stories about Winchester at this early stage was superstition. "The belief exists when work of construction ends disaster will result, and it is rumored among the neighbors that this superstition has resulted in the construction of domes, turrets, cupolas and towers covering territory enough for a castle," one writer reported.[2] The only plausible explanation, said the newspapers, was that she feared bad luck if she finished the house.

The outbuildings also implicated the widow in superstitious practices: "There are many buildings besides the house, and they, too, show the effects of the owner's odd belief. Summer-houses and conservatories are made with the most picturesque of pinnacles and there are many unexpected niches where groups of statuary are hidden. Even the barns and the granaries are built with the same prevailing idea and they are full of L's and T's which suggest that they were made in parts and are ready at any time for a resumption of the work of improvement."[3] Within a short time, Winchester's supposed fear of bad luck mushroomed into a full-out phobia of death. Winchester's few defenders were quoted but opted to remain nameless. One, who was identified as "a close friend of the Lady," said, "The story about Mrs. Winchester being superstitious, and believing that she is going to die when the house, or rather all additions are completed, is all nonsense. She is not superstitious, but is an unusually sensible woman," one person contributed.[4]

The earliest newspaper reports about Winchester's house contain important clues about what precipitated the legends. Apparently, Sarah Winchester snubbed her neighbors. "When she first went into the neighborhood," one newspaper reported in 1897, "people in the vicinity dutifully called on her but she never returned a call and seldom recognizes any of her neighbors." A local promoter cautioned the public about spreading rumors and gossip. "If people come here with fortunes and are inclined to spend it, I do not think it is wise to circulate reports that they are 'cranks' merely because they do not get 'thick' with the neighbors."[5] Nevertheless, when Winchester did not acknowledge or reciprocate friendly overtures, and when she disregarded questions and invitations, she unwittingly laid a sturdy foundation for years of wild speculation.

Shortly after the turn of the twentieth century, the most damning and enduring layer of gossip topped all the theories about Winchester's huge house. Newspapers declared that not only was the mysterious Winchester superstitious, she must also feel powerful guilt about the deaths caused by the repeating rifle. One writer summed up the thinking: "Mrs. Winchester to the most imaginative of the storytellers was a mysterious dweller in a house of 500 rooms toiling at some impossible task and fearing to die because of the destruction wrought by that most ingenious of firearms, the Winchester rifle." Most publications, with very few exceptions, named her as the widow of the inventor of the famous rifle. "She is no relation to that family," one defender claimed.[6] The rifle was invented by Benjamin T. Henry, and true enough, she was no relation to his family. At the very least, she could have clarified that the founder of the Winchester Repeating Arms Company had been her father-in-law, rather than her husband. This denial by a person close to Winchester interviewed by the reporter seemed a disingenuous refusal to admit association with the rifle company. The perception of dishonesty invited more criticism.

This concept of gun guilt emerged out of progressive social ideals prevalent at the turn of the twentieth century. Up until then, weapons were perceived as a necessity for survival and as symbols of an American identity. As the nation transitioned from an agrarian society to an urban one, widespread gun ownership became a challenge to public safety. Later progressives favored curing violence with legislation rather than with the weapons that had hitherto managed the job. Populations swelled in densely occupied cities, and the task of hunting for sustenance retreated to the background.[7]

It is highly unlikely that Sarah Winchester felt responsible or guilty for the manufacture of firearms that killed people or for inheriting money from it. People associated with the Winchester Repeating Arms Company and those who wrote about it most often looked at it as an American success story. A sense of pride was more likely than one of guilt. Moreover, the gun had always been a tool of survival and progress in America, and lately the Winchester itself captured the imagination enough to become a recognizable icon.

Yet the press superimposed guilt on Sarah Winchester after the turn of the century. Since she benefited from the repeater, she would also be considered responsible for it. It was as if she personified a conscience, one that was so guilt-racked over countless violent deaths that she suffered her way into madness in a burgeoning and ghost-infested mansion. The image of wandering souls of brutally killed cowboys and American Indians at the hands of settlers with repeaters provided lurid fodder for an already substantial hyperbole. If Winchester expected to live with her inheritance without mention of the rifle, she was sadly mistaken. Her aversion to publicity, to making a statement in her own defense, ensured that gun guilt became her persistent companion. Whether for her politics, her physical attributes, her religious practices, or her personal lifestyle, by the turn of the twentieth century Sarah Winchester was considered an obsessive and superstitious dowager. She could have mitigated the gossip, but chose to remain silent. In the face of increasingly outlandish stories, she never discussed her connection to the Winchester Repeating Arms Company and she never answered questions about her large San José house. Even the more realistic columnist, Merle Gray, had to depend on "a close friend" of Winchester's, rather than the widow herself, for information.[8] If Winchester had answered some questions, the rest of the story may have turned out differently.

When the press claimed that Sarah Winchester was superstitious, the logical rejoinder was that she was a spiritualist. By the turn of the twentieth century, adherence to spiritualist practices and attempts to communicate with the spirit world had been debunked, and the Fox sisters in New York had admitted to making up their conversations with the dead. Where previously spiritualism had been held in high regard, as almost a scientific enterprise, now it began to be viewed as simple superstition. Belief in spirits and superstition became one and the same.

Sarah Winchester's upbringing had been loosely Baptist, resulting from the conversion of her parents from Congregationalism. Even though neither Sarah's name nor that of her husband appears on the roles of a

New Haven church, the weddings and funerals in her family, including her husband's memorial service, were Baptist. Her mother-in-law was a consistent benefactor to the Baptist Church in New Haven. From the time she arrived in California, though, Winchester had had a religious affiliation with the Episcopal church, and beginning in about 1905 she attended the parish of St. Paul's in Burlingame.[9]

Despite these facts, it is not beyond the realm of possibility that while funding traditional religious causes Winchester may have been participating in spiritualistic practices. Spiritualism reached its zenith in popularity in the middle to late nineteenth century—at the same time that Winchester's dearest relations died. Many would-be believers, in the throes of grief, sought solace by gathering with a medium to ask for contact, comfort, assurance, and instruction from deceased loved ones. At this point, spiritualism was believed to be scientific, offering to bridge the gulf between life and death by communicating with those who had died. It was not considered antireligious or superstitious, but a positive thing. Perhaps it was to have been the next scientific frontier. Many adherents found no contradiction in their belief in God or traditional religious expression and spiritualist practice. Here was cutting-edge religion. Where electricity or telegraphy offered new and mysterious inroads in communication, it was not that much stranger to think that science was fast approaching the final hurdle, the chasm between this life and the next. Even the eminently respectable Stanfords had visited a psychic in an attempt to have contact with their deceased son.

If Sarah Winchester had wished to explore spiritualism, she would not have needed to look far to find associates. San José had an active and open spiritualist community made up of a collection of moderately wealthy forward thinkers. The First Spiritual Union met at a hall on South First Street beginning early in the 1890s, directed by a Mr. and Mrs. Stowe. San José's Mrs. Stowe was a medium and demonstrated psychic abilities as she worked as an itinerant lecturer throughout California. Her husband managed her career and established a spiritualist following in San José.

The Stowes shared spiritual convictions with George and Nancy Roberts, a couple who lived near Winchester. Since her childhood in New York, Nancy had believed that she had psychic abilities and had "been gifted as a healing medium." The Robertses' Stockton Avenue home, not far from Llanada Villa, became known as the White Temple. There, on the first Sunday of each month, Nancy Roberts hosted the "Orders of the Angels of Light," in which she received instructions from "the angel world" and performed cures. At one of these séances, Roberts received instructions to build a temple, a task her husband carried out. The Roberts

Spiritualist Temple at North Fifth and Saint John streets adjoined property where they also built a home. Today the Robertses' Spiritualist Temple is a Christian church.[10]

Another local woman, Mrs. Wesley Fanning, was also a believing spiritualist. When she had her portrait taken by San José photographer W. W. Wright, he was astonished that the cabinet-card image revealed not just a smiling Fanning, but five other women as well. Fanning believed "that the forms surrounding her in the photograph were those of her spirit friends who are able to make themselves visible to be photographed through the mediumistic power that she exerted upon them." The skeptical photographer declared that he had "never been a believer or even an investigator of Spiritualism, and he was as much surprised as any one else could be at the revelations." He assured the public that he "did not connive to produce any fraudulent spirit pictures."[11]

The True Life Church was founded and hosted by Mary Hayes Chynoweth, matriarch of the Hayes family. An avowed healer and spiritualist, Chynoweth held services in a large chapel she had designed at her home, where she laid healing hands on the infirm and discontent. Remarkable cures of elderly people and of children were reported. It appeared that when she interviewed the sick or injured, she took on their malady for a brief time. One man came to her with a rash on his back. She did not examine him, but very quickly held out her own hand, which erupted in blisters. "The spots on your back look like this," she said. The man left her relieved of his condition.[12]

Sarah Winchester could have found support among these women if she had desired. She would have been welcomed, as would any financial contributions she wished to make. But there is no evidence that she interacted with these spiritualists. At its most fundamental, spiritualism is a social religion. A séance, for example, is a social affair, where people gather to receive messages from spirits of deceased persons. One does not have a séance alone, but with a group of like-minded individuals who have an interest in hearing messages from people who have died. Seated at a table, perhaps clasping hands, the parties focus on the leader to channel messages from the dead. The messages may take the shape of automatic writing or levitation or dramatic noises. Furthermore, séances are most likely held in the evening, in a parlor or living room where one entertains on other occasions as well. To suggest, as tour guides at the Winchester Mystery House do, that Winchester held a solo séance in an interior closet of the house misrepresents the social nature of the ritual and misunderstands Sarah Winchester. Her desire to work was the root cause of the structure and floor plan of her enormous house. Her interest in landscape design, horticulture, architecture, and woodworking found satisfaction in her sprawling, ever-changing San José property. She did not need input from spirits.

Some people denied their links to spiritualism and others embraced them. Leland Stanford, for example, admitted having visited a spiritual medium, but explicitly denied that the founding of the college dedicated to his late son was in any way the result of the visit. Jane Stanford was a bit less forthcoming. Mary Hayes Chynoweth openly admitted a profound belief in the spirit world. From the time that newspaper articles first suggested Sarah Winchester was a spiritualist, she began receiving thousands of letters from all over the country asking for money or spiritual favors.

Belle Merriman was far less traditional in the practice of religion than her sister. While Sarah was an Episcopalian, Belle espoused Bahaism, an Iran-based Universalist faith that combines Christian and Islamic principles. When a news story labeled Sarah "the Spirit Saver of the Carpenter's Union," a sarcastic reference to the many woodworkers at her ranch, it noted that "Mrs. Merriman is equally famous as the prophet of Abdul Baba [*sic*]."[13] Belle had befriended a Bahai leader named Abdul Baha Abbas, and had been invited to take charge of an orphanage in Iran. Honored by the request, she briefly considered moving there, but ultimately decided against it.

Sarah Winchester's reluctance to appear in public made her a mysterious woman. At least one contemporary claimed that Winchester was extremely self-conscious because she had almost no teeth and because her hands were misshapen from rheumatoid arthritis. If she was required to venture out, she most often covered her face with a veil and her hands with gloves. Phyllis Moulton Merrill recalled that when her parents sold a house to Winchester it was clear that she "did not like to mingle with people. She always wore a little veil, like a mantilla."[14]

People wondered about Winchester and presumed that she kept herself hidden for superstitious reasons. When she was summoned for a court appearance, the newspaper proclaimed that she must "throw her cloak of mystery aside" to testify. In short order, an alleged mysterious aura settled over the huge house, which was often referred to as the "house of mystery near Campbell."[15]

Newspaper stories about Winchester are more mean spirited than reports of Chynoweth or Stowe or Roberts. Each of those women went public with her spiritualist beliefs. Winchester fueled gossip and criticism by refusing to participate in society after about 1900, by ignoring the press, by limiting dialogue with neighbors, and by shutting herself off from the world. The Winchester repeating rifle and the fortune it produced made her more of a target for vindictive stories. The fact that

Fleet of Winchester cars and carriages. In the foreground is the widow's green 1909 Renault limousine, customized with two square side lamps and a mahogany toolbox attached to the running board and equipped with state-of-the-art Michelin tires. This auto cost $8,425. Among the other vehicles are two phaetons, or open carriages, with large wheels. Black trotters pulled the phaetons and the more exclusive Victoria coach. Courtesy History San José.

Sarah Winchester's attorney, Samuel Franklin "Frank" Leib, 1903, while serving as Judge of Superior Court. Leib specialized in land-title claims. He and Winchester maintained a professional relationship for almost thirty years, and his careful record keeping was the single most important source for this biography. Courtesy Marian Leib Adams.

Sarah Winchester's Atherton home, officially photographed by A. G. C. Hahn for a program for the Panama Pacific Exposition held in San Francisco in 1915, as an example of one of the finest homes in the Bay Area. This was Sarah Winchester's full-time home from 1910 to 1922. Courtesy San Mateo County History Museum.

An interior view of Sarah Winchester's Atherton home, circa 1915. Courtesy History San José.

Frederick A. Marriott III, who married Sarah Winchester's niece, Marion "Daisy" Merriman, in 1903. Marriott acted as Winchester's agent in the purchase of automobiles. In 1916 Fred and Daisy filed for divorce, but they later reunited. Photograph from San Francisco News Letter, September 5, 1925.

Tudor-style cottage purchased by Sarah Winchester in 1907 located on lot number one of Burlingame Park, at the County Road (El Camino Real) and Oak Grove Avenue. Winchester stayed at this house while overseeing the dredging project to create sea channels for her houseboat, which was docked on San Francisco Bay at the end of Oak Grove. When she sold the cottage in 1912, the furnishings were included in the sale price. The house was razed in the mid-twentieth century. Courtesy History San José.

Moon bridge at Sarah Winchester's houseboat property circa 1909. The bridge was placed over a creek near the railroad tracks, giving entry to the ark. Winchester may have gotten the idea for the bridge at the 1894 California Midwinter International Exposition in San Francisco, where the Japanese Tea Garden was built and remains to this day in Golden Gate Park. It is unknown whether Winchester imported her bridge from Japan or had a copy built locally. Courtesy History San José.

Sarah Winchester's ranch foreman, John Hansen, with his wife, Nellie, and sons, Carl (left) and Theodore. This photograph was taken at Winchester's San José ranch, Llanada Villa, circa 1913. John Hansen worked at the ranch from the late 1890s until the widow's death in 1922. Carl and Theodore Hansen were born and raised at the ranch. Courtesy History San José.

Carl (left) and Theodore Hansen, the children of Sarah Winchester's ranch foreman, in one of Winchester's autos in front of the barn at the San José ranch circa 1912. Courtesy Richard Hansen.

Two pages from one of ranch foreman John Hansen's daybooks, where he jotted notations about Sarah Winchester's San José ranch operations from 1907 until 1922. These pages note that Winchester came to the ranch on Friday, September 15, 1911, and left with 343 eggs, and that she came again the following Wednesday. The daybooks indicate that a prodigious supply of eggs was coming out of the ranch and going with Winchester or her niece to Atherton, but it is unknown what the women did with the thousands of eggs they took off the ranch between about 1910 and 1920. The pages also indicate that Hansen took various things to "F.O." (meaning Fair Oaks, the early name for Atherton). Courtesy History San José.

Margaret Marriott, flanked by Carl (left) and Theodore Hansen at Sarah Winchester's Llanada Villa circa 1912. Daisy and Fred Marriott adopted Margaret in contentious court proceedings. Courtesy History San José.

Winchester's head gardener, Tommie Nishihara, who worked for her from about 1910 until 1922, holding his granddaughter, Ida Winchester Nishihara, named for Sarah Winchester, circa 1914. Nishihara and his son and family lived at the Winchester ranch until he died, just months after Winchester. Courtesy History San José.

Winchester employee Ito Nishihara with her baby, Ida Winchester Nishihara, and the Hansen boys, Carl (left) and Theodore, circa 1912. Nishihara, her husband, Ryoichi Nishihara, and her father-in-law, Tommie Nishihara, all worked for Winchester, who provided a house for them. Courtesy History San José.

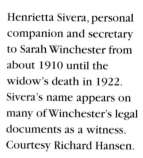

Henrietta Sivera, personal companion and secretary to Sarah Winchester from about 1910 until the widow's death in 1922. Sivera's name appears on many of Winchester's legal documents as a witness. Courtesy Richard Hansen.

Chynoweth's sons owned the *San Jose Mercury and Herald* could also account for the fact that no untoward stories about their mother's spiritualist beliefs appeared in print. Winchester's refusal to participate in society contributed to her misunderstood personality, but gun money coupled with silence, at least in the eyes of the press, added up to a mysterious misfit.

Sarah Winchester was not nearly so preoccupied with preventing her own death as she was with remembering her late husband. Through the building arts, not mystical séances, she was able to keep the memory of her husband alive. William Winchester loved the field and practice of architecture, and the more Sarah built and the more she enjoyed it, the more she recalled the life she had shared with William.

By 1906, Sarah Winchester had been in California for twenty years and had been a widow for twenty-five. Her wealth continued to grow by virtue of about a 30 percent share of the Winchester Repeating Arms Company, which had $10 million in net sales that year.[16] As of 1906, Winchester owned almost a dozen properties in the San Francisco Bay Area. Her San José ranch approached 140 acres, with the haphazard castle, a caretaker's house, several barns and outbuildings, and various and sundry houses occupied by tenants and gardeners. She owned two homes in Atherton, each on about four acres, and an additional thirty undeveloped acres. Forced by the railroad to sell part of *El Sueño,* she was in the process of liquidating the remainder, but officially still owned the Merriman house until 1908. "The Pasture" in Burlingame had about a hundred acres with the completely outfitted houseboat. She owned rental houses in Palo Alto and one on San José's Stockton Street. Winchester roamed from one property to another, depending on her desire and the season. But up until 1906, she spent most of her time and money on the San José ranch, except for months-long periods when she chose to live nearer to Daisy.

Winchester corresponded with Leib several times during the early part of 1906 about real estate problems in Burlingame and with the Merriman ranch. She encountered serious obstacles to getting legitimate title to the Burlingame land. She put Leib on the case, and it required a painstaking study of obscure Mexican-era maps and surveys. Both Leib and Winchester had been ill, she with a "bronchial trouble" that kept her "quite closely indoors."[17] At sixty-six, Winchester was considered elderly. She was significantly affected by rheumatoid arthritis, and her overall health was fragile. She was under a doctor's care.

The pattern of Leib's letters and phone conversations with Winchester at her various properties during the weeks leading up to the San Francisco earthquake of April 18, 1906, leaves some doubt as to whether she was at the San José house during the earthquake. Letters indicate that at least from April 4 through April 7, 1906, she was in Atherton. On April 7th, Leib spoke to her by telephone there. In a letter he wrote the same day, he referred to the phone conversation and apologized for not reaching her the day before as she had requested, but he had been in court all day settling Jane Stanford's estate.[18] They set a meeting to discuss the Burlingame land purchase. The dispute had been going on for well over a year, so Winchester would not have begrudged Leib's attention to Stanford's estate, particularly given the disquieting circumstances of her death. The press hinted that Stanford had been poisoned, and since Leib had been her personal attorney, his counsel would have been very much in demand.

It is unclear whether Winchester went to San José sometime after April 7 and before April 18. Regardless of which of her houses she was at during the earthquake, it would have been a profoundly disturbing event for her. The earth's convulsions under the San Francisco Bay Area at 5:12 a.m. on April 18, 1906, changed how the world viewed the city and how California viewed itself. Not since the Gold Rush had so much far-reaching attention been focused on the Golden State. Idyllic California was violently awakened that morning by unprecedented disaster, and both its image and its infrastructure suffered a catastrophic blow. The magnitude 7.8 or so earthquake,[19] the worst in the state's history, tore open almost three hundred miles of the San Andreas Fault, from the Mendocino coast south to San Juan Bautista. The impact on San Francisco was huge: more than 3,000 people died and property damage was estimated to be in excess of $500 million (in 1906 dollars); images of the fire that followed have been imprinted on our historical memory.

The quake's force in the Santa Clara Valley, fifty miles to the south of the city, is not so well known. Almost two hundred people died in the valley, over half of those at the Agnew Asylum for the Insane five miles from Winchester's Llanada Villa, when the four-story hospital collapsed, trapping doctors and patients alike. More people died at Agnew than at any other single location, including in San Francisco, giving it a dubious distinction and one that is not often reported in history books. Dozens of buildings were destroyed in San José and many fires erupted there as well.

Stanford University also suffered heavy damage, and two people died there. The gigantic Memorial Arch, gateway to the campus, toppled, as did the Memorial Church belfry. If Jane Stanford had not died the year before, she would have been horrified by the destruction of the priceless

Italian mosaics she had had commissioned for the façade of the chapel. Thousands of valley residents camped outdoors after the quake, afraid to reenter their damaged homes. The glow of fire in the night sky to the north was a frightful notification of the fate of San Francisco.

A local newspaper proclaimed, "The world stands aghast at the great catastrophe which has come upon San Francisco, Santa Rosa, San Jose, . . ." It noted that many brick-and-stone buildings in San José were apparently damaged beyond repair. The new, $300,000 Hall of Justice was a "mass of ruins." Two 60,000-gallon water tanks toppled in Campbell, instantly flooding the immediate surroundings. Virtually every chimney tumbled, and most windows broke. The biggest local fire was put out, and by April 27, residents were reportedly "getting down to hard work, with eyes fixed on the future, more determined than ever to conquer."[20]

One of Winchester's Atherton houses, a stout house built by Frank Moulton, survived but required restoration and repair. Next door at the Moultons' new house, "the earthquake took the chandeliers, which were leaded and hung down, swung them back and forth and snapped them right off the ceiling, and dropped them on the floor."[21] Even so, it was obvious that Moulton's construction methods held up better than Winchester's.

Llanada Villa was severely damaged. The seven-story tower tumbled in a heap, leaving a gaping hole at about the third level. Shingles, wood, and glass collapsed into rooms on the lower level. Most of the several chimneys fell, either to the ground or through roofs. The third- and fourth-floor additions were wrecked, an entire wing of New England—style porches lay in ruins, and three Tudor turrets broke to bits. All the painstaking plaster work that Winchester had described in such detail to her sister-in-law crumbled beyond repair. Twenty years of meticulous wood and tile craftsmanship were destroyed by the devastating temblor.

Although Winchester's house was half wrecked, Frank Leib knew nothing about it even two weeks later. The attorney sent a letter about other business to Winchester at her San José house at the beginning of May and concluded his letter with, "Did the earthquake damage you to any considerable extent? I sincerely hope it did not. I received only my share of damages." His chimney had fallen and some plumbing fixtures had snapped, and he ordered a thousand bricks for repairs, retaining a mason, a plumber, and a painter to repair his home.[22] In the last week of April, Leib noticed Winchester's name on a list of donors to the "San José Relief Fund" as having given $150. Leib would have known if Winchester had been injured or if she was disturbed more than others by the earthquake. Yet the quake took a psychological toll on most people, so presumably it affected Winchester, too. It is unusual to live through an earthquake of that magnitude and not suffer post-traumatic stress to a greater or lesser degree.

The city of San Francisco and its promoters were confronted with a choice. Would it allow the earthquake the final word, and give in to its power? Or would it try to vanquish Mother Nature and rise optimistic in rebuilding bigger and better than ever? Coincidentally, just days before the earthquake, the renowned city planner and architect of Chicago's Columbian Exposition of 1893, Daniel Burnham, had submitted a detailed urban design plan to the City of San Francisco. His grand plan called for a San Francisco to outshine even the amazing Washington, DC, and city officials were considering Burnham's plan when the earthquake occurred. Afterward they opted to build more quickly (and cheaply). They rushed to reassure banks in the East that the city would return to a vibrant economy. San Francisco, they insisted, would rise from the ashes in record time. It was a shortsighted but popular plan.

When Winchester looked at the massive shambles at Llanada Villa, she was faced with choices of her own. Should she plot out a strategy to rebuild bigger and better, as the city planned to do? She found it very tempting to throw in the towel and gave serious consideration to razing the entire structure. She decided not to tear it down, but arranged for fallen debris to be cleared away. She showed no hesitation to leave the place a shadow of its former self and no compulsion to remedy its ghastly shortcomings. As a result, after the rubble was cleared and the place made safe, second-story doors opened out to thin air where there was once a balcony, and water pipes protruded where window boxes had been. Rubble from the fireplaces was hauled out and chimneys sealed off, some below the ceiling level. Staircases leading to the upper floors were left intact even though whole levels were swept into the rubbish heap. According to Daisy's husband, Fred Marriott, Winchester herself thought the post-earthquake house "look[ed] as though it had been built by a crazy person."[23] There is no doubt that Winchester's building practices were unusual and not up to precise and professional standards, so it was not, perhaps, surprising that the great California earthquake of 1906 inflicted near-fatal injury to Llanada Villa. Winchester opted to basically leave her castle in its transformed state after the earthquake, with merely fundamental repairs, rather than rebuild according to her previous exacting requirements.

Winchester was forced to confront her own limitations as an architect, and she was not very forgiving. Her designs, instructions, and careful plans did not hold up against natural forces. She took no comfort in the fact that she was in good company, as many other, more expensive and famous buildings suffered the same fate. One neighbor reported, "Sarah was so heartbroken after the earthquake damage in 1906. Everything was so neatly kept and all those beautiful windows studded with precious stones were damaged."[24]

The great San Francisco earthquake of 1906 was a defining moment in the history of the state, and it was also pivotal for Sarah Winchester. Confronted with the vagaries of life in the Golden State, she decided to be realistic. Any semblance of a California dream that Winchester had once imagined was shattered. She also knew she would never escape a social landscape that quaked with ridicule and judgment of her. If she found legal contests harrowing, she must have been stunned by the earthquake. At the time of the earthquake, she had no way of knowing that her private choices would engender newspaper stories with accusations of insanity that would end up haunting her life and her memory. Her decision to leave the house as it was after it was damaged caused the most enduring and damaging turn in the labyrinth of legends: Sarah Winchester was deemed a madwoman because of her pessimistic and recalcitrant reaction to the earthquake. Articles about her after the earthquake proposed that only someone who was insane would refuse to rebuild, and since she did just that, the wealthy widow Winchester had to be certifiable.

After the earthquake, tiny villages hugging the coast around San Francisco Bay mushroomed into full-blown towns with displaced city dwellers. Burlingame, for example, a scant fifteen miles south of San Francisco, saw its population jump from a pre-earthquake total of about two hundred to five times that number within a year. The town had been named for Anson Burlingame, an American diplomat to China under Abraham Lincoln. In 1866, when he purchased a thousand acres there, he envisioned a "large planned community after the English country style, which allowed for the building of substantial cottages in an exclusively residential setting, with winding roads and much space between homes."[25] Burlingame died in 1870 before accomplishing his plans, but a fairly accurate portrayal of his dream was built as the exclusive Burlingame Park. Two years before the Great San Francisco Earthquake of 1906, Sarah Winchester purchased over a hundred acres about a half mile from Burlingame Park. It proved a timely and profitable investment.

Sorting out the exact boundaries of her latest acquisition proved exceedingly troublesome and ultimately consumed two years. Surveys that had been produced in the middle nineteenth century were less than reliable. Aggravating the problem, marshy bayside land shifted and eroded with the tides. A slice of eighteen acres remained in limbo with uncertain ownership. Frank Leib wondered whether an entirely new survey should be undertaken, telling her, "I made one or two endeavors to

... stop off and see the premises for the purpose of determining whether it would be advisable for us to have a re-survey of it. . . . I shall do so at the very earliest time."[26]

Winchester had three reasons for establishing exact boundaries. First, the land was priced by the acre and she did not want to pay for more than she was getting. Second, she needed to locate the land's boundaries so she could fence it against encroaching livestock and fishermen. And finally and perhaps most important was having the ability to sell it in the future free from encumbrance or questionable title. Winchester was quite persnickety about legal documents and made absolutely certain than every one of her dozens of land purchases was officially recorded, a practice not required by law at the time and costing extra fees. With California's history of murky land records, her practices fell on the better side of prudence.

Leib's years of experience in California land law, which included some widely publicized cases that came before the Supreme Court, were trumped by this purchase. He declared, "Without exception this is one of the most complicated titles and the hardest to locate with the data that I have at hand, that I have ever tackled, and I have passed a great many titles in my time."[27] After almost two years of painstaking work, in late March 1906, Leib believed he had solved the complicated legal puzzle. He invited Winchester to meet with him to see documentation. In the meantime, the purchase was finally recorded at the county courthouse on March 30. "You have had more than your share of trouble about all these matters," he told her, although he had attempted to shield her from them. "I only wish I could do more in that direction."[28] Two weeks later the massive earthquake struck.

Not surprisingly, of all Sarah Winchester's properties, the one to suffer the least earthquake damage was the houseboat in Burlingame. The land where the boat was docked lay mostly undeveloped, and since a boat is designed for jostling, it came out unscathed. Personal items were thrown to the floor, but after the glass was swept, there was no visible damage. Winchester and the Marriotts took refuge at the houseboat during late April and May 1906 while their respective homes were repaired.

As Leib made minor repairs on his home, he believed Winchester's tangled title mess was solved and he sent a bill for his fees. In June, he received a visit from a man who represented the San Francisco title company. Leib was informed that all documentation that had been submitted on behalf of Winchester, including the original abstract of title, had burned up in the fire after the earthquake.[29] Leib would have to reconstruct the entire chain of title for his client once again. He put off telling Winchester for a little more than a week, but finally telephoned her with the news, following up with a letter confirming the conversation. There is no record of her response.

In the days immediately following the earthquake and fires, newspapers published images and accounts of unimaginable destruction. The following week more-optimistic pieces ran, underscoring acts of heroism and predicting a quick recovery. San Francisco officials and bankers feared the quake would ruin the financial prospects of the city if they did not assure the public and financiers in the East that the city would emerge from the catastrophe more vital than ever. They grasped at the biggest life preserver within sight and latched on to the Panama Canal project as the perfect panacea to save San Francisco. The $40 million Panama Canal Act of 1902 promised a huge increase in trade with San Francisco since merchant lines would be able to sidestep the arduous and dangerous southern tip of South America. If San Francisco could be rebuilt and ready for business by the canal's projected opening in 1911, then the city would have a gloriously prosperous future.

Small communities around San Francisco Bay leapt onto the Panama bandwagon and imagined their insignificant selves as players in the international trade game. Redwood City, East Palo Alto, and Sunnyvale, among dozens of others, built wharves and dredged marshlands to provide access to the bay in preparation for steamers and schooners from ports of call around the world. Warehouses cropped up as roads were laid to the bay's edge. Each town and business diligently prepared for the predicted traffic jam of ships in San Francisco Bay.

Sarah Winchester did not ignore the impending influx of traffic owing to the canal, either. Floating in her houseboat after the earthquake, she contemplated visitors' sailing directly to her bayside home, situated perfectly to become the most exclusive personal port on the entire West Coast. Between 1906 and 1910, Winchester unleashed her architectural ambitions, plotting a coastal estate where personal docks and sloughs would welcome visitors coming to California via Panama. The project offered an entirely different set of parameters than her house-building at Llanada Villa. She designed and directed the construction of an elaborate system of canals and locks with floodgates to safely harbor expensive yachts. There is no doubt that this project was far more unusual than the labyrinthine San José house, but fewer people knew about her proposed harbor, and neighbors there did not care much what she did. "She had a basin dug with a system of canals (moats)," one local recalled. She put the ark in dry dock, then water was allowed to flood around it. One channel led to the bay to a floodgate located about in the center of the property on the concrete retaining wall."[30] The distinctive Japanese moon bridge spanned a creek that ran near the craft.

Winchester hired contractor and nurseryman Edgar W. McLellan to build a concrete dike and dredge a channel in the bay. McLellan was a well-known businessman on the peninsula and had greenhouses and nursery grounds along Burlingame's marshy bayside land. He saw an opportunity to use Winchester's land for his own business, and in return he would appease the old woman. She paid top dollar for the dredging and dike. He set to work carrying out her unusual instructions and at the same time agreed to lease one hundred acres of her pasture to store nursery supplies and construction equipment.

Winchester could not very well occupy the houseboat during the muddy construction, so she purchased another house. It was a small but expensive—$35,000—Tudor-style cottage in Burlingame Park, located at County Road (El Camino Real)[31] and Oak Grove Avenue, on a two-acre parcel just a half mile from the houseboat's docking station. From the comfort of the well-appointed house, Winchester kept watch over the channel dredging. Each day, coachman Frank Carroll helped her into a sporty phaeton and drove her black trotters down Oak Grove Avenue, past the entry to the Carolans' Crossways Farm and polo fields, to the houseboat and construction site.

By the end of 1908, McLellan had completed an amazing concrete sea-retaining wall over 1,100 feet long.[32] Underestimating Winchester's precise attention to detail and her ability to monitor him, he had made a side deal by subleasing the hundred acres to a third party, who used it for grazing livestock. McLellan did not realize that Winchester was finicky about land-use practices and was strictly opposed to livestock grazing on her land. In all the years she owned the property she made only one exception by allowing Mrs. Bakewell, a widow with two children, to pasture her horses and cow there.[33] When she objected to this third-party use, McLellan was annoyed, but he appeased her by promising to remove the third party. He never did. She was disturbed not only because he broke the guidelines of the lease, but also because his workers had harvested literally tons of sand and gravel from her property for roadbed-construction projects. Huge ditches had appeared along her waterfront where sand had been collected. She even caught one person red-handed.

One particular morning she asked Frank Carroll to drive her down to the bay. While still in her coach, they encountered a young man in the process of loading his wagon with sand and gravel. She demanded to know what he was doing. He was on a mission of mercy, he claimed, saying that he had noticed her driveway was full of chuckholes, so he was collecting the material to fill them in for her. She thanked him for his concern for her road, and watched as he smoothed out her path.

She knew very well that as soon as she was gone he would load his wagon once again. Sarah Winchester was not imagining this disappearance of gravel. A local resident recalled that it was common knowledge that "half the sidewalks in Burlingame were made from sand stolen from Winchester's beach by a well-known contractor at the time."[34]

Winchester wished to carry on with her plans for the canals, so she retained McLellan as her contractor, but not as a tenant. When his lease was up, she did not renew it. Again, he placated her, but made matters worse by continuing to collect rent from a third party and not paying any rent himself. She lost patience with McLellan and ordered him off the premises, but he did not comply. Winchester sued Edgar McLellan for back rent, property damage, and stolen property. Court documents state that without permission or consent McLellan had taken large quantities of gravel and that he "still continues to remove" it to the "damage and detriment of the entire property."[35] Ultimately she won her claim, and McLellan vacated the premises.

Winchester had to resort to the courts to settle other troublesome disputes, too. Late in 1906 her groundskeeper informed her that a local developer who was building a nearby subdivision had laid a sewer line across her property so that it emptied into the creek near the Japanese bridge leading to the ark. It was not hooked up to anything. She was furious and indignant, and she wrote to Leib, "It is being laid across my property to empty into the creek at a point where it is dry in the summer! It seems to me an outrage which should be immediately stopped."[36] Frank Leib was informed independently about Winchester's sewer problem. A property manager he occasionally worked with in San Francisco wrote that "the stench was awful."[37] It took a year before the developer was required to install closed sewer pipes.

Articles about the disputes appeared in the Burlingame, San Mateo, and San José newspapers. All of them highlighted Winchester's odd reputation and reclusive preferences and sympathized with the defendants. "Heiress to Millions Decides to Throw her Cloak of Mystery Aside," one reported because she would have to appear at the court proceedings.[38] McLellan was clearly in the wrong, but the public sided with him because of his standing in the community. Winchester's legitimate claims against McLellan and other real estate developers were barely mentioned, and the papers inferred that she was an unstable and miserly old widow. The journalists dreamed up reasons for her many construction projects, surmising that the houseboat and moats were built out of fear of an earth-destroying flood, like the one that befell Noah in the Bible. The Sarah Winchester mythology reached new heights, and still she offered no response.

With the sewer issue solved and McLellan safely removed, Winchester took a respite from Burlingame and in October 1909 returned to Llanada Villa. While she was there, Frank Carroll died unexpectedly of an apparent heart attack.[39] He was fifty years old and left his wife, Mary, with three children ranging in age from eight to twenty-one, living at the San José ranch. Frank had been her most faithful courtier, her loyal coachman and personal valet, since she left New Haven. He was the only person in California outside her family who had known her husband. His death was particularly shocking because he had seemed so healthy. She had fully expected that he would outlive her, and she would have been pleased to leave him a generous inheritance. How would she manage without him carrying her about? The loss of Frank Carroll shook the foundations of her imperial lifestyle and jarred her into reevaluating the distribution of her fortune.

Winchester arranged for a Catholic burial and paid for funeral services for her beloved Irish driver. He was buried just down the road from Llanada Villa at the Santa Clara Mission Cemetery, an annex to the old mission property. Afterward she assured Mary Carroll of her continued financial support. Mary could have considered returning to New Haven, but she had been in the Santa Clara Valley for twenty years, and two of her three children had been born there. She accepted Winchester's gift of a house a short distance away on Williams Road. Mary established a fruit farm there; between that and a regular support payment from Winchester, she was able to make a modest living. The Carrolls had fond feelings for Winchester, and years later they were among those who were deeply disturbed when her house was declared haunted and turned into a tourist attraction.

Without Frank to escort her about Burlingame, Winchester lost interest in the personal yacht harbor. She abandoned the idea of a private wharf, and the little houseboat with its acres of grassland sat isolated in the fog for many years. She visited the ark very seldom, and found it necessary to install a full-time caretaker to secure the place. She hired Ida and Henry Kohne, an elderly German couple, and their presence discouraged further plunder of the sand and gravel. They ensured that Mrs. Bakewell was the only tenant on the property. The Kohnes remained for ten years.

Winchester toyed with selling the San José ranch. In fact, the *San Francisco Examiner* reported in April 1908 in an article entitled "Woman Defies Ghosts in Selling Her House" that it had been sold to "a wealthy magnate" and that "in all probability the sale will be shortly consummated." It is not clear if there was an actual buyer, and no property records or letters to or from Frank Leib indicate an interest in selling. It is possible that Winchester could not bring herself to sell the house where she had placed so many hopes and invested so much time. She spent most of 1908 in Burlingame or Atherton and made only modest improvements at the ranch. She dispatched a gardener to plant sunflower beds near an artichoke patch.[40] The newspaper claimed that Winchester planned "to brave the wrath of the spirits and sell her palatial villa." This story is the first to specifically mention "spirits," and angry ones at that, although other superstitions had previously been attached to the widow, this article became the basis for countless future references that lifted the exact wording from this reporter's version. After this, Winchester was described as "braving the wrath of the spirits" for *any* decisions about her big house. A cadre of ghosts and spirits allegedly prowled about her gangly house, whispering directives. These spirits supposedly revealed to her how she should construct the edifice. By this time, Winchester had ceased making additions to her San José house.

In about 1910, the legends about Winchester's superstitious belief in ghosts instructing her in the design of her San José house were superimposed onto all her properties. A San Francisco newspaper reported that she believed that "she was not to dispose of any of her country homes" or she would die. The Atherton houses were evidently monitored by ghosts as well. "Her occult friends declare she must brave the wrath of the spirits," claimed the latest article in 1911 as Winchester prepared to sell one of the Atherton houses, referring to "occult friends" as a hint that Winchester might be a witch of sorts.[41] Neither Winchester nor the new owner ever reported paranormal activity at the home.

The little houseboat could not escape becoming involved in the legends, either. An article in *Sunset* magazine incorrectly claimed that Winchester bought her "ark" after the great earthquake (she really purchased it two years before) because she feared that the earth was about to be destroyed by a great flood, the likes of the biblical one. "Mrs. Noah never dreamed anything like this," the article said. All subsequent reports of Winchester's houseboat, of which there are a dozen or more throughout the twentieth century, repeat the mistaken date and paranoid reason for her purchase. The actual date of purchase and the fact that dozens of other houseboats also floated on the edges of San Francisco Bay were not reported.

Malignant rumors about Winchester spread so quickly that no amount of truth-telling could rein them in. The press implied in the clearest possible terms without libeling her that Winchester suffered from mental instability. Insanity kept company with superstition, guilt, and fear. A writer for the *San Jose Mercury and Herald,* Merle H. Gray, attempted to give a more balanced account of Winchester in 1911. Gray wrote a lengthy article outlining many rumors but for the first time providing logical rejoinders to them. Winchester's building activities, he asserted, came from "a taste for architecture and [she] devoted her time in the study of this art to the utter exclusion of social pleasures. She read the best literature on this subject to be obtained and was a subscriber to many technical magazines in both English and French. Carpenters were employed and they carried out her ideas. She built slowly and planned each staircase, window and wing in the establishment. She considered the place her workshop and was such an ardent devotee to her art that she had little time left to make new acquaintances."[42]

Gray clarified that Winchester's late husband was the son of the founder of the Winchester arms company, and he highlighted many of Winchester's accomplishments. "Mrs. Winchester is an accomplished pianist and is a good performer on the violin and organ. She had composed for the entertainment of her tiny coterie of friends. She is also a French scholar and has one of the most complete French libraries on the Pacific Coast."[43] Never before had personal information about Winchester made it into a newspaper. Gray stated unequivocally that Winchester was "not a Spiritualist . . . but is of an orthodox faith." The author wrapped up the article with a list of Winchester's philanthropies, including a multi-million-dollar gift to a hospital in New Haven. Evidently no one in New Haven read the *San Jose Mercury and Herald.* The half-million-dollar gift remained "anonymous" there for several years. Most of the accurate information in the article was quickly forgotten, while the more entertaining storylines remained intact. Another five years went by before Winchester's name was mentioned in connection with the New Haven hospital in either San José or New Haven.

Accounts differ as to Winchester's reactions to the ghost stories. One maintained that as the stories spread across the state, she planted high hedges to block public view of her house.[44] Her house was in fact hidden from view by thick greenery. An unnamed friend reported that Winchester was reluctant to have her rudimentary skills as an architect inspected, and that "in spite of her seeming callousness to public opinion, Mrs. Winchester is really a tender-hearted, shrinking woman, and public inspection of her work has been evaded by discouraging all visitors."[45] Others pointed to her physical disabilities as her reason for shunning the public. Afflicted with severe arthritis, she was rarely able to manage her pain. A tile setter who worked at the house said, "I always felt sorry for her because she was deprived normal use of her limbs."[46]

Her arms and hands were curled and cramped. She also had lost many teeth.

Winchester had found a substitute for her late coachman, Frank Carroll, in a new chauffeur, Fred Larsen, who recalled, "She wasn't crazy. She was a plenty smart woman, and she had all these people pegged as plain busybodies." Larsen admitted that he did wonder about Winchester's sanity once. He could not fathom that she ordered an extensive wine collection smashed at the beginning of Prohibition. Other than that incident, he never thought her unusual.[47] Larsen's view was confirmed by Ted Hansen, who lived at the ranch his entire childhood. He argued, "I believe Mrs. Winchester found these stories quite humorous, and that she cared less what the general public thought of her."[48]

Much later, after Sarah Winchester's death, her relatives, employees, servants, and gardeners scattered across California. None of them ever claimed that Winchester was superstitious, guilty, mad, or a spiritualist. A few tried to make a public statement in her defense. Attorney Frank Leib had nothing but compliments and courtesy for Winchester. In his eyes, she was a smart and good woman. His son and law partner, Roy Leib, stated unequivocally in the summer of 1925, "Mrs. Winchester was as sane and clear headed a woman as I have ever known, and she had a better grasp of business and financial affairs than most men. The commonly believed supposition that she had hallucinations is all bunk." He declared, "She did not hire a single carpenter after her house was damaged in the earthquake of 1906."[49]

In 1910, Sarah Winchester was seventy-one years old, past the average life expectancy for American women by twenty years. Even as she aged, ridicule and sensational press surged ever forward with no apparent end in sight. For the final twelve years of her life, between 1910 and her death in 1922, she sank deeper into health problems and shrank further from the public eye. In her final years, the intimate bonds she held with Daisy Marriott and Belle Merriman both comforted and confounded her. But Winchester no longer depended on either relative for day-to-day assistance. Instead she built a sturdy support staff of employees including a nurse, a dresser, a secretary, a couple of maids and cooks, property caretakers, chauffeurs, and a number of short-term workers for farm work and housework. Winchester was well taken care of in her final years.

CHAPTER 9

Health and Welfare

A FTER THE SOUTHERN PACIFIC RAILROAD SPLIT THE MERRIMAN RANCH, Sarah Winchester sold it in a few pieces. The Merrimans remained at the old house until 1907, when Winchester agreed to buy a lot and build them a new home in Palo Alto. Winchester believed that land near Stanford would only increase in value, and Palo Alto's accessibility by rail to San Francisco thirty miles to the north made it a highly desirable location. She had already made a tidy profit buying and selling a half dozen town lots there. When she bought a lot for Belle a short walk from Daisy and Fred's Waverley Street home on the new Melville Avenue, she knew what she was doing.

The builder's detailed list of amenities for Belle's house is among Frank Leib's papers. Plans for the house called for a seven-room frame cottage, with a roof of redwood shingles and dormer windows on the north side. Special colonial-styled doors were requested, with "slash grain sanded pine casings." Belle made some special requests for the interior. She wanted the attic to be finished into a twelve-by-twelve-foot room, with a dormer window. She ordered a cooling cupboard in the pantry and a china closet "to be the same as in Mr. Marriott's house," or copied from her daughter's dining room. A double fireplace would throw heat from living to dining room, and in the back of the house a small toilet room was built. Belle's house cost $5,000, and was one of hundreds under construction in 1907, the year after San Francisco's devastation. Builder J. F. Parkinson promised to complete the project within sixty days.[1] That the work was complete within two months of signing a contract testifies to the quick pace of construction in the town.

Belle moved into the house just as her husband's health disintegrated. Louis was in and out of hospitals and sanitariums between 1900 and 1908. He is so rarely mentioned in relation to his family, it is unclear whether any ties between them remained. If he lived at the Melville

Avenue house, it was only very briefly. On October 30, 1908, he was checked into O'Connor Sanitarium, a hospital in San José, with pneumonia, and died fifteen days later. The seventy-three-year-old had chronic kidney disease along with the pneumonia. Belle did not act as informant for Louis's death record; instead, their son, Willie Merriman, signed the document. The remains were handled by a San José undertaker, cremated and inurned at Cypress Lawn Cemetery in Colma. A death notice never appeared in the newspaper, and if there was a service for Louis, there is no record of it. Daisy had distanced herself from her father years before. Willie alone is linked with Louis; he had stayed close to his ailing father as his health declined. Willie had married at about the same time that Daisy had, but with little fanfare. He and his wife lived in Pacific Grove, and Willie worked as a teamster, hauling goods from the coast to the valley. He maintained a good rapport with his mother and aunt, and helped them from time to time.

Belle created quite a life for herself in Palo Alto. An ardent progressive reformer, she sought public notice at least as much as her sister shunned it. Belle worked for humane causes, including racial equity, child welfare, and animal rights. Since her girlhood days when the cause of abolition caught her attention, she had lobbied for rights for black people. When the local chapter of the National Association for the Advancement of Colored People came to Palo Alto, Belle Merriman was its first white member. Winchester's feelings about racial equity are more difficult to determine. There is no record of her employing anyone of African American heritage after she left New Haven. In California, adhering to local custom, she paid Asian employees less than white workers. She employed more Asians, however, than did others of her race and class. When she supplied housing to employees, the white workers were given houses, and the Asians were loaned them.[2] This practice may not be the insult that it appears, however. Exclusion laws in California disallowed property ownership by Asians to the middle of the 1920s.

Letters between Belle and Sarah have never been located. They may not even exist since the two saw each other often. Sarah's letters to others suggest the widow's opinions about Belle's causes. Like Belle, Sarah was an animal lover and had a variety of pets. At one time she had a favorite dog named "Snip," and later, another called "Zip." She distinguished between workhorses and riding horses, and the best of her herd were Black Frank, Bessie, and Flower. She made special accommodations in the stables for the proper upkeep of carriage horses. Daisy boarded horses and dogs at her aunt's ranch.[3]

Winchester's concern for animal welfare extended further than the farm pen or doghouse. When the paper boy asked Winchester permission to hunt robins on her property with his air rifle she refused, but only after a lengthy explanation on the entire life cycle of robins. She emphasized the birds' need for the warmth of the valley landscape before venturing back to summer in the Sierras. That boy grew up to be a lawyer, and never "drew a bead on any feathered songster." Nor did he forget the lecture he got from Mrs. Winchester.[4]

Ironically, Belle's defense of animals and children was the most vociferous at the same time that the Winchester Repeating Arms Company shifted its sites to market hunting rifles to children. Winchester historian Herbert Houze writes, "It was the company's hope that youngsters who used Winchester .22 caliber rifles would upon their majority elect to use larger bore arms produced by the firm. To that end, in 1904, the Winchester Repeating Arms Company instituted an advertising program which actively promoted the concept that a child who first used a Winchester would eventually become a customer for a Winchester centerfire rifle or shotgun."[5]

Neither Belle nor Sarah objected to hunting for food or sport. They objected to cruelty and waste. Saidee, their late sister Estelle's daughter, took it a step further. She ardently opposed hunting and lobbied Californians against the use of animals in scientific experimentation. Saidee, not to mention Belle, Daisy, and Sarah, received substantial income from those rifles. There is no evidence that Saidee turned down a monthly allowance from Aunt Sarah. Saidee had married before 1900 and by 1912 was divorced. She married Henry "Harry" Ruthrauff, a writer who was about her age. Saidee's writing career took off after marrying Ruthrauff. Most of her poetry and essays were about animal rights.

Belle devoted most of her time to the Humane Society, a group dedicated to humane treatment of children and animals. The year she moved onto Melville Avenue, she took up the animal rights cause with a fiery enthusiasm that was typical of Belle and was anathema to Sarah. In June 1908, Belle was elected along with Alice Park, an outspoken women's rights advocate, to the board of directors of the Palo Alto Humane Society. Among the board's first tasks was to help establish a statewide organization, resulting in the State Humane Association of California. Board members were issued badges signifying their role as humane officers in the community. Dues were set at $1, and the membership roll was stacked with Belle's relatives: her daughter, Daisy; son-in-law, Fred; and Fred's sister, Adele.

Belle did not hesitate to brandish her state-issued badge, and on at least two occasions made citizen's arrests against men she believed were being cruel to animals. When a two-car circus rolled into town to give a performance, Belle believed the circus man was cruel to his animals.

She promptly called for authorities to arrest him. Local police noted that he had not paid the requisite licensing fees and issued the citation for that, but they did not cite the fellow for animal cruelty.[6] Belle's activities raised eyebrows when she caused the arrest of the most popular butcher in Mountain View. She insisted that charges be pressed against the butcher for leaving his horse unattended and stuck in a muddy hole. Butcher Blanchard was found not guilty, but the court's response did not deter Belle from fighting for animal rights. She voiced her objections to cruelty to animals constantly and loudly.

In 1910 Belle created a spectacle when she arrested "two society belles of San Francisco who have been spending the summer near Palo Alto and whose fathers are prominent business men of that city." A local paper described how the two young women "were arrested the other day by Mrs. Merriman, the humane officer of the college town, while driving a poor old emaciated horse covered with sores and trembling from old age and overwork."[7] The girls were distraught and their fathers dismayed, but they were released without consequences. Nevertheless, Belle believed her point was made that mistreating animals would be reported under her watch.

Belle was named the director of the Santa Clara County Humane Society. She hobnobbed with progressive leaders and attended the state conventions, among them one held in Pasadena in 1910. Under Belle's directorship, the Santa Clara County Humane Society began advocating for child welfare as it had for animals. "Mrs. I.C. Merriman, who for years [has been] connected with the Juvenile Court work, has given her time and strength to the uplift of children, and now, in this new capacity will serve without remuneration." The county society, it was reported, "has been a mighty factor in the prevention of cruelty to animals, has taken up a still greater work—the prevention of cruelty to children."[8] Even though Belle held official positions, she was not paid for her work and remained financially dependent on Sarah.

Belle became the Special Humane Officer for the investigation of children's cases in the county. She began in earnest to rescue "unfortunate girls" and abused children. Acting as a social worker and as "one of the most trusted attachés of the juvenile court," she placed foster or abandoned children in private homes. She advocated for adoption and over the years, took a number of young girls into her Palo Alto home, where they stayed in her upstairs dormer-windowed attic. She rescued two young brothers whose "bodies bore marks of bruises and ill treatment, starvation and general misuse," and placed their guardians, self-described religious fundamentalist "Holy Rollers," under arrest. At one time she had as many as a dozen boys and girls staying at her home.[9]

Daisy and Fred had been married for five years but had not had any children. When Belle brought home one little girl from the Santa Clara County Juvenile Court, she particularly captured Daisy's attention. In 1909, six-year-old Margaret Cozza had been brought before the county court for neglect and severe abuse. Reportedly, Margaret's father "would knock her down and trample upon her."[10] The childless Daisy and Fred Marriott fell in love with her and took steps to adopt her.

The girl's biological parents agreed to have the Marriotts adopt Margaret—until they discovered that the adoptive parents were related to the wealthy Sarah Winchester. Because of the kinship between Mrs. Marriott, Mrs. Merriman, and Mrs. Winchester, the parents did their best to change the terms of the adoption, to include a demand for cash and periodic visits, a practice that is commonplace today but virtually unheard of at that time. As legal negotiations played out over a period of three years, Margaret lived in the Marriott home as the long-awaited child. She was showered with every possible good thing, including riding privileges of a pony at Aunt Sarah's.[11]

The California Supreme Court stunned the Marriotts in 1911 by awarding custody of Margaret to the birth mother, Filomena Sutori. By this time, Margaret had lived with the Marriotts for three years. Shortly after the verdict, an "amicable" meeting was held at the Marriott home in Palo Alto between the Marriotts, the birth mother, and her attorney. At that meeting the biological mother suddenly signed relinquishment papers and gave custody to the Marriotts.[12] There is no way of knowing whether cash changed hands, but a very unusual transaction shows up in Sarah Winchester's financial records just two weeks before the fateful meeting. Winchester gave a small bungalow that she owned on Stockton Avenue in San José to Daisy Marriott, as the deed says, "in consideration of the love and affection which the said party of the first part has and bears unto the said party of the second part [Marion I. Marriott], as also for the better maintenance, support, protection, and livelihood of the said party of the second part."[13] Did Winchester give Daisy the house to convince the birth parents of her financial support? Did Daisy use the house as collateral to win custody of Margaret? There is no proof of either of these things. However, Winchester never signed over any other property to Daisy Marriott, or to any of her relatives, before or after this. Even the Marriotts' home on Waverley Street was owned by Sarah Winchester until her death, when it was bequeathed to Daisy. It is very curious that just as a negative verdict came down regarding Margaret's adoption this financial anomaly shows up in Winchester's records, and specifically names Marion I. Marriott as the beneficiary.

By 1912, when Margaret's adoption was made official, the child was nine years old. She personified Daisy's and Belle's reformist ideals. They had rescued a child from the grip of abuse and supplied her with all the good things in life. Convinced of the possibility of changing the world one child at a time, each reveled in Margaret's adoption. As did most reformers of the period, the women ardently believed that placing a child in a safe environment changed the outcome of a life, made a good citizen, and developed a thoughtful person. They fashioned a little charmer out of Margaret. Psychological aftereffects of trauma in early childhood only surfaced as the girl grew toward adulthood. Margaret never successfully maintained warm relationships, and she often displayed impulsive and aggressive behavior. Eventually she became an alcoholic.

Fred Marriott's role in the child's adoption appears peripheral. He displayed fondness for Margaret, and his name is attached to Daisy's in court records. But most public mention of the adoption case includes Belle's and Daisy's names, only occasionally linking Sarah Winchester to the adoption. Headlines ran "Little Margaret to be Reared as Heiress," setting up fairy-tale expectations, and Margaret was not too young to believe that she was indeed an heiress.[14]

As adoption proceedings played out in court, Sarah Winchester amended her latest will to include language explicitly allowing adopted children "of either Marion Marriott or William Merriman" to be considered "as normal issue."[15] Winchester anticipated that although neither Daisy nor Willie had biological children, Belle's work in child protective service would supply any desirable grandchildren.

Margaret's induction into the Marriott ranks added to a troop of children who found Winchester's Llanada Villa an enormous playground. Daisy and Fred brought Margaret for visits at the villa, and in spring and summer, the family spent even more time there. Carl and Ted Hansen, the caretaker's two sons, were built-in playmates. The three recruited coachman Frank Carroll's daughter, Mabel. A girl named Minnie Yeager bounced over from across the street, and she was exactly the same age as Margaret. "Oh! What fun we kids had on the place," Yeager recalled. "It was like a child's paradise, so many places to scamper and climb. We were like monkeys in the trees. The Hansens sort of adopted me because they had no little girls of their own."[16] All attended Meridian School, except Margaret, who went to school in Palo Alto.

Sarah Winchester's health had been unpredictable and problematic since her New Haven days, following the death of her husband. Frank Carroll's wife recalled that when William Winchester died, Sarah

Winchester's "health was affected. Her doctor prescribed a change of climate and a vigorous hobby ... [suggesting] that she develop her latent interest in designing."[17] Winchester found the climate in California quite agreeable, and was able to take her doctor's advice and work on architecture and interior design.

Once in California, Winchester engaged Dr. Euthanasia Meade as her personal physician. Meade was very helpful during Estelle Gerard's illness and death. But Meade herself died within a couple of years after that. Winchester turned to Dr. Charles Wayland, a California man who had gone to the East for his medical degree. Upon his return to San José, he worked in association with Dr. Helen Lee, a gynecologist. Wayland's partnership with a female physician made him unusual in the American medical profession but in Winchester's eyes may have given him more credibility. Later, Wayland's son, Dr. Clyde Wayland, took over and served as Winchester's personal physician. She came to trust the young doctor implicitly.

Winchester reported health problems to relatives in the East. "For years it has only been at long intervals that I have been able to do more than sew on a button without suffering. Since I have given up drinking coffee my hand has been much better although not yet normal." She tried a number of homeopathic remedies for pain and insomnia. "I have been more or less troubled with insomnia but for two or three weeks I have been so sleepy all of the time that I find it difficult to summon enough energy to do anything. At the same time I am continually very tired and listless. I don't know what to attribute this very somnolent condition, unless it is the result of having left off drinking coffee." She was an insomniac for most of her remaining years. "These days I find it prudent to be economical of strength and energy. ... I sincerely hope I shall soon feel more wide awake and develop more energy and enterprise," she commented after subscribing to the Corrective Eating Society, which laid out a course in scientific eating based on food chemistry. The society claimed that America had become a "nation of stomach sufferers" because the combination of certain foods resulted in digestive problems.[18] Winchester did not report in her letters whether her subscription to the program helped.

By 1903, when she purchased land in Atherton, Winchester was seriously afflicted with rheumatoid arthritis, which limited the use of her arms and hands.[19] The disfiguring effects of the disease made her extremely self-conscious. She was also losing her teeth, so she made arrangements with Dr. Robert Payne of San Francisco to build a set of dentures. Payne traveled by train to San José, hired an assistant, and used a local dentist's office to construct the dentures. Evidently his efforts were not wholly successful or Winchester would not have disputed his bill. When he submitted an invoice for $8,750, Winchester went apoplectic. In a fury she sent Leib to negotiate the invoice. The dentist threatened to sue if the bill was not paid; Leib offered $2,500 with a carefully worded letter outlining all the possible costs the dentist could have incurred, including "material, equipment, upkeep, railroad fares, assistants, and office rental." Winchester ended up paying $3,000, and then looked for a new dentist. Perhaps Payne's name could have been a clue that all would not go well. The incident may confirm that she was reluctant to be seen in public and often wore a veil over her face.[20]

Business correspondence required more paperwork than Winchester was able to accomplish. Frank Leib acknowledged that he knew it was painful for Winchester to write, and he offered to send a stenographer to Atherton to take dictation. "I note what you say that even writing is a painful task, and it may be possible that I could save you more or less trouble and strain by taking the data from you in person, which I would gladly do . . . or send down my stenographer. . . . anything stated would be kept by her absolutely confidential." During the last half of 1908 and in the early months of 1909, Winchester was quite ill. When Leib asked to see her to discuss business matters, she refused. Only months later did he write, "Today came a note from your niece explaining your illness . . ."[21] It did not say what her illness had been.

In 1911, however, Winchester enjoyed remarkably good health. In her early seventies, she enjoyed a reprieve from many chronic complaints. Leib wrote, "I am very glad to hear your health is so much better, and that you are feeling so well." Several months later he also noted, "I am very glad to hear of your good health. In fact, I did not need to have you say so to know it was a fact, as it was apparent from the tone of cheerfulness in the letter itself." John Hansen noted in his daybook "sent Mrs. W. her sewing machine to F.O. [Fair Oaks, or Atherton]."[22] That she was able to sew was a marked improvement. For some reason at precisely this same time the newspapers reported that Winchester was dangerously close to death. In June 1911, the *San Francisco Call* stated that the widow was "not expected to live." The notice was picked up and repeated in the *New York Times*. It went on to explain that she "suffered from a nervous breakdown at the time her mansion was partially destroyed by the disaster of 1906 and became afflicted with neuritis, which grew worse."[23] Neuritis, an autoimmune disease, is not necessarily linked to mental illness, and the concept of a nervous breakdown in 1911 did not mean the same thing as such a diagnosis would mean today. It is impossible to determine whether indeed she had a nervous breakdown, but questions about Winchester's mental competency emerged after the earthquake and after she had declined to rebuild her large San José house.

When the newspaper story appeared, her employees in San José were barraged with questions about the widow's health. The ones at the ranch knew she was in Atherton, but began to wonder if something was indeed wrong with "Madame." John Hansen telephoned the Atherton house to verify Winchester's well-being, and was assured she was fine. Dr. Lee reiterated to the press that the widow was well. "Doctor Helen Lee, assistant to Dr. Wayland, says reports of Mrs. Winchester's near fatal illness are false," one local paper reported. About a month later, a long article about Winchester appeared in the same newspaper stating that "at the present time [Winchester's] health is better than it has been for several years, but she is still a semi-invalid."[24]

Five months later, Daisy fell ill. Fred rushed Daisy to Palo Alto Hospital, where she almost died. Dr. Samuel Van Daisem diagnosed acute appendicitis and proceeded to operate. Daisy's prospects did not look good, and the evening paper ran an article headlined "Mrs. F. Marriott May Not Survive Operation." Winchester called in Dr. Wayland from San José, and after he made his way to Palo Alto to examine Daisy he declared, "Mrs. Marriott is very low." The next day a follow-up noted that "little hope was entertained for her recovery." The terrifying ordeal brought home to Winchester once again that age is not necessarily a requirement for death. Daisy was forty-two, almost exactly the same age that William had been when he died.[25]

— ⋙◆⋘ —

Daisy fought off infection and slowly recovered. Her illness made Sarah Winchester realize how much she depended on her niece to carry out business correspondence and banking. With Daisy in a weakened condition from the appendectomy, Sarah needed to look elsewhere for personal and business help. She constructed a new scaffold of employees to surround her carefully ordered world. The staff she built remained remarkably stable for her remaining years.

John Hansen captained an unlikely team of employees. If Winchester had hired a police officer to guard her she would not have done better than the sharp-eyed Hansen. He was hired as a farm laborer in the 1890s, and just after the turn of the century he married Nellie Zarconi. The young woman's brother worked as a carpenter at the Winchester place. John was promoted to ranch foreman after Ned Rambo died, and the Hansens made a home at the carriage house just behind the main house at Llanada Villa. They raised two sons, Theodore (Ted) and Carl, who brought life and playmates to the property. Ted and Carl lived their entire youth at the Winchester place. The Hansen family photograph album and scrapbooks provide visual documentation of life at Llanada Villa with glimpses into the workaday world of the ranch. Nellie worked as most farm wives in the valley did, at cutting and drying fruit, and feeding farm help. Hansen's management of the orchards, hiring of seasonal workers, and selling the crops kept production in gear. Things would have come to a grinding halt without the Hansens. Whenever Winchester was away from the ranch, John went through the entire house, room by room, making sure everything was secure and safe.

Nellie Hansen struck up a warm friendship with Winchester's newest hire, Henrietta Sivera. The Hansens and Henrietta worked well together for more than a decade. Sivera acted as Winchester's secretary and personal companion, placing phone calls and making any appointments that she required, taking over where Daisy left off. Her signature on documents shows that Winchester trusted her enough to make her privy to private business transactions. The relationship between Henrietta and the widow was one of fondness and some humor, but Henrietta always called the widow "Mrs. Winchester" or "Madame."[26] At the end, Henrietta was the widow's most trusted employee.

Winchester's different houses required distinct kinds of help. Maud Merrill served as a nurse, and another single woman, Mae Shelby, kept house. Most were foreign born. Charlie Yen was older than Winchester, but managed the landscape at Atherton. The anti-Chinese movement in California late in the nineteenth century reduced the supply of Asian farm workers. Japanese immigrants were allowed in to fill that gap, and mostly men arrived to work in the valley orchards. In the coming years, women followed, sometimes as picture brides, and families were established. In 1900, there were just under 300 Japanese in the valley. Within ten years, the number rose to 2,200.[27] Sometime before 1910, Winchester hired a Japanese couple to work at the Atherton house. Rikitaro and Tomo Ushio came from Japan together, making them somewhat unusual. Tomo worked as Sarah's personal maid, while Rikitaro landscaped and gardened, helping Yen. A man named Mr. Nakano ran her Atherton kitchen.[28]

The Ushios had worked for the widow for about five years when she hired Misa Hirata as a dresser. Hirata sewed and mended, and deftly managed the decorative stitching that Winchester was no longer able to make her fingers manipulate. Misa worked for Winchester until the widow's death. The Oyamas, another Japanese family, lived in a house Winchester owned near the San José ranch, where they worked.

By 1911, Winchester had hired Tommie Nishihara, a gardener who managed all the decorative landscape features at the San José and Atherton homes. That same year, Tommie's son, Ryoichi, arrived in the Santa Clara Valley from Japan with his new wife, Ito. She was hired at once for the San José house. Winchester loaned one of the houses that had belonged to the Laederiches to the Nishihara family. Tommie's first grandchild was born at that house in 1913, and the little girl was named Ida Winchester Nishihara, an obvious gesture of respect and affection for Sarah Winchester. Photos of the child and her mother appear in the Hansens' family scrapbook.

Hiring so many people from Japan made Winchester different from most of her wealthy contemporaries in California. Both Jane Stanford and Mary Hayes Chynoweth died in 1905, too early for a valid comparison of their hiring of Japanese workers. The Hayes sons, however, provide a comparison. They lived in the large mansion that was rebuilt after a fire in 1899 destroyed the one their mother had built. In 1910, Winchester had at least six Asian workers, and her workers lived at her respective properties with their families. Jay Hayes and Everis Hayes had no Asian servants on a staff of more than twenty. The Carolans, whose large San Mateo County estate and polo field sat next to Winchester's houseboat, hired no Asian workers. They had a French stable man, and the cook, laundress, gardener, butler, and valet were all English or Scottish.[29] The presence of Japanese workers cast a new shadow of suspicion on Winchester. Beginning at this time, stories in the newspapers claimed that Sarah Winchester hosted unusual religious rituals in her home. "One of the latest yarns is to the effect that religious services of a strange character are conducted in the house and that Orientals participate in them," one newspaper reported.[30] Winchester's appreciation for Japanese culture and willingness to hire Japanese workers added to her reputation as an oddball.

* * *

During the first decade of the twentieth century, Americans were introduced to the automobile, particularly after Henry Ford's Model T rolled off the assembly line. But even by 1910, only people of means owned autos. Fred Marriott was both passionate and knowledgeable about the new contraptions. He put his passion for automobiles into print, writing a new automobile section of the *News Letter.* Fred had never been as enthralled with the newspaper business as his father and grandfather had been, so he had tried other businesses, but always wandered back to the newsroom. A happy marriage of the news business and the dawn of the auto age, the new section of the Sunday paper suggested driving excursions for Californians. Fred found moderate success as the auto editor. He appeared in Palo Alto on the weekends, and spent time driving any one of a handful of Winchester's new autos. Her finest car was a

1909 green Renault limousine with a thirty-horsepower engine, customized with two square side lamps. The long brass-tubed horn sounded a warning to horses in the way, and a mahogany toolbox was attached to the running board. Sarah ordered two extra forward-facing seats, and the state-of-the-art Michelin tires made the ride smooth. Winchester also requested an electric enunciator so that the driver could hear instructions from the passengers. The total cost for this amazing piece of automotive machinery was a whopping $8,425, and she had Fred Marriott take delivery of it.[31] He drove the Renault from the San Francisco dealership to Atherton, and had use of it quite often.

Keeping the limousine in good working order was quite challenging. Winchester searched out an auto mechanic to maintain the car. After a series of mishaps where the expensive machine would not start, she found Fred Larsen, a man who immigrated from Denmark in 1904. Eventually she cajoled him into a full-time job chauffeuring and servicing what became a small fleet of autos purchased by Fred Marriott with Winchester money. In April 1911, John Hansen noted in his daybook, "Mrs. W. got new auto," but he did not specify which it was.[32] Her fleet of cars began to grow. Most of the cars turned heads, but the gray Pierce-Arrow "flat-roof suburban" with a hairline lavender stripe was so distinctive that when people spotted it, everyone knew the widow Winchester was out and about. Larsen skillfully kept the temperamental mechanisms in the cars on working. Winchester's mobility was increasingly limited, and she had an additional running board attached to one of her cars so that she could more easily step into her seat.

Larsen quickly won the widow's trust. For Christmas in 1913 she gave him a matchbox and a wallet. That holiday season she jotted ideas for Christmas gifts in a tiny, black leather book measuring two by three inches and embossed with gold letters reading "Winchester Repeating Arms Co., New Haven, Conn." The inside page shows a fluid signature in perfect classic script: Sarah L. Winchester. Next, in faded pencil, is a list labeled "Christmas 1913." The list suggests holiday remembrances of simple elegance with a nod to utility. Besides Larsen, she gave Ito Nishihara a flashlight, perhaps to make her way home in the evenings. A hat brush was designated for Henrietta, to keep her small collection of felt hats fresh and clean. Her gift for the Hansens was an elegant silver-plated vase. Another entry on the list is a work box for Misa Hirata. The list does not specify what kind of work box, but some kind of sewing box is a possibility since the woman handled Winchester's clothing. She also noted gifts for family members. For Daisy, Winchester ordered two dozen monogrammed towels. She planned to give a thimble to eleven-year-old Margaret. Perhaps Margaret was learning to sew. Winchester's prolific orchard and fruit-drying operation provided gifts to be sent east. She gave her brother's daughter, Sadie Pardee, California-grown nuts and glacéed fruits.

Sarah Winchester's staff of employees, hailing from Denmark, Japan, China, Ireland, and California, grew into an unlikely community. Some, like Larsen and Sivera, had been hired to work at Atherton, but traveled with Winchester when she visited San José. Others, like Charlie Yen and Mr. Nakano, remained at Atherton. John Hansen was undoubtedly the leader, and worked for Winchester the longest. While he hired and paid orchard pickers and cutters, he had little to do with household servants, and nothing at all to do with Winchester's other properties. Hansen and his wife, Nellie, developed cordial and warm relationships with the Nishiharas, the Oyamas, Henrietta Sivera, and Fred Larsen. Sivera and the Hansens exchanged letters for many years after leaving Llanada Villa. Larsen left Winchester's employ in 1917, married, and started a family. He managed his own fifty-acre prune orchard on Moorpark Avenue. The remarkable congeniality among the workers in Atherton and San José is documented in the photographs taken and preserved by the Hansen family and by the fact that after Sarah Winchester died, none of them spoke a bad word about her.

CHAPTER 10

Changing Fortunes

ADVANCING AGE AND FAILING HEALTH MADE SARAH WINCHESTER RETREAT from construction projects that had occupied her time up until about 1910. And the death of Frank Carroll derailed her plans for a harbor at Burlingame. She no longer worked on the San José house except for adding an elevator in 1916 and having odd maintenance jobs completed. Instead, she launched an entirely new type of enterprise. Her construction efforts from here on out would be confined to ledgers and account books as she dedicated her time to building an investment portfolio.

Winchester redrafted her will, reshuffled her investments and real estate holdings, established a new primary residence, and formalized her financial support to relatives. In a letter to her New Haven attorney, Charles Morris, she wrote, "You have in your possession a will I made some time ago. I have recently made another will in which I revoked the one you hold, and which I wish to destroy."[1] Morris sent the original to attorney Frank Leib, who turned it over to Winchester.

She was far more successful constructing an investment portfolio than a mansion, and her portfolio rested on a substantial foundation of stock in the Winchester Repeating Arms Company. In 1910, for example, Winchester received $260,000 in stock dividends. The previous year had earned her slightly less, but the next two years reaped the same amount. Sometimes she sought advice, and occasionally implemented it. She grew her money by shrewd investments in stocks, bonds, real estate, and by farming ventures. She assembled a diverse financial scheme with skill and wisdom beyond most other Americans'—male or female. Sarah Winchester rarely lost money.

Winchester invested in municipal bonds from the City of San Francisco amounting to $50,000, and she also bought school bonds, all the while keeping bonds she had purchased in New Haven. Leib cautioned that California law did not conform to Connecticut's, and he advised Winchester to select a trustee in the East to monitor her interests there. "I never thought it was wise to see how near one could walk to the edge of a precipice," he warned, "and not fall over."[2] He wanted her fully protected in both states.

Winchester's real estate portfolio did not remain static. Among her most irksome real estate problems was coping with issues of eminent domain or easements. Llanada Villa was trimmed on its south side in 1906 by the incursion of Moorpark Avenue. The Interurban Railroad demanded a strip of land on the north along Stevens Creek Road, and she resisted as long as she could. The rail company planned to expand the line running from Bird Avenue to Meridian Corners along Stevens Creek Road, but still angry about the Interurban's dissection of the Merriman ranch, she ignored repeated requests to give construction crews access to begin work. The rail company sued, and when Frank Leib, who was on the railroad's board of directors, read about it in the newspaper, he wrote, "I noticed in the morning paper that the Railroad Company has brought suit against you to condemn the strip along Stevens Creek Road, which they desire for railroad purposes. I held off the bringing of the suit as long as I possibly could, but they would not wait any longer."[3] Leib walked a thin tightrope between his board position with the railroad and his fiduciary obligations to Winchester. Overall, he managed to maintain good relations with both. Winchester did not hesitate to implement tactics of her own. "Mrs. Winchester is too clever for deputies," the newspaper reported. "It appears that a corps of expert summons servers have been on Mrs. Winchester's trail, but without success."[4] A subpoena floated from one unsuccessful messenger to another as Winchester hid out behind loyal servants and locked doors.

Meanwhile, Winchester added to the Atherton property which stretched from today's El Camino Real (the County Road) south to today's Inglewood Lane. It edged Atherton Avenue, part of which was taken from her acreage, east to Isabella Avenue. In 1907, Winchester purchased a second house from the Moultons on an adjoining property. When a newspaper reported in 1904 that "Mr. & Mrs. F. Moulton are erecting a beautiful dwelling house on Atherton Avenue.... Mr. Moulton thinks he will be suited this time and will devote himself to horticulture,"[5] it was mistaken. For although Sarah Winchester had been residing in the Moulton house she bought in 1903, she offered to buy the newer one in 1907. The first one had suffered more earthquake damage than she wanted to live with and it was too close to the increasingly busy County Road. The second Moulton house, at 44 Inglewood Lane (although at the time it was an Atherton Avenue address), became her permanent and full-time home. The interior was finished with mission- and Craftsman-style décor. Photographs of it show book-laden shelves, doily-covered tables, and an oak desk with papers strewn across it. A bottle of wine peaks out from a glass-doored curio cabinet.

One wonders what motivated the Moultons to build houses only to sell them to Sarah Winchester. Evidently Frank Moulton was a better builder that money manager. The newer house was saddled with mechanics' liens and mortgages, and Winchester's cash allowed him to get out of debt. She vacated the first house and moved into the one off Atherton Avenue.[6] Two years later she bought yet another house nearby, this time from a family with six boisterous children. A neighbor surmised that the noisy children may have been motivation enough for Winchester to buy them out.[7] In reality, the family could no longer shoulder the $10,000 mortgage. By 1910, Sarah Winchester owned three houses and about forty acres in Atherton.

Winchester had no intention of occupying the latest addition, but had eyed it with a plan to house servants and a watchman. Lately she had become more conscious of security breaches. Her concern was not simply a matter of paranoia. On a chilly February night in 1912, when she happened to be in San José, an intruder broke into her new Atherton house and, in the style of Goldilocks, chose one of the finely appointed feather beds to have a good night's sleep. Inadvertently he left behind a satchel. Finding himself without even a change of clothes, he broke into another house nearby, "Byde a Whyle," the home of Lucie and Louis Stern, the nephew of blue jeans millionaire Levi Strauss. The intruder replaced his lost satchel with a newer one belonging to Lucie, and changed tattered and dirty clothes for one of Louis's most expensive suits, silk stockings, and handcrafted leather shoes. Later, the Redwood City police identified the burglar. The presence of a prowler, even if he did not inflict serious harm, was enough to make Winchester hire more help.

She installed a property overseer named James Bogie, who, with his wife, Sarah, kept doors locked, gates latched, and watchful eyes open. The Bogies were a childless couple approaching fifty years of age. Since James arrived in the United States from Scotland, he had worked as a gardener. With the Bogies, Winchester got the best of all possible combinations—a watchman, a gardener, and a quiet neighbor. The couple lived right next door, so she and a maid or two still had the house to themselves. The setup worked well for over ten years.

Sarah Winchester's new Atherton home was the epitome of modernity and respectability. No one could criticize its design or décor. It matched the landscape of the old Atherton woods, with a Mission Revival style, its interior favoring Craftsman detail—giving no evidence of Victorian over-decoration or Queen Anne fussiness. When Leib saw it, he commented, "I had the pleasure of dining in your immediate neighborhood yesterday and your place was pointed out to me as I drove past it. It struck me as being a very beautiful home."[8]

The house was so attractive, in fact, that it was officially photographed and featured in a publication for the Panama Pacific International Exposition in 1915.[9] The exposition signified the rebirth of San Francisco after the destruction of the great earthquake, but also heralded the end of the Gilded Age. As at previous international fairs, the Winchester Repeating Arms Company had great exposure at the Panama Pacific International Exposition, where it was awarded the highest honor, the Grand Prize, for rifles and ammunition. That Winchester's home appeared in the official program of the exposition identified it as among the Bay Area's finest. Sarah Winchester had finally moved into the twentieth century and shed many Victorian tendencies. This marked a major departure from the widow's association with the cumbersome house in the Santa Clara Valley.

From this modern platform Winchester settled into old age. Canceled checks from this period reveal some of her personal interests and preferences. She shopped for clothing and linens by mail from New York retailer B. Altman & Company. She kept apprised of events in New Haven and the East with subscriptions to the *New York Herald* and the *New Haven Register.* The magazines she received reveal diverse interests: *Architectural Record, Vogue,* and the *Science Press.*[10]

Winchester's philanthropy was as carefully calibrated as her real estate transactions, and most was precisely plotted with an eye to future returns. What donations would generate the most good for the longest period of time? She was deluged with requests for money from all sorts of charities and individuals. She had developed a strict policy of rejecting all requests. When she found a philanthropic cause worthy of a donation, which she sometimes did, she usually gave a check to someone she trusted to make her donation anonymously.

The "Save the Redwoods" campaign, which established California's first state park at Big Basin in the Santa Cruz Mountains, contacted Winchester through local landscape artist and photographer Andrew P. Hill. He was the group's spokesman and leading advocate for saving the giant, old-growth trees. Winchester supported the cause, but even for Hill, would not give the money directly. Instead she wrote a check for $500 to Dr. Clyde Wayland, who in turn wrote his own check to the Sempervirens Club. Dollars and political support that the club collected at that time saved the redwoods from the logger's ax. The park has grown from its 3,000 acres early in the twentieth century to its current 18,000 acres.

Winchester's wish to remain anonymous made her very different from other American heiresses. Although women were not admired for earning money in the early twentieth century, they were often lauded for giving it away. Historian Ruth Crocker explains that "women who made money or who enjoyed investment or speculation risked being considered unnatural." If women gave money away, however, they "confirmed Victorian gender expectations."[11] Sarah Winchester was a speculator who gave away a great deal of money, but no one knew about it. As a result, she was viewed as a miserly female money-grubber, a combination that made for bad press.

Undoubtedly, Winchester managed her vast income very well. But what sets her apart from others of her time is her knack for real estate investment. Each of her large real estate investments turned into significant civic or private developments in the twentieth century. The San José ranch included land that became today's Interstate 280 interchange at Winchester Boulevard and the Santana Row retail development. The Burlingame houseboat land was absorbed by the San Francisco International Airport and Bayshore Highway 101. The combination of her Atherton land purchases is a residential subdivision with some of the most expensive homes in the Bay Area. The Merriman ranch has become the City of Los Altos, and the house is the town's oldest. Winchester's purchases show her to be a tenacious investor who set herself apart from others of her class and gender with unrelenting property acquisition and incisive business savvy.[12]

Winchester was not in the habit of selling property, particularly that in proximity to her own house, but in 1911 she made an exception. The earthquake damage to the first of the Moulton houses had been repaired, and she sold it to Delia Fleishhaker, a wealthy Jewish widow from San Francisco. Fleishhaker and Winchester happened to be exactly the same age (the two would have lived the precise lifespan had Winchester lived a few months longer). Fleishhaker was born in New York and educated in Albany. She had not been born into wealth, and had high regard for hard work. Winchester and Fleishhaker shared a number of personal and philanthropic values. They understood each other and afforded each other privacy. The two were neighbors for the next twelve years, although Fleishhaker was often in San Francisco. Upon purchasing the house, Fleishhaker hired a contractor to add "two verandas and several sleeping porches."[13] Her sons owned houses nearby.

Next, Winchester reassessed her Burlingame properties, deciding to keep the houseboat and surrounding acreage since she believed it would increase in value. In 1912 she put the little Tudor cottage she had bought in 1907 on the market, and it sold promptly to a San Francisco doctor and his wife. The newspaper noted that it had recently been improved at considerable cost, and that the house was sold fully furnished.[14] The doctor's finances complicated the transaction somewhat, and it did not proceed as quickly as Winchester desired. She threatened to deal with other parties if the negotiations were not completed in a timely manner. To satisfy

Winchester's demands, the buyer's agent purchased the house as an intermediary before turning it over to the doctor when his mortgage request was approved.

Winchester worried about security at her houseboat property. As long as Ida and Henry Kohne resided there, she believed poachers and vandals could be kept at bay. After Ida Kohne died in 1917, Winchester gave the matter serious consideration, and within two years, Henry Kohne was also dead. She called Rev. Brewer in Burlingame, and he arranged a service at Stead's Chapel for Kohne. A burial took place at Cypress Lawn Cemetery. The ark sat empty.

Winchester offered the caretaker position at "the Pasture" to her niece, Saidee Gerard Ruthrauff, and her husband, Henry. The Ruthrauffs agreed, and moved into the little houseboat in Burlingame. Saidee was more like her aunt Belle than her mother or her aunt Sarah. She had become one of California's most ardent anti-vivisection writers. She and Henry transformed Winchester's "Pasture" into the "Royal Band of Mercy," an animal shelter with horses, goats, chickens, rabbits, and dozens and dozens of cats. They set up a makeshift tented classroom, and children from Oak Grove School walked there on field trips to learn how to take care of pets. Saidee instructed the children on humane treatment of animals, and when one or other suggested he preferred fishing or duck hunting, he was promptly hushed. One boy recalled mentioning that he had fished for clams on the seawall and that "[Mrs. Ruthrauff] gave me the devil for being cruel to sea life." Duck hunters were shooed away by a screeching and broom-wielding Saidee.[15]

The Ruthrauffs lived a bohemian life, and the foggy seaside boat was the perfect muse. The eucalyptus-sheltered property inspired Saidee to write poetry published in *Sunset* and other magazines. Henry Ruthrauff did not share his wife's passion for animals nor her politics. In fact, he was a registered Republican, countering her Progressive Party registration. Henry had served in the Spanish-American War, and his work often reflected bitter wartime memories.

The Ruthrauffs became well known in the neighborhood. Henry befriended one neighbor whom he allowed onto the property to collect manure to fertilize his garden; the Ruthrauffs had a prodigious supply produced by their many furry and feathered friends. The couple kept Winchester's little houseboat safe and secure. She could rest easy about it.

Winchester explained to Leib, "There are several individuals to whom for a long time it has been my custom to send monthly remittances and sometimes I find myself unable to attend to it promptly, so I thought to relieve myself of the task by creating trusts."[16] Winchester mapped out a unique plan, and Leib was not sure it could be carried out. "The reason I selected a trust company," he explained, "was because what you proposed to do was in the nature of a trust, and is beyond the powers of a bank." He went on, "I do not know of any other institution which will agree for so much money paid to it to pay a given amount to any one else during their life time, except an insurance company, and even then I do not think they issue any such annuity policy, except upon agreement that upon the death of the party the principal shall belong to it, instead of anybody else."[17]

Winchester shared her wealth with family members, but always within precise boundaries. She seemed suspicious of the benefits of inherited wealth. Her husband's nephew Ollie Dye was an example of someone who was given money only to waste it on dissolute living. Winchester believed in work, in its intrinsic value as well as its ability to give a person purpose. She herself had experienced the positive power of work first-hand. But with Leib's help she established accounts with the First Federal Trust Company of San Francisco to hold securities for distribution to a number of personal and institutional beneficiaries. At the end of 1908, Winchester deposited three large checks with the company. Two were in the amount of $45,000, and the third was for $60,000. Each beneficiary was to receive $150 per month, except Nettie Sprague, to whom for some reason $200 was extended. Winchester included provisions to "withdraw or change the conditions of the trusts at any time."[18]

As Winchester aged, so did her siblings, and one by one, she heard news of their deaths. Her brother, Leonard, and his wife both died between 1910 and 1912. Nettie Sprague died in 1913, her husband, Homer, lived until 1918. Sarah received a telegram just after Christmas in 1916 informing her that her sister Nettie's daughter had died in New York. Winchester added a handwritten notation at the bottom of the message: "I received this at 9:10 pm December 27, 1916, SLW."[19] That day was sixty-two years since her two sisters had their double wedding in New Haven. Only Belle was left.

In about 1909, Winchester read a news story in her New York and New Haven newspapers that piqued her interest: doctors of the General Hospital Society of Connecticut had issued an appeal for money to establish a tubercular ward in New Haven. The Society had been chartered in 1826, and the renowned architect Ithiel Town, who was from New Haven, designed a building that opened seven years later. It was spacious both inside and out, and indeed the building and grounds were much larger than was needed. But by the Civil War, when upwards of 25,000 patients were treated there, the expansive property was a godsend. After the war, new wings were added, as was a nursing school. Between the Civil War and World War I, the hospital society formalized an association with Yale's School of Medicine, and the university purchased land adjacent to the hospital. During the 1890s, modern new buildings were added, and indeed, Sarah Winchester's sister-in-law, Jennie Bennett, donated funds for the construction of the Jane Ellen Hope Building there in 1901 in memory of the senior Mrs. Winchester.[20]

Sarah's most heartfelt desire was to create some kind of memorial to William Winchester's memory, and the tubercular ward in New Haven seemed exactly the right project. The request from the hospital's board of directors outlined the need for accommodations for the treatment of tubercular patients. According to Dr. Samuel C. Harvey, a New Haven physician, in the mid-nineteenth century, "the treatment of pulmonary tuberculosis was probably at its worst. The precepts of avoiding fresh air, of exercise, of depletion by bleeding and restriction of diet, was the antithesis of what we know to-day as the proper therapeutics."[21] Winchester read the reports from New Haven and responded to the appeal with an anonymous donation of $300,000, a sum that stunned hospital administrators and doctors alike. She dispatched Frank Leib under strictest confidentiality to deliver the money to Eli Whitney, grandson of the great inventor and president of the board of directors of the hospital. Leib told Whitney not to disclose her name and said that "if she is willing to have it announced before her death, she will notify you to that effect." Leib also intimated that additional money would be forthcoming if progress was made toward establishing the tuberculosis ward.[22] Over the next ten years Winchester donated more than $1 million, and she placed no restrictions on the use of the money.

The board was shocked by the large donation and set up a committee to locate a good site to build an annex to New Haven Hospital. Committee members visited several tubercular sanatoria in the United States as they set plans for a new clinic, and they chose a fifty-eight-acre site on Campbell Avenue in West Haven. When it was purchased in 1911, the anonymous donor gave another $300,000. The architect for the new hospital was Scopes & Feustmann of New York. Construction did not get under way until 1916, and the estimated cost to build was $271,085.00. A piece of adjacent land was added to the original, and another $300,000 was forthcoming from the donor.[23]

In addition, Winchester sent a $25,000 special gift. "The disposition of the especial fund of $25,000 was given over to the taste and discretion of the distinguished landscape architect, Mrs. Beatrice Farrand, who designed the Campbell Avenue front and gateway." Farrand had been born into a socially prominent family thirty years after Winchester. She turned a passionate interest in garden design into a profitable career. Among her notable clients were Theodore Roosevelt, J. P. Morgan, and John D. Rockefeller. When she was hired to design an entry to the new tubercular hospital in New Haven, she had been working on a landscape project at Yale. As design proceeded, the identity of the anonymous donor was made public, and the hospital was named in William Winchester's honor. While the tubercular clinic operated as an annex to New Haven Hospital, it was located five miles away and was separately identified. The intricate arched metalwork inset with "William Wirt Winchester Hospital" was a fitting entry that acknowledged the site as a memorial. Hospital records noted that "the donor expressed approval" of both the entry and the gateway, but that she expressed "especial pleasure with the gateway which indicates to whom the entire memorial is dedicated."[24]

Thomas Bennett wrote to Sarah, "The gateway (perhaps you have seen a photograph) is fine and I like your tablet also." He was complimenting the choice of words that Sarah had had inscribed on a bronze plaque.[25] When Winchester had placed the order from the Gorham Manufacturing Company in Providence, Rhode Island, she requested that the plaque say,

IN MEMORY OF
WILLIAM WIRT WINCHESTER
THIS ANNEX OF
THE NEW HAVEN HOSPITAL
TO BE USED FOR THE CARE
OF PERSONS
SUFFERING FROM TUBERCULOSIS
WAS ERECTED AND ENDOWED
BY HIS WIFE.[26]

Before the official dedication even took place, the United States government had leased the new hospital for casualties of World War I. On April 4, 1918, the William Wirt Winchester Hospital was formally dedicated, with appropriate accolades and speeches.[27] Sarah Winchester was not well enough to attend, and would not have liked the public spectacle anyway. Some of her friends and relations were sent engraved invitations, including the Hansens at the San José ranch, Belle, and Daisy.

The Bennetts attended the dedication in her place, and the following day, Thomas wrote,

My dear Sallie,
    We were all very much interested yesterday in the ceremony of dedication of the hospital. It seemed to me appropriate, graceful and

dignified. There was good attendance—all the hospital board and all those you named. . . . we saw all the appointments and conveniences said by the commandant and the architect to be the best in the world. In my time soldiers were not so well taken care of. To see the elevators, electric lighting, heating, ventilation, sterilization, cooking, washing and ironing machinery was in itself a liberal education. I regret you could not have seen it yourself.[28]

When all was said and done, just after the hospital was dedicated in 1918, Leib wrote her, "Your contribution to the Tuberculosis Fund of the hospital is nearly equal to the sum total of all the other contributions to the general hospital itself. My dear Mrs. Winchester, you are a wonderfully generous woman, and as I am one of the very few [in California] who know what you have done, I wish to thank you in the name of humanity for your great generosity."[29]

By the time the hospital was built and dedicated, the United States was embroiled in war in Europe. When the United States entered World War I, emotions in California were running high as local citizens of German ancestry were being treated with hostility and suspicion. On an April morning in 1917, Belle Merriman caught the ten o'clock train to San José. She overheard two passengers commenting on the progress of the war, one man defending Kaiser Wilhelm. "I tried not to listen," she claimed, "but I could not help myself. The more I heard the more my blood began to boil. Finally I could stand it no longer and I got up and walked over to that man and grabbed him by the nape of the neck. I shook him as hard as I could." The conductor reported that Belle "trounced" the passenger so severely that he got off at the next stop. Her actions were met with a round of applause by the other passengers, and she was not charged with assault.[30]

During World War I, Belle "declined to claim" political party, although before the war she had been registered as a Democrat. Despite her display of patriotic tendencies when she beat the German sympathizer on the train, she was not pro-government in all cases. Later, when she believed the U.S. Army had trashed leftover foodstuffs when it vacated Menlo Park's Camp Fremont rather than donating them to a good cause, she reported it to the Attorney General for investigation and called the press to make a fuss about it. Belle Merriman was alternately the source of surprise and dismay for her sister and her daughter.

Perhaps the most peculiar escapade that Belle instigated happened in 1915, when she kidnapped a patient from the county hospital. The story began when an older man who had forgotten his name checked in for medical attention. He could not remember anything of his past. Doctors, hospital officials, and the police attempted to determine the identity of the man, and based on markings on his clothing, suspected that he had come from some kind of medical institution. County Humane Officer Merriman complained that the officials were "pestering the life out of him," so she took him home. "Mrs. Merriman made no attempt to conceal the fact that she had brought [him] to her home. She said she had done this to save his life and to protect him from vultures." It took about a week before the man was identified as a Mr. Harry Williams, who had gone missing from an asylum in San Diego. His wife was contacted, but she did not want him back. She had no means of caring for him or supporting him. A doctor had encouraged Merriman to check the man back into the hospital, which she did. She planned to escort him to San Diego to "confront his wife." When she went to the hospital to make final arrangements, Williams was gone.[31]

Williams's mental condition was not the only one in question. Belle's behavior around the Williams case made some wonder about her stability. At age seventy-two, she had, even for her, acted without thinking through the possible outcomes. Daisy took her mother to Gardner's Sanitarium in Belmont, an institution that specialized in the treatment of nervous disorders.[32] It is unclear whether Belle was free to come and go from Gardner's or not, but she stayed for several months. (Strangely, when Daisy reached about the same age, her daughter, Margaret, attempted to have her institutionalized, too.)

Fred Marriott dipped in and out of military service after serving the army in the Philippines during the Spanish-American War. In 1911, with the rank of captain, he was given command of a California National Guard unit going through machine-gun corps training in Palo Alto. Having actively trained and drilled, Marriott's contingent was mobilized as part of the Fifth Infantry in June 1916. The same month, Daisy filed for divorce.

Fred Marriott was presented with divorce papers claiming he had not lent financial support to his wife and adopted daughter. He did not contest the divorce, but he wanted custody of Margaret, who in 1916 was thirteen years old. He claimed that if he were awarded custody, he would allow Daisy to visit the child whenever she wished. Daisy likewise demanded custody, but she refused to allow Fred any visits with Margaret. The custody battle lasted a year. Daisy told the court that Fred was unfit as a father because "he took [Margaret] on automobile rides and took her to cafes."[33] The court sided with Daisy, at least temporarily, deciding that after one year, Fred could present to the court reasons why he should be granted visits. Fred shipped out to Europe for the duration of the war. The week that the divorce was finalized and reported in the Palo Alto newspaper, Daisy sent Margaret to visit her old friend Grace Adel Linscott, who lived in Santa Cruz. Grace also had a daughter, a little younger than Margaret, and the two girls enjoyed the summer beach while the unpleasantness of the divorce got worked out at home. Margaret also knew her father was gearing up for full-time military service.

Sarah Winchester may have noticed something amiss with her sister. Early that year she notified Frank Leib to change her trust account so that Belle's support payment was redirected, explaining, "For good reasons I am very anxious to have the check which should come [to Belle] on or before the first of February sent to me. For reasons which I cannot explain, I know that this would be the best disposition to be made of it."[34] For the next two years, Belle Merriman did not receive a monthly check from her sister. Sarah did not explain to Leib why she chose to suspend Belle's allowance, but he did not need an explanation after Belle's behavior in the Williams incident and subsequent entry into Gardner's were reported in the newspaper.

Winchester had been so scrupulous about her finances that when Frank Leib received a letter from her in the summer of 1917, he was surprised to read, "I would like to change nearly all of the trusts that I made some years since."[35] He believed her affairs were in fine order, and wondered what she would want to change. He had an answer after meeting with her: she wished to change everything. First, she added to the accounts she had in the First National Bank of New Haven, eliminating some beneficiaries and establishing others. One intriguing change was to Daisy's trust, which, under new terms, would no longer extend to Margaret. A trust of a lesser amount, the same as those for Winchester's other grandnieces and grandnephews, was set up for Margaret. Once again Leib reviewed the widow's financial plan, account by account, bond by bond. His work was cut out for him. Winchester had concerns about other investments, too.

She meticulously followed the finances of the Winchester Repeating Arms Company. At the end of 1914, as war erupted in Europe, the United States claimed neutrality. However, Winchester Repeating Arms Company posted over $16 million in military orders of guns and ammunition from Britain, Belgium, and Russia—all on the Allied side. By the end of the following year, orders reached almost $50 million. The huge backlog overwhelmed the factory, and company officers hired hundreds of additional workers for second and third shifts. Between 1914 and 1917, Winchester employment rolls exploded from about 5,000 employees to over 17,000. On the brink of war, it appeared that Sarah Winchester's fortune would skyrocket again.

World War I fulfilled Oliver Winchester's greatest aspirations for his company—it brought large government wartime contracts for weapons. The company founder had ensured that the Winchester Repeating Arms Company was built on solid footing, and Thomas Bennett had carried it through tumultuous and highly competitive years. The aging Bennett had been grooming his son, Winchester Bennett, to take over as president of the company. Neither Thomas Bennett nor Oliver Winchester would have guessed that a world war, the "war to end all wars," with huge military contracts, could dismantle decades of success. But in fact it proved the company's undoing.

Thomas Bennett wrote to Sarah a few times each year with a financial summary, and she monitored the value of the stock dividends. Stockholders had not received a dividend since 1915 owing to the war. Income was being set aside for even more expansion, and the federal government set regulations to tax wartime profits. She also kept apprised of the company's large orders, and knew, for example, that in 1915 and 1916 almost 300,000 Winchester muskets were sold to the Imperial Russian government.[36] At the end of 1917, company balance sheets showed that her stock was worth almost $10 million.

At first, high sales figures indicated good news for company coffers. In the summer of 1918, Thomas Bennett informed Sarah Winchester that "the matters of Winchester have progressed favorably so far as our U.S. Gov't. contracts are concerned. This year we shall make probably 8,000,000 dollars and this sum would with our present cash assets put us nearly out of debt."[37] Just a few months after Bennett's letter, when an armistice with Germany was signed, all orders for weapons came to a screeching halt. Company management had been so engrossed in war production that they had made virtually no plans for how the company would survive after the war. Winchester Repeating Arms Company had an enormous, empty factory, one that occupied over three million square feet of floor space on more than eighty acres, and had to let thousands of workers go.

Added to that, the most likely and presumptive successor as president of the Winchester Repeating Arms Company, "Win" Bennett, had returned from the war in ill health. "After a month's illness was operated on for abscess of the liver," Thomas told Sarah. "We had a week of great anxiety. . . . the doctors say he should not work for some months." Win Bennett would not be well enough to take over leadership of the family enterprise. Thomas ruefully noted to his sister-in-law that he was seventy-three years old, well past the usual retirement age, and he could not retire.[38]

In the same missive, Bennett enclosed a copy of a telegram from the management company Kidder, Peabody & Company. It outlined a shocking recommendation that he endorsed: it suggested that the Winchester family withdraw from control of the company. The proposal called for Winchester stockholders to turn over their stock to the management company, which would in turn create a holding company to become the owner of the facilities and debts of the arms company. In return, the stockholders would be given 7.5 shares of stock in the new holding company for every share they held in the old company. In plain terms, the value of Winchester Repeating Arms Company, reported at $20 million including facilities, would be compensated by Kidder, Peabody & Company with $7.5 million. In this scenario, Winchester's fortune in Winchester Repeating Arms Company stock would be reduced in value from $10 million to less than $3.75 million.[39]

It is possible that Frank Leib was more disturbed by this news than Sarah Winchester. When she asked him to review the terms of the agreement, he obliged, and he told her that in his mind at least, the company had been grossly undervalued. Leib was astonished to discover that the arms company was $10 million in debt from building wartime additions to the factory. New buildings had swallowed wartime profits. Leib put his questions on paper to Thomas Bennett, who pointed out to him that "the larger part of the $20,000,000 of which you speak is in buildings, . . . largely a burden rather than an asset."[40]

Leib took the matter under consideration. He knew the debt must be paid, but counseled Winchester against signing the documents submitted by the company. His analysis, the subsequent negotiation, and Winchester's response time ended up taking about two years. Leib tried to protect his client's fortune, and he wanted to make perfectly clear that she should not shoulder any debt that the company had incurred or would in the future incur. Frank Leib was not the only person with serious reservations about turning the arms company over to Kidder, Peabody & Company. Bennett received letters from minority stockholders who had only read about the plan in the *New York Tribune*. One irate man wrote, "If the newspaper is correctly informed, I hereby serve formal notice that I shall at once instruct my attorney to apply for an injunction restraining the 'Committee' from presuming to further represent stockholders."[41] While the majority stockholders were given details of the proposed changes, minority stockholders were not.

By the spring of 1919, Bennett was absolutely convinced that the holding company was the best choice. Furthermore, it had become obvious that Win Bennett would never be healthy enough to work full-time. Jennie Bennett signed her stock certificates, a fortune roughly equal to Sarah Winchester's, over to Kidder, Peabody. Those who promoted the reorganization realized they could not get 100 percent cooperation from stockholders, so they amended their plan to maintain the Winchester

Repeating Arms Company within a new corporate holding company called the Winchester Company. This bought more time to convince more stockholders of the necessity of the new plan. On April 16, 1919, the holding company was incorporated by the State of Connecticut as the Winchester Company. Thomas pointed out to Sarah that it had to be done; otherwise, he maintained, "we should be in bankruptcy because we had no working capital to go ahead. Now all our debts are paid and we have plenty of money to take care of current expenses and go ahead."[42] In the space of one year, the value of Sarah Winchester's interest in the Winchester Repeating Arms Company went from about $10 million to about $3.75 million. Thomas Bennett remained on the board of directors and Winchester Bennett was a vice president. The new ownership directed a restructuring of the product line as well. It added hardware and a whole variety of sporting goods—including knives and cutlery, ice and roller skates, and fishing gear—to firearms and ammunition.

In the spring of 1920, Jennie Bennett died at age seventy-two. A funeral was held at the house on the hill, the mansion where Sarah and William Winchester had left their hearts and where the Bennetts had resided since the death of Jane Winchester. The funeral was presided over by a minister of the Center Church, and a quartet of musicians rendered quiet hymns. Jennie's death left Sarah as the single largest stockholder in the company. But she was frustrating officials at Kidder, Peabody and at Winchester because she had never signed over her stock certificates. If she died before signing, the future of the company would be in an indefinite limbo.

Frank Leib knew the parties in the East were frantic because Sarah Winchester had not responded for more than a year. He also knew that she was in such ill health that she was putting off meeting with him—which went on for another whole year. Nevertheless, when a vice president of the Winchester company showed up unexpectedly on his doorstep in February 1921, Leib was disturbed. The widow's inability or refusal to address the financial problems of the company had stalled negotiations in the East, and the official was instructed to get Winchester to sign the stock certificates and bring them back to New Haven. Leib was alarmed by the tactic, and informed his client that he thought she was being pressured. He counseled her to take whatever time was necessary to address the problems. He had possession of Winchester's stock certificates—the bulk of her fortune—in the vault in his law office.

Leib and Winchester met to confer on Thursday, March 31, 1921. A week later he wrote to her, "I dictated to my stenographer all the matter printed on the face of the certificates of stock and then, during the succeeding day, have compared the same with the previous correspondence and agreements between myself and the Eastern parties. I am sending you a copy of such matter printed on the face of each certificate of stock." In the final paragraph of an eight-page summary of the events to date, he wrote, "I was equally bound to protect you, (to the best of my ability), from dangers that *could* happen, unless I made it *impossible* for them *to* happen. And this I have done my very best to accomplish."[43]

She signed the stock certificates and sent them to the East, her fortune receding to one third of its former self. She paid Frank Leib huge fees during those years, but he had earned them, spending hours and hours poring over documents and corresponding on the widow's behalf with company and financial officials in the East. In 1919, she wrote a check to Leib for $15,500, and one for over $20,000 the following year. In 1921, his bills were even higher, and he wrote, "I do not wish you to feel for a moment that I am charging more than what I honestly believe I have earned, and to which I am fairly entitled. If, nevertheless, you have the slightest feeling to the contrary, I beg you to say so and to fix the amount yourself."[44] If his 1 percent was $21,000, then he transferred property valued at over $2 million in that year alone.

Early in 1920, Winchester had Leib draft a new will. He suggested that since Dr. Wayland had witnessed the previous version, she should ask him to witness again. Leib explained that all of her household employees were named as beneficiaries, so none of them could witness the will. Frank Leib, his son and partner Roy Leib, and Clyde Wayland witnessed Sarah Winchester's last will and testament.

Sarah never expected to outlive her younger, more robust sister, but Belle died unexpectedly of a massive stroke at her Palo Alto house on June 13, 1920, at age seventy-seven. Daisy was notified immediately, and she called Aunt Sarah at Atherton. The two agreed on funeral arrangements, and a small service was held at Palo Alto's Alta Mesa Cemetery rather than Cypress Lawn, where Belle's husband and sister had been buried. They rented two carriages and two autos, and requested a special burial robe. Sarah paid Belle's funeral expenses, which amounted to about $800. Newspaper notices of Belle's death praised the many efforts she had made in behalf of the helpless, both human and animal. One admirer penned a poetic tribute and a memorial essay on Belle that the *San Jose Mercury Herald* published, pointing out, "Her last years were most cruelly saddened by malicious attacks made upon her character and work by some who probably have never achieved the smallest fraction of the good for humanity that she did." Sarah wasted no time and sold Belle's house in September. It sold for less than the cost to build it thirteen years earlier.[45]

In 1920, Daisy was fifty-one. She and Fred Marriott had reconciled and lived together again in the Palo Alto house. In the spring of 1922, Margaret Marriott married a Stanford student named Richard Smith. Daisy and Fred Marriott may have felt she was too young at only age nineteen, but Margaret's teenage years had been stormy ones, so perhaps they hoped marriage would help her to mature. Aunt Sarah was too feeble to attend the wedding, but the Hansens went. The newlyweds lived with the Marriotts so that Richard could finish his education at Stanford. Then Fred gave him a job at the *News Letter.*

Sarah Winchester was venturing out very little by this time, and when she did, either Daisy, Henrietta, or a new employee named Frank Glennon drove her. She arranged to have her best car, the gray Pierce-Arrow with the lavender pinstripe, put in storage. The dealer sent her a note to tell her, "We regret to learn that you have decided to lay the car up for the time being but should you at any time in the future want a good chauffeur to drive your car we would appreciate a call from you."[46]

Throughout the 1920s, Thomas Bennett continued to serve on the Winchester board of directors, but was not part of the day-to-day operations of the company. Perhaps the problems created during World War I could have been handled better if he had found a successor earlier. He had been a good and faithful servant. His loyalty to his wife, her family, and the company carried it from Oliver Winchester's death in 1880 to 1920, when his wife died. Thomas Bennett did well by Jennie, his children, his in-laws, and Sarah Winchester, to whom he sent warm and informative correspondence. Bennett resided at the old house on Prospect Hill, the home built by Jane and Oliver Winchester with design and architectural help from Sarah and William Winchester, until his death in 1930. He did not live to see the former Winchester Repeating Arms Company, the company he gave his life to, go bankrupt.

The evolution of the Winchester Repeating Arms Company and the many incarnations of the repeating rifle present us with a sense of amazement at the emergence of one of America's great arms companies. They engender respect for the power of the weapon itself. After World War I, the company floundered in debt. It survived by being bought out by a holding company, and a new management team expanded Winchester products to sporting goods, household items, and camping gear. The company failed early in the Great Depression in 1931 and was purchased by Olin Industries, which used the Winchester name to market guns and ammunition. The plant in New Haven closed in 2006 and began undergoing redevelopment.

CHAPTER 11

Trapped in a Mistaken Legacy

⊰◈⊱

S ARAH LOCKWOOD PARDEE WINCHESTER, VARIOUSLY KNOWN AS THE heiress to the Winchester rifle fortune, a recluse, a spiritualist, and "Aunt Sallie," hovered between life and death the first week of September in 1922. Ravaged by years of rheumatoid arthritis, her body slowly shut down. The household staff knew it. Tommie, the aged Japanese gardener, knew it. Her nieces and nephews knew it. Frank Leib knew it. And most clearly of all, her doctor, Clyde Wayland, knew it. Belying years of infirmity, the invalid widow had been a force to reckon with as an aunt, as an employer, and as a client. But her final day had drawn near.

It was difficult to imagine that Winchester had been a beauty as a young woman. Petite in the extreme, not even reaching five feet tall, Winchester at her most robust had approached one hundred pounds. No longer the bright-eyed, sophisticated pixie that Isaiah Taber had photographed so many years earlier, Winchester showed a different picture altogether as she lay dying, her fingers and toes knurled and knotted from years of destruction by the painful arthritis.

Nevertheless, Sarah Winchester orchestrated her death much like her life: privately, efficiently, elegantly. Her explicit instructions were followed to the letter. She dispatched Frank Leib to pay expenses out of one of her several bank accounts. On September 1, while still in Atherton, Winchester wrote a check to Misa Hirata, her maid. This was the last known document signed by the widow.[1] As she lay bedridden, she arranged to have herself driven the twenty miles to the ranch in the valley. Aware that her final days were approaching, she wanted to be close to Clyde Wayland, her trusted San José doctor. If she was seeking immortality, as some would later claim, it was not apparent to those closest to her.

Dr. Wayland made a house call at the ranch to look in on Winchester on Sunday, September 3, 1922.[2] The doctor rather liked Winchester and thought the press was mean spirited in its treatment of the old lady. He was led to the bedroom where she lay, tiny in a large bed, white against white bed linen, inert, with joints locked in place. After the doctor left that day, he never saw her again. Sarah Winchester took her final breath two days later, on Tuesday, September 5, at 10:45 p.m. Later Wayland recounted that she was mentally alert to the last. The doctor was somewhat defensive of Winchester. He had known her his entire life because his father had been her physician in her earliest years in California and then he had taken over as her personal physician, caring for her till her death. Wayland hoped her death would lay to rest all the neighborhood gossip about communicating with the spirit world, but he was disappointed. Over the next fifty years the house's subsequent proprietors embellished the tales until they were institutionalized as gospel. Wayland claimed that he "just saw red" whenever he heard Winchester legends and the strange beliefs she purportedly held.[3]

Henrietta Sivera, Winchester's personal companion, was with her when she died. She called the county coroner and acted as informant for the official death record. Henrietta gave correct data for most of the standard questions, identifying birthplace, parents, and maiden name. But she got Winchester's age wrong, stating that she was seventy-nine, when in fact she was over eighty-two. Henrietta also made the imaginative claim that Winchester's occupation was "housewife." The cause of death was given as myocarditis, a chronically weak heart.[4]

For someone who had generated so many newspaper articles in her life, Sarah Winchester's death notice was quite small. Placed next to trumpeted news of the American Legion convention in San José that week, and set against long reports of the death two days earlier of Western landscape artist and photographer Andrew P. Hill, the scant three-inch column "Sarah Winchester is Summoned by Death" seemed barely a whisper. She had resided in California for thirty-six years, but had uniformly restricted social interaction to a handful of relatives, a few professionals, and a small circle of household servants. So despite her great wealth and aura of celebrity, her passing went almost unnoticed. The little news report did, however, make a big announcement of something that was only too apparent to her financially dependent relatives and staff: "many . . . have lost . . . a benefactor."[5]

Daisy was notified immediately, and she set in motion the carefully planned funeral arrangements. On Wednesday, a black, horse-drawn hearse transported Sarah's body from her deathbed to the George W. Tinney & Sons Mortuary in Palo Alto. It was the same funeral home Winchester had hired to hold a memorial service for Belle two years earlier. Her body was embalmed, dressed and gloved, and laid in an intricately decorated bronze casket. The funeral home invoiced for some standard charges—$50 for embalming, $20 for the hearse, and $7.50 for a floral casket cover.[6]

On Friday morning, September 8, the undertaker delivered the casket to Daisy's Palo Alto home, where it was placed in the front parlor. Mourners congregated as two o'clock approached, and the collection of nieces and nephews lined up to pay final respects to Aunt Sarah. First, of course, were the Marriotts—Daisy, Fred, their daughter, Margaret, and her new husband, Richard Smith; then Daisy's brother, Willie Merriman; Estelle's children, Saidee and George, each with spouse; and one of Nettie and Homer's children, Dr. William Sprague, who lived in San Francisco. All of the cousins, having been born within five years of one another, were about fifty years of age.

Most of Winchester's household staff members also came to the small, private service, including Henrietta; Tommie, with his daughter-in-law, Ito; the Hansen family; Misa, the maid; the caretakers of the Atherton home, James and Sarah Bogie; and Winchester's former chauffeur, Fred. The professionals in Winchester's life also made an appearance at her memorial service: Frank Leib, with his son and law partner, Roy; Dr. Clyde Wayland; and Reverend William Brewer. The Episcopal clergyman had recently visited with Winchester, recounting their twenty-year acquaintance. At the service, Brewer intoned prayers over the remains and spoke briefly of Winchester's philanthropies. After murmured condolences, the casket was carried from the front room of Daisy's house to the hearse waiting in the street.

Despite Winchester's careful preparations, the weather was one eventuality that she could not control. September 8 was the hottest day of 1922, with temperatures soaring near one hundred degrees. The odor of fermenting fruit hung over the valley as tons of prunes succumbing to the heat lay on the ground. The Santa Clara Valley produced more prunes than any other spot on the globe. The yield from an estimated 7.5 million prune trees, worth more than $30 million, was due to be picked within the week, and the extreme heat threatened the crop. A healthy harvest at Llanada Villa also awaited picking.

The small congregation of mourners, sweltering in full funeral regalia, climbed into four rented carriages for a procession to Alta Mesa Cemetery two miles to the west. A chauffeured and rented automobile was reserved for the Marriotts. A few others drove themselves. Any bystander in Palo Alto that day, taking notice of the modest funeral cortege of four carriages and a few autos, would never have guessed that this was the final farewell to one of California's wealthiest residents. It was nothing like the outpouring of grief for the popular (but penniless) artist Andrew P.

Hill that very same week. The modest entourage entered the cemetery gates to bid adieu, and Brewer, in a black wool suit, sweated through the requiem ritual.

Each mourner brought personal memories, worries, or suspicions, depending on the history and relationship shared with Sarah Winchester. Frank Leib was only too aware that some of those sniffling at the funeral would be sorely disappointed by Winchester's will. He knew where the money was and where it was going. He knew who truly cared for the old lady. Leib suspected that the nephews would begrudge any bequests to employees, but Winchester had stipulated that anyone who contested the will would receive nothing.

Besides Daisy, the most emotionally distraught person at Winchester's death was Tommie Nishihara, the head gardener at Llanada Villa and Winchester's Atherton home. A small man with just a slightly larger frame than Winchester herself, Nishihara was old and almost toothless. He had worked at the Winchester place since 1910, living in a house on the ranch. He spent years executing gardening plans drawn up by Winchester. He was so distressed by Winchester's death that years later one of the neighbors even recalled, "I remember Tommie was so grieved when Mrs. Winchester died."[7] Tommie Nishihara was one of a very few who did not expect anything more from Winchester. For him, losing her was personal. He did not live long enough to know that she had named him in her will. Nishihara worked until the day he died, within a year of Winchester's death. The $800 that he inherited when the will was finalized in 1925 went to his son.[8]

Henrietta knew Winchester intimately, having been her personal companion for more than ten years. She had grown fond of the old lady, but harbored no illusions. Henrietta had penned some of the widow's correspondence to Leib, and had a good idea of the lady's plans for her money. She did not expect anything but a perfunctory gift from Winchester's death. Henrietta needed a job, though. Her elderly mother was quite sickly and had no means of support. Henrietta required employment in the not too distant future.

The Bogies were old and stooped. They had dedicated themselves to Winchester's Atherton home, and it was smartly maintained, although it had not been updated or improved upon for a long time. It showed wear, like the Bogies themselves. John Hansen, on the other hand, had a number of farming years left in him. His boys were grown, but at fifty-six years of age, he could not hire out very easily. He might have wondered whether Leib would continue to pay him to tend the Winchester orchards, or whether he might be able to buy a farm for himself and his wife, Nellie.

A small band of relatives survived Winchester. The only one of her own generation was her brother-in-law, Thomas Bennett. By this time he was an elderly widower himself in New Haven, and he did not travel to attend her funeral. None of Sarah's five siblings were living. The several nieces and nephews represented the Pardee family.

Winchester had instructed in her will and Daisy Marriott knew that her aunt wished to be buried in New Haven in the family plot she had purchased so many years before. Leib negotiated with Alta Mesa Cemetery to hold Winchester's remains until arrangements could be made to transport them to Connecticut. The cemetery accommodated the coffin in vault number 12 from September until the following April, charging a fee of $28.[9]

Daisy also arranged for the remains of her mother, Belle, who had been buried two years earlier at Alta Mesa, to be prepared for transfer to the East. On April 14, 1923, the casketed remains of Sarah Winchester and Belle Merriman were taken by hearse from Alta Mesa Cemetery to Tinney & Sons Mortuary. The following day, the crated caskets were delivered to the Palo Alto train depot and put in a luggage car for the 3,000-mile journey back to New Haven.

Daisy accompanied the caskets to New Haven. Neither her husband, Fred, nor her daughter, Margaret, went with her, but she traveled in the comfort of a Pullman car. Over and above her train fare, she accumulated receipts for $125 in meals and almost $50 in taxi fees, all costs reimbursed from Sarah's estate.[10] Upon arrival in New Haven, the caskets were claimed by local undertakers Lewis & Maycock and transferred to Evergreen Cemetery. Daisy arranged a brief ceremony, and invited some New Haven relations, including Thomas Bennett. Belle was buried in the Pardee lot, near her parents, a brother, and a sister. Sarah's body was buried in lot number 52, beside William and their infant daughter, Annie.[11]

What became of Sarah Winchester's fortune, the cash and stocks that the Winchester rifle enterprise generated and her collection of California real estate? The simplest and truest answer is that it went to the William Wirt Winchester Hospital in New Haven. But as with everything Winchester, from her homes to her investments, the fortune traveled a circuitous route before arriving at its intended destination.

A month after Winchester's death the *San Francisco Chronicle* noted that the "announcement of the terms of the [Winchester] will, awaited with interest by many to whom Mrs. Winchester had long been a figure of mystery, caused some surprise that the total value of the estate should be so few millions." The estate was valued at just under $3 million, although the press reported that it was closer to four. Either sum was paltry considering how much the widow was thought to be worth. The article suggested that Winchester frittered away her inheritance on the San José house: "There must have been a severe tax on the fortune to keep going that unceasing building activity by which the widow thought to prolong her life."[12]

Immediately after Winchester's death, Frank Leib proceeded with the disposition of her property as he had been directed. A trust company would manage the estate's dissolution, but until then Leib held the reins. Leib knew most Winchester family secrets, although on occasion Winchester had made alterations to her will without offering him an explanation. He could identify which relation or employee lived in a house owned by Winchester, and the list was long—Daisy, Saidee, Tommie, the Hansens, and the Bogies. His work for Sarah L. Pardee Winchester was by no means over.

Sarah Winchester drafted at least four wills during her lifetime. The first was just after her husband died, while she was still in New Haven. Leib drew up the second one in 1909, when she first made substantial contributions to the General Hospital Society of Connecticut in honor of her late husband. The third was in 1917, and her last will and testament, which was filed in Santa Clara County Superior Court by Frank Leib upon her death, had been drafted in 1920. The executor and trustee of the trusts it created were one and the same: the Union Trust Company of San Francisco.

The first provision of her will provided for funeral expenses, a common beginning to such documents. An attachment indicated her concern about the consistency and quality of cemetery care. She declared that $3,000 should be invested by New Haven's Evergreen Cemetery to pay for perpetual care of her cemetery lot, "for keeping said lot as beautiful as may be and free from weeds and from other undesirable growth." She stipulated that "no interments other than my own shall be permitted therein."[13]

Next, she named five employees and declared a sum of money that each should inherit. Her personal companion and secretary, Henrietta Sivera, was given $3,000. The caretakers of the San José ranch and the Atherton home, John Hansen and James Bogie, were each given $2,000. Misa Hirata, her maid, was likewise given $2,000. Gardener Tommie Nishihara came last, with $800. Two charities were named to receive cash payments. The Visiting Nurses Association of New Haven was given $4,000, and the Home for the Friendless, also of New Haven, was given $3,000. The only provision for a charitable organization in California was $250 set aside for "furnishings for one room in San José Hospital as per agreement with Lucy M. Wayland, Chairman of the Woman's Auxiliary Board to said hospital."[14]

Sarah Winchester's Heirs

(Heirs shown in bold)

LEONARD PARDEE (1807–1869) ══ SARAH BURNS (1808–1880)

- SARAH E. PARDEE (1831–1832)

- MARY AUGUSTA PARDEE (1833–1884) ══════ William W. Converse (1834–1889)

- ANTOINETTE E. "NETTIE" PARDEE (1835–1913) ══════ Homer Baxter Sprague (1829–1918)
  - **Charles Homer Sprague** (1856–?) ══ Jennie L. Starbuck
  - Sarah Antoinette "Nettie" Sprague (1858–1916) ══ William W. Davis
    - **Mary Converse Davis** (1882–1968) ══ 1. Edgar R. Marsh (1884–1912)
      ══ 2. Glover P. Prout (1878–1918)
      - **William Davis Marsh** (1907–1974)
      - **Bryant Risley Marsh** (1910–1965)
  - **William Pardee Sprague** (1860–?) ══ Louise Velbert
  - **Goldwin Smith Sprague** (1869–?) ══ Isabel

- LEONARD MOREHOUSE PARDEE (1837–1910) ══════ Sarah H. Domkee (1838–1912)
  - **Sarah "Sadie" Catherine Pardee** (1870–1956) ══ 1. Eugene Beecher
    ══ 2. William T. McLean
    - 1a. **Hazel Beecher** (1902–1991)
    - 2a. **Anita Sarah McLean** (1914–2010)
  - Louise Beecher Pardee (1872–1922)

- SARAH LOCKWOOD PARDEE (1839–1922) ══════ William Wirt Winchester (1837–1881)
  - Annie Pardee Winchester (1866)

- ISABELLE CAMPBELL PARDEE (1843–1920) ══════ Louis A. Merriman (1835–1908)
  - **Marion "Daisy" Isabel Merriman** (1869–1949) ══ Frederick A. Marriott III
    - **Margaret Marriott** (1903–1961) ══ 1. Richard C. Smith (divorced)
      ══ 2. Donald Robesky (divorced)
      ══ 3. ? Gale
      - 2a. Donald Robesky
  - **William Winchester Merriman** (1872–1959) ══ 1. Fannie R.
    ══ 2. Chrissie W.

- ESTELLE L. PARDEE (1845–1894) ══════ George Lyon Gerard (divorced)
  - **Sarah "Saidee" Louise Gerard** (1868–1925) ══ 1. Arthur Bugbee (divorced)
    ══ 2. Henry "Harry" Ruthrauff
  - **George Leonard Gerard** (1869– before 1940) ══ 1. Grace M. (divorced)
    ══ 2. Katherine Wade

The third provision of Winchester's will named family members who were to receive lump sums. Nieces Saidee Ruthrauff (Estelle's daughter) and Sarah McLean and Louise Pardee (Leonard's daughters) were each given $2,000. None of her nephews were left cash separate from a trust account. Belle was left $3,000 in cash, although she had preceded Sarah in death by two years. Daisy was given $3,000, and since Winchester had retained ownership of Daisy's Palo Alto home, she gave the house to Daisy. In addition, Winchester left all the "pictures, furniture, household goods, jewelry and paraphernalia" from her San José house and her Atherton house to Daisy. She also left her niece the 1917 Model Pierce-Arrow valued at $1,500 and a four-cylinder Buick truck worth about $250. Daisy was never wealthy, although she could have been since Winchester left all the contents of the Atherton house and the huge San José house. Appraisers estimated the value of the contents at about $11,000. They were scattered to time and auction. Of all the heirs to her aunt's estate, Daisy alone was bequeathed a $200,000 trust (Belle was named in the will to receive an equal trust, but she had died before Winchester did), which delivered about $600 per month, a substantial sum in 1922, along with personal and real property free from the trusts. Sarah also bequeathed the Waverley Street house in Palo Alto to Daisy, who sold it and moved with Fred a few blocks away, to 1060 Lincoln Avenue.[15] Eventually the Waverley Street house was razed; today an apartment building occupies the spot.

At the time of her death, Winchester had about $150,000 in liquid cash. The Union Trust Company of San Francisco held most of her money in trust. She had set up funds to be invested, and the returns were to be sent to a variety of individuals for their lifetimes. Upon the death of each, the principal was to revert to the General Hospital Society of Connecticut. Once again, Daisy and Belle were first, and each were to receive the investment returns on $200,000. Next, funds of $50,000 each benefited three of her nephews and three nieces: William Merriman, George Gerard, William Sprague, Sarah McLean, Louise Pardee, and Saidee Ruthrauff. One of Nettie's sons, Goldie Sprague, had a fund of $40,000, and his brother, Charles Sprague, had one for $30,000. Both had borrowed money from her.[16] None of her nieces or nephews were left out of the will.

Winchester also remembered her grandnieces. Eighteen-thousand-dollar funds were set up to benefit Daisy's adopted daughter, Margaret; the daughters of Sarah McLean, Hazel Beecher and Anita McLean; and Nettie's granddaughter, Mary Prout. Eight-thousand-dollar funds were set up for each of her two grandnephews, William Marsh and Risley Marsh, who were Mary Prout's sons.

The most important provision of the will outlined the guiding purpose of the last forty years of Sarah Winchester's life, her wish to memo-
rialize her husband:

> I desire and direct that such General Hospital Society of Connecticut
> use the funds derived from the gifts and bequests above given to
> it for charitable purposes in the furtherance of the best interest of
> the William Wirt Winchester Annex of said Hospital Society, (which
> Annex is owned by said General Hospital Society of Connecticut,
> and such Annex having been purchased and endowed with funds
> which I furnished), and especially for giving the best possible care
> and treatment to tuberculosis patients, who at my death may have
> then been admitted, and to those who may thereafter be admitted,
> to said Annex.[17]

On the final page of the document was a short but precise warning. If
anyone for any reason contested the will, "he or she or they shall receive
no part whatever of my estate, and I hereby revoke any devise, gift or
bequest herein made to anyone who so contests or disputes the validity
of this will." Winchester did not want squabbling over her money.

Winchester's will was finalized in the summer of 1925, three years
after her death, but the case was not closed until the last of her heirs,
her brother's granddaughter, Anita McLean, died in 2010. By the time the
legal referee was appointed by the court in June 1925, others involved
in the case or named in the will had also died, including Frank Leib,
Tommie Nishihara, and Saidee Ruthrauff.

According to the report of the treasurer of the hospital for March 31,
1926, Sarah Winchester's gifts with accumulations of interest and rentals
to the William Wirt Winchester Hospital were summarized as $925,000
in land, buildings, and equipment, and $2.2 million in cash and securities.
In addition, the hospital was made residuary legatee of other securities
available upon the termination of certain life annuities that made her gift
undetermined in value. In her lifetime, she gave between $1.3 and $1.8
million. All the bequests she left to more than a dozen relatives were
trusts for life, and upon the deaths of those people, the principal of their
trusts reverted to the hospital. In this way, Winchester kept the endowment growing.

The William Wirt Winchester Hospital remained under government
jurisdiction from World War I until 1927. Between 1928 and 1940, it was
the tuberculosis clinic of the New Haven Hospital, and during World
War II it was once again used for veterans. In 1945, the General Hospital
Society of Connecticut and Grace Hospital Society merged, resulting in

the Grace—New Haven Community Hospital. It sought a ruling from the courts in Connecticut, asking permission to sell the William Wirt Winchester Annex in West Haven. It argued that between 1900 and 1940, deaths from tuberculosis dropped from 186.7 to 35 per hundred thousand people. The hospital argued, moreover, that those who required hospitalization for tuberculosis in 1945 had a stay that was shorter than those of patients decades earlier. This facility was the only strictly private tuberculosis treatment center in Connecticut, and it cost more than twice the weekly rate of the state institutions to keep patients there. Grace—New Haven stated that it would run deficits into the foreseeable future and deplete all bequests.

The Superior Court of New Haven County allowed the society to deviate from the terms of the Sarah L. Winchester trust and authorized the sale of the facility. In its ruling it instructed that the Hospital Society of Connecticut must apply "the proceeds of such sale to providing and operating a building or buildings, or a distinct and separate part or parts thereof so designed and constructed as to maintain an individual identity, to be called and known as the 'William Wirt Winchester Annex,' as a worthy, distinctive and enduring memorial to William Wirt Winchester, the husband of said Sarah L. Winchester to be used for the care and treatment for patients suffering from tuberculosis and for no other purpose."[18]

In 1948, the grounds and buildings were sold to the Veterans Administration. Sarah Winchester's endowment was absorbed into the Yale School of Medicine's pulmonary clinics as the Winchester Chest Clinic at Yale—New Haven Hospital. By that time, the "white plague" that she had fought ferociously with her checkbook was all but eliminated. Today, VA Connecticut on the onetime Winchester Annex property operates in association with Yale.

Sarah Winchester's archenemy was not her own death, as legend has insisted; rather, it was tuberculosis, the disease that took her husband from her. She began making major financial contributions to build a hospital dedicated to the treatment of the malady in 1909. The eradication of tuberculosis was beyond her hopes; she wished only that patients with it would receive good treatment. Today's Yale—New Haven Hospital is the most enduring of Winchester's legacies. In it she perpetuated her concern for pulmonary patients and her abiding love of her husband. It is the clearest and simplest manifestation of the values, goals, and love of her life, yet it is a legacy that is mostly unknown.

CHAPTER 12

Capitalizing on Spirits

The Mystery House

O NE BY ONE, SARAH WINCHESTER'S PROPERTIES WERE SUBDIVIDED, sold, and developed. The land in Burlingame was thought to be worth $65,000, but the houseboat was worth very little. The ark was offered for sale in 1924, with a notice in the *Burlingame Advance* stating: "A modern ark, built along the lines of Noah's famous houseboat, is offered for same by the syndicate which recently purchased the Winchester estate. . . . although no animals could be housed in the boat in case of a deluge, it is an up-to-date model of its ancient ancestor with hardwood floors and other modern conveniences."[1] It sold the following year and was occupied by a single woman for a while, but was set afire in 1929 by transients. In a historical coincidence, Saidee Ruthrauff's animal safe haven is currently owned and occupied by the Humane Society. Thirty-five acres near the boat dock were subdivided in 1925. The state built the Bayshore Highway on the land and took with it a piece of "The Pasture," while another 100-plus acres was developed later. Today's Winchester Avenue in Burlingame is a reminder of Sarah Winchester, but most of the property is occupied by hotels adjacent to the San Francisco International Airport.

The Atherton property cluster was worth about $40,000. To get the Atherton house ready for sale, Roy Leib signed a contract for $7,000 worth of work on it, including roofing, plumbing, carpentry, plastering, and installation of a hot-water system.[2] The property along with thirty acres sold promptly and was subdivided. In the 1960s, the land was subdivided again. There is also a Winchester Avenue in this subdivision.

The rambling San José house and surrounding property proved more difficult to divide and sell. Frank Leib wrote to John Hansen that it was "appraised as of no value."[3] It survived to tell quite an unusual tale, however, and within nine months of Winchester's death, it opened as a tourist attraction.[4] Even she, who had been the subject of countless spooky stories, could never have conjured such an eventuality. What led to this unlikely incarnation of the labyrinthine old house?

Leib wrote to Hansen on November 16, 1922: "This will introduce you to Mr. E. A. Barker. Please give him any information he wishes about the Winchester lands and improvements, and allow him to inspect the same. He does not wish to see the residence, as that it is appraised as of no value; so you will not admit him inside the house."[5] An official description stated that the house was "a large frame dwelling in bad state of repair and outbuildings, small pumping plant and gardens."[6] Sixty-eight acres went along with the house, thirty-two of which were planted in prunes and apricots. The land was valued at $125,000.

Beginning on November 27, 1922, the bidding process was opened on Llanada Villa. A few days later, Daisy Marriott and Henrietta Sivera arrived at the house to go through personal items.[7] Leib informed them that the house and surrounding property had sold, and the women arranged for the removal of the contents of the house. Some objects too heavy to move, including the large safe, and some items that belonged to the house, such as unused windows, doors, wall coverings, and moldings, were left behind. There is no evidence in the Leib-Hansen correspondence or in Hansen's daybooks that the Winchester Mystery House tour script is correct when it claims "the house was three quarters furnished at the time of her death and it took the movers eight truckloads a day for six and a half weeks to empty the house." Leib wrote to Hansen, "As you are aware the property of Mrs. Winchester near San José is being sold. The return of sale will be heard on the 15th of December next and on that day the sale will be completed and the new owner go into possession within a few days thereafter."[8] San José real estate developer T. C. Barnett was acting as trustee for a group of investors intent on buying the property. It was divided into a ninety-acre parcel and a sixty-six-acre piece, and the latter included the house. The developer had no problem selling the larger piece.

Between January 1 and April 1, 1923, Barnett tried unsuccessfully to sell the old Winchester house and grounds. Only one viable customer stepped forward. John H. Brown wanted the property, even the old house, but he did not have the capital to buy it. The trust company and Brown worked out a deal whereby he would lease the premises with an option to purchase at some future date. By the middle of April, Brown and his family were at the house, and the sixty-six acres around it had been subdivided and sold. "Winchester Half Acres" held a large portion, and Brown's "Winchester Amusement Company" was the proprietor of the house and immediate surroundings.

John Brown and his wife, Mayme, had most recently lived, along with two daughters, in Alameda, California. They had come from Pittsburgh, Pennsylvania, where John learned the building trades. Intrigued by rail boxcars used in the Pennsylvania coal mines, Brown manipulated those designs into roller-coaster cars. He invented one of the earliest roller-coasters, the "backity-back," an amusement-park ride that thrilled riders by rolling both forward and backward. He built and installed the $50,000 coaster at the famous Crystal Beach Resort on the Canadian side of the shores of Lake Erie, not far from Niagara Falls. The coaster was featured in advertisements for the resort in 1909 and 1910, and it drew visitors from Canada and the States during the summer months.

The Browns had been married in 1907, and their first daughter, Edna May, was born at Crystal Beach. In June of 1910, a young woman was killed when she was thrown from the backity-back. It is not clear if Brown was blamed for the accident, but later that year the family was in Pittsburgh again, and a second daughter, Mildred, was born. Sometime thereafter, the Browns moved to California, where John sought work building amusement devices in both southern and northern California. He perceived an opportunity in Sarah Winchester's old house. The Crystal Beach Resort had had a "house of mystery," and it had drawn large crowds. Brown knew that people were intrigued and thrilled by the mysterious and unknown, and the Winchester house came with a built-in story line and name recognition. The "fun house" required very little alteration.

The Browns leased the Winchester property in the spring of 1923, just six months after Winchester's death, and by May 20 of that year, the house was open for business. To get the proverbial marketing ball rolling, the Browns invited a few journalists to tour the house. Columnist Ruth Amet could not have been a better choice for Brown. The *San Jose Mercury Herald* ran her sixty-column-inch description of "the Winchester House." Bemused and amused, Amet made dozens of references to the odd and mysterious. She declared, "There is something of the awful 'House of Usher' about it." She offered suggestions about how to tour the house: "I, for one, would tremendously like to give a Hallowe'en party in this old home. First each guest would be given a lighted candle. They would be started off in foursomes at given intervals a la golf tournament." Amet's article sparked local curiosity into a firestorm of visitors to the house. "Unfurnished, and mainly undecorated, with even the wall surface stripped from them, [the walls of the house] are nevertheless teeming with atmosphere for those who would a-ghosting go."[9] The Browns were in business.

Besides luring contemporary locals for tours, Amet's article left important clues for those of us who came so many years later to view the house. Why, for example, for all the detail of Amet's article as she described the house room by room, appliance by appliance, and each window and door, did she never make any reference to the number thirteen? Today's tours inform the public that the widow's favorite number was thirteen. The answer to this question was given by a carpenter who worked on the house for many years, James Perkins, who asserted that references to the number thirteen were later additions: "The number 13 in chandeliers, the number of bathrooms, windows, ceiling panels and other things were certainly put in after Mrs. Winchester died." [10] The first mention of the use of the number thirteen in the Winchester house did not appear in print until 1929, [11] and after that, Winchester's supposed obsession with thirteen is mentioned in almost every article.

One thing is certain, Sarah Winchester's lengthy history of choosing and having made impeccable pieces for her house would never have allowed for a beautiful chandelier imported from Germany and hung in the great ballroom to be so poorly amended to include a thirteenth candle. If she had wished to add a thirteenth candle, she would have had it accomplished with precise workmanship or even as part of a custom design, and it would not look, as it does today, as if it were added by a stage crew for a tourist trap. Perkins also averred that "the more irregular features, which have made the house a world-famed oddity were built after Mrs. Winchester's death." [12]

In 1924, the Browns invited Harry Houdini, the great magician and escape artist of the early twentieth century, to visit the house. Houdini claimed to be bent on exposing tricks, and he had set out to debunk the existence of spirits in speeches critical of spiritualism. His visit to San José accomplished quite the reverse. Not only did he endorse the Browns' tourist venture, he went to the house at midnight very close to Halloween and claimed that he saw that "Mrs. Winchester has a vast wardrobe of variously colored robes, and she uses a different robe for each spirit." [13] Houdini's midnight examination only inflated and entrenched the aura of a spectral presence at the house.

The Browns knitted together a confused persona of Sarah Winchester, with her family history of gun-promoting relatives and her bizarre building practices, to entice tourists to visit the house. They laced the stories with persisting inferences of spiritualist leanings and invited ghosts of the old West along for good measure. They were in business, and the house provided them with a modest income. By 1931, the Browns had purchased the property, but they never admitted ownership, even decades later. When the *San Jose Mercury News* printed the names of the owners in 1997, reporter Jake Batsell asked why they wished to keep their names out of the public eye. The senior owner replied, "Because we get too many pests."[14] In the early years the Browns had reason to fear more than pests. During the Depression, children of well-known people were targets for kidnappers, including Charles Lindbergh's baby and, closer to home, the college-aged son of department store owners in San José. Both baby Lindbergh and Brooke Hart were murdered.[15] If the Browns' worry was excessive, at least they kept their daughters safe.

Security at the house was sometimes an issue. People occasionally broke into "the largest haunted housing project in history," sometimes as a lark and sometimes in a real attempt to steal things. One of the Tiffany windows was stolen early in the 1940s.[16]

Mayme Brown was the original tour guide for the Mystery House and enjoyed showing tourists a "solid gold passkey," purportedly one that Sarah Winchester used to enter the countless rooms. Brown also showed two water buckets filled with keys to hundreds of doors and cupboards. The keys and locks may have been part of the tour, to discourage would-be thieves. With large numbers of people passing through on tours, items from the house sometimes go missing. Pieces of hardware are the most commonly stolen item. Mystery House manager Shozo Kagoshima said that many stolen objects are anonymously returned in the mail with notes confessing that the thief experienced bad luck since taking the object.[17]

Sarah Winchester's former employees and neighbors read articles about the Winchester house from time to time. Henrietta Sivera, who married and moved to Santa Monica, saw the stories. She sent a copy of one that ran in *Coronet* magazine to John Hansen, telling him that her husband, a southern California doctor, was tempted to expose the Browns as frauds. She explained, "What disturbs Doctor Noé is that the Browns are making money out there by telling a lot of falsehoods, and that is obtaining money under false pretenses, which is against the law." Sivera corresponded with Minnie Yeager Hall, who as a child lived across the road from the Winchester place, telling her, "It just made my heart sing to know you understand all that is going on at dear Mrs. Winchester's home which is not the truth."[18]

For years Hall stewed about the stories swirling around the Winchester house. In old age, when she could stand it no longer, she gave a lengthy interview that addressed many fables. She explained, "I knew Mrs. Winchester. In all my years there never did I ever see multitudes of servants and workmen. I knew everyone who was employed on the Winchester place. She really had no servants here, at her Atherton estate, yes, but here was just her cook, secretary, and whoever cleaned her bedroom."[19]

As the Browns aged and their daughters grew up and married, it became apparent that they needed to hire a manager for day-to-day operations. They hired Bill Rebello to assist with management. Rebello rang the old bell in the tower each Friday the 13th at 1300 hours thirteen times. The little ritual became a tradition. John Brown died in the late forties, and Mayme Brown died in 1951.

Of all the employees of the Winchester Mystery House over the years, Keith Kittle, general manager from 1973 until 1996, had the biggest impact. After flunking out of college in the early 1960s, Kittle moved to California, where he worked at Disneyland for a time, then, when he came to San José, went to work for Frontier Village, a family-run Western-style amusement park. Kittle immersed himself in the mythology of the old West, absorbing historical anecdotes and substantial romantic notions. For years Kittle played piano in the Silver Dollar Saloon, entertaining guests into believing they were sipping sarsaparillas (or stronger) in a real frontier watering hole.

In 1973, Kittle left Frontier Village to become general manager at the Winchester Mystery House. It was in serious disrepair, and the employee culture of the place had degenerated to where smoking and drinking on the job were commonplace. Kittle enforced new rules and sought out historic landmark status for the old house. He instigated the addition of a Winchester rifle museum to the attraction. Perhaps Kittle's most significant contribution to the success of the mansion was the advertising campaign he initiated that put huge red, black, and white billboards up beside highways.[20]

A latter-day John Brown, Kittle had a knack for getting publicity. He also knew human nature well enough to inject a bit of the macabre into Winchester stories to jump-start attendance numbers. Both men had been described as "carnival hucksters," both fostered respect for the old house, and both were good storytellers. Kittle's grasp of California's tourist industry and John Brown's instincts for drawing the public lived out the notions first hinted at in the promotional books Sarah Winchester saw before moving to California. Charles Nordhoff's *California for Health, Pleasure, and Residence, A Book for Travelers and Settlers* (1872) first formulated the perception of California as a tourist destination. If Nordhoff, Brown, and Kittle had lived at the same time, the three would have found many things to discuss about the Mystery House. It successfully weaves together nostalgia, history, and a superstitious kind of religiosity with American cultural symbols, giving it a significant place in California's tourist industry.

Kittle also believed that as one tourist attraction went, so went the others. To that end he brought together the managers of other venues in a cooperative, cofounding the Northern California Attractions Association, and was active in the San José Convention and Visitors Bureau. In 1997, within two days of being inducted into the California Tourism Hall of Fame (at the same time as the Beach Boys, no less), Keith Kittle died of complications from AIDS. He left the Mystery House with a sturdy reputation.[21]

The current general manager of the Winchester Mystery House, Shozo Kagoshima, worked with Kittle and has been employed at the house since the 1980s. Kagoshima does not mind saying that he has never experienced any paranormal activity at the house. But he adds that he has worked with people who sincerely believe that they have. "So who are we to say?" he asks. "If Sarah Winchester wanted to live forever, maybe she lives in the stories generated from the house."[22] The current owners never responded to my requests to be interviewed for this book.

Through the years, tour guides have been given a carefully written script and told not to deviate from the story line too far. In more recent years, guides are required to sign commitments of confidentiality, promising not to disclose the identities of the Mystery House's owners or give attendance numbers. Most of the tour guides are not privy to this information anyway.

The Winchester Mystery House is a carefully packaged product that is heavily advertised with, among other things, massive billboards along California's roadways. The image of a human skull superimposed over a silhouette of the Winchester mansion has little to say about the house or its builder. As with any brand-name product, we recognize the packaging or can hum the jingle without real knowledge of what is inside. It is incumbent upon the consumer to question and read labels carefully before adding our dollars to the balance sheet of the product's bottom line.

The house has sometimes been used to promote other products or services. *Thirteen Ghosts,* a B-rated horror film from 1960, capitalized on the superstitions involving the number thirteen and showed an extremely rundown Winchester house. In 1966, the house was the backdrop for an album cover for a local rock group, the Count Five. That album has become a valuable collector's item because the song "Psychotic Reaction" from it took its place among the most important punk songs in rock history. The movies and music were unwitting advertisements for the old Winchester house in San José. The roadside haunted house stayed open and supported yet a new generation.

In 1911, journalist Merle H. Gray, critical of Winchester's treatment by the press, distilled the Winchester mythology into one statement: "Mrs.

Winchester . . . was obscessed [*sic*] with the idea that she would live as long as she continued building and that as soon as the work was discontinued she would die." What is startling in retrospect is not that Gray reported the legend, but that a dozen years before the Mystery House opened for business, he correctly pointed out that "younger generations accepted this version from their elders without a doubt as to its authenticity and have repeated it as the truth, and in time to come it will probably remain a legend explaining one of the most curious structures in the valley."[23] Gray was dead-on.

The mysterious and the promise of an eerie spectral presence are quantifiable in dollars if not in matter. According to a marketing survey at the Winchester Mystery House, the most important factor attracting visitors to the house is the connection between Sarah Winchester and spirits or ghosts.[24] For this reason, one that most locals find utterly unaccountable, when visitors arrive in San José from another part of the country, one of the first places they want to see is the Winchester Mystery House. It has far-reaching cachet.

The elusive watermark in anything about Sarah Winchester or her mysterious house is the Winchester repeater. The rifle's story is distinctly American, from its invention and the emergence of the huge company, through its evolution into hundreds of models and iterations, down to its symbolic value in Hollywood movies. After the rifle was no longer needed on Civil War battlefields and, later, after legitimate law enforcement overtook outlaws in the West, the capabilities of the repeater became a source of popular entertainment. The repeater's appearances at the great world's fairs and in Wild West shows brought it swiftly and definitively into the entertainment industry. Celebrities from Buffalo Bill and Annie Oakley to Jimmy Stewart and Chuck Connors pulled the repeater out of reality and made it an almost charming and nostalgic symbol. Sarah Winchester's role in the story is to shoulder the guilt for the violence and death inflicted by the repeating rifle, and to answer for all those thorny questions about death and life after death. A shadow of herself plays the role very well every day at the Winchester Mystery House.

Winchester rifles financed the original construction of the house, and today hold up the Winchester Mystery House's premise that a guilt-ridden widow was pestered by countless spirits of those killed by them. It is ironic that the utterly private Sarah Winchester drew so much attention to herself for over 110 years because of the big, gangly house. Since her death the house has undergone many alterations to ensure its viability as a tourist destination: room additions and deletions, paint, carpet, a supposedly seven-mile-long fire sprinkler system, the addition of thirteen coat hooks—not to mention many other references to thirteen, and random furnishings including an office with inexplicable Russian references that even the tour guides point out have nothing to do with Winchester. But through the years and alterations, Sarah has not evolved or changed. She, much more than the house, remains trapped in myth and legend.

Perhaps someday more letters that Sarah Winchester exchanged will surface. She noted, "As I keep most of the letters which I receive, I have accumulated many boxes and baskets of them and have never yet sorted them out as I have often thought of doing."[25] But for now, we have the Hansens and Leib to thank for lending at least some form and fabric to the woman who was Winchester.

NOTES

━┼─ ⚞◇⚟ ─┼━

The names of repositories and people frequently cited in the notes are identified by the following abbreviations:

CHC   Stocklmeir Library and Archives, California History Center, De Anza College, Cupertino, California
CHS   Connecticut Historical Society, Hartford, Connecticut
HSJ   History San José Archives, San José, California
LDS   Latter Day Saints Family History Library, Salt Lake City, Utah
SFL   Samuel Franklin Leib
SLW   Sarah L. Winchester
SUA   Stanford University Archives, Stanford, California

PREFACE

1. Bruce Spoon, "Sarah Winchester and Her House," 19–20.

2. Ted A. Hansen to Helen Arbuckle, May 10, 1972, Arbuckle Collection, CHC; Richard Hansen, telephone interview with the author, March 13, 2008.

3. U.S. Department of the Interior Historic American Buildings Survey, CA-2107, Winchester House, 1981.

INTRODUCTION

1. The Winchester was a modified "Henry," patented in 1860 by Benjamin T. Henry.

2. Oliver Winchester's 4,000 shares were to be divided between William Winchester and his sister, Jennie Bennett, when their mother died. So by 1898, when Jane Winchester died, Sarah Winchester had inherited the stock her husband owned, half of his father's, and a small number from her mother, totaling about 2,777 stocks, nearly a third of the 10,000 total stocks in the Winchester Repeating Arms Company.

3. SLW to Hannah Jane "Jennie" Bennett, June 11, 1898, Bennett Family Papers, CHS.

4. "A Woman Who Thinks She Will Die When Her House Is Built," *San Jose Evening News,* March 29, 1895, 4.

5. For example, Catherine Gittings, "The Lady and the Ark"; Ruth Amet, "Mystery Novel Atmosphere Dominates Web of Rooms."

6. *San Jose Mercury,* September 7, 1922, 1.

CHAPTER 1, NEW HAVEN'S DAUGHTER

1. Charles Dickens, *American Notes,* 70.

2. Jedidiah Morse, *The 1797 American gazetteer, exhibiting in alphabetical order, a much more full and accurate account of the civil divisions, rivers, harbors, Indian tribes, &c. on the American continent....,* 362.

3. The best published genealogy of the Pardee family is Donald Lines Jacobus, *The Pardee Genealogy.*

4. Charles J. Hoadly, ed., *Records of the colony and plantation of New Haven, from 1638 to 1649,* 135.

5. Edward E. Atwater, *History of the Colony of New Haven to Its Absorption into Connecticut,* 289.

6. Jacobus, *Pardee Genealogy,* 75.

7. Ibid., 76.

8. See, for example, Leib correspondence for the year 1905. Winchester's interest in woodworking is attested to by the intricate woodwork in her San José home and the number of woodworkers she employed.

9. Revolutionary War Widow Pension file, number 16519, Revolutionary War Pension and Bounty-Land Warrant Application Files, National Archives, http://www.archives.gov/index.html.

10. John Woolman Brush, *A History of the First Baptist Church in New Haven, 1816-1966,* 18-21.

11. Ann Braude, *Radical Spirits: Spiritualism and Women's Rights in Nineteenth-Century America,* 36, 201.

12. Jacobus, *Pardee Genealogy,* 245.

13. *Vital Records of New Haven 1649-1850.*

14. Research Publications, New Haven, Connecticut, 1840-1860/61, Series, City Directories of the United States: segment 1 through 1860, fiche no. 817-838:6.

15. J. Knight, "An Introductory Lecture to the Course of 1849-50, in the Medical Institution of Yale College," 440.

16. *Vital Records of New Haven 1649-1850.*

17. Rollin G. Osterweis, *Three Centuries of New Haven, 1638-1938,* 292.

18. Sarah Winchester's precise birth date has not been determined. However, an examination of U.S. Census records for 1850, 1860, and 1870 confirms that she was born between July and October of 1839. Later census records indicate different birth years, but they are less reliable because no one in her immediate family gave the census taker the information.

19. See, for example, William Converse to SLW, May 16, 1888, Leib Collection,

HSJ; SLW to Jennie Bennett, May 14, 1898, Bennett Family Papers, CHS; SLW to Jennie Bennett, June 11, 1898, Bennett Family Papers, CHS; Thomas G. Bennett to SLW, April 5, 1918, Leib Collection, HSJ.

20. See, for example, information about Sarah's sister Belle's work with the Humane Society in "The Humane Society and Its Work," *San Jose Mercury and Herald,* June 5, 1910, 6; and notes about her advocacy for African Americans in Anne Whitney Wakefield, "A Tribute to the Memory of Isabelle C. Merriman." Belle was the first white member of a local chapter of the NAACP in Palo Alto, California. Homer Sprague was fired from for his abolitionist speeches.

21. U.S. Census records from 1850 and 1860 (New Haven County, Connecticut) indicate that Belle was born in 1843 and Estelle in 1845.

22. Research Publications, New Haven, Connecticut, 1840-1860/61, Series, City Directories of the United States: segment 1 through 1860, fiche no. 817-838:6.

23. Ibid.

24. Robert W. Rydell, John E. Findling, and Kimberly D. Pelle, *Fair America: World's Fairs in the United States,* 14.

25. U.S. Census, New Haven County, Connecticut, 1860.

26. Osterweis, *Three Centuries of New Haven,* 348.

27. *Boston Transcript,* March 23, 1918; Charles L. Ives, "Statistics of the Class of 1852 of Yale College," 52.

28. *New York Times,* January 1, 1855.

29. Homer Sprague was asked to leave Worcester, Massachusetts, High School in 1860; Adelphi Academy, Brooklyn, New York, in 1875; and Mills College, Oakland, California, in 1886. The reasons that he left the Connecticut State Normal School in 1868, Cornell University in 1870, and the University of North Dakota in 1889 are unclear and may also be examples of conflicts with boards of trustees.

30. Isabelle (Pardee) Merriman's obituary describes events in her early life, including that Henry Bergh was "for long periods a guest in the home of her childhood." *San Jose Mercury Herald,* June 18, 1920.

31. Osterweis, *Three Centuries of New Haven,* 230.

CHAPTER 2, MARRYING INTO THE WINCHESTER FAMILY

1. Thom Peters, e-mail message to the author, September 28, 2004, citing information from the Hopkins School Archives, Hopkins School, New Haven; Research Publications, New Haven, Connecticut, 1840-1860/61, Series, City Directories of the United States: segment 1 through 1860, fiche no. 817-838:6.

2. Lucius R. Paige, *List of Freemen of Massachusetts 1630-1691* (Baltimore: Geneaological Publishing Co. Inc., 1978), 15.

3. C. H. Simmons Jr., ed., *Plymouth Colony Records,* vol. 1, *Wills and Inventories, 1633-1669* (Camden, ME: Picton Press, 1996), 310.

4. Fanny (Winchester) Hotchkiss, *Winchester Notes,* 19.

5. Research Publications, New Haven, Connecticut, 1789-1860/61, Series, City Directories of the United States: segment 1 through 1860, fiche no. 115-73.

6. Hotchkiss, *Winchester Notes,* 24.

7. *New Haven Register,* December 11, 1880, 1.

8. Boston city directories, 1818–1825; U.S. Census, Boston, Ward 12, Suffolk County, Massachusetts, 1820.

9. The Bretts moved to New Haven just after Oliver and Jane Winchester. The U.S. Census, New Haven County, Connecticut, 1860, shows that neither of the Bretts had an occupation or owned real estate. The Mary Ann (Winchester) and Cyrus Brett family are interred in Oliver Winchester's family plot at Evergreen Cemetery in New Haven.

10. William Wirt (1172–1834).

11. U.S. Patent 0005421, O. F. Winchester, 1848, Method of Cutting and Fitting Shirts, filed date unknown, issued February 1, 1848.

12. *New Haven Register,* December 11, 1880, 1.

13. Osterweis, *Three Centuries of New Haven,* 254.

14. U.S. Census, New Haven County, Connecticut, 1860.

15. Ibid.

16. Harold F. Williamson, *Winchester, the Gun That Won the West,* 393n4.

17. United States Passport application, July 26, 1858, New York, New York; Passenger Lists of Vessels Arriving at Boston, Massachusetts, *Niagara,* 1820–1943, www.ancestry.com.

18. See, for example, the *New Haven Daily Register,* March 8, 1881, which says that William had "a retiring disposition"; and Herbert G. Houze, *Winchester Repeating Arms Company: Its History and Development from 1865 to 1981,* 63, which describes Oliver as a "ruthless competitor."

19. U.S. Census, New Haven County, Connecticut, 1860.

20. Preston Maynard and Marjorie B. Noyes, eds., *Carriages and Clocks, Corsets and Locks: The Rise and Fall of an Industrial City—New Haven, Connecticut,* 29; Winchester & Davies Shirt Manufactory advertising broadside, circa 1860, in Houze, *Winchester Repeating Arms Company,* 242.

21. Williamson, *Winchester,* 21; Houze, *Winchester Repeating Arms Company,* 23.

22. U.S. Census, New Haven County, Connecticut, 1860.

23. SLW to Jennie Bennett, May 14, 1898, Bennett Family Papers, CHS.

24. Jacobus, *Pardee Genealogy,* 245.

25. James B. Coit, *Second Connecticut Volunteers.*

26. Osterweis, *Three Centuries of New Haven,* 351.

27. Homer B. Sprague, *History of the Thirteenth Infantry Regiment of Connecticut Volunteers, during the Great Rebellion,* iv.

28. Ibid., 9.

29. Record of Births in the Town of New Haven, vol. 15, LDS microfilm #1405860.

30. Ibid.

31. Braude, *Radical Spirits,* 39.

32. Record of Marriages in the Town of New Haven, vol. 16, LDS microfilm #1405860. The U.S. Census, New Haven County, Connecticut, 1880, states that Isabelle was thirty-three when she was actually thirty-seven. The U.S. Census, Santa Clara County, California, 1900, states that Isabelle was born in 1853, ten

years after her real birth year. It says Lewis Merriman was born in 1845, also ten years later than his actual birth year.

33. Connecticut Probate Court, New Haven District, vol. 121, pp. 137–38 (Genealogical Society of Utah, Salt Lake City, 1984, microfilm #1405899).

34. SLW to Jennie Bennett, May 14, 1898, Bennett Family Papers, CHS. The original clipping was found in the safe at her San José house after she died.

CHAPTER 3, "THE GUN THAT WON THE WEST"

1. Houze, *Winchester Repeating Arms Company,* 14.

2. Dean K. Boorman, *The History of Winchester Firearms,* 12.

3. Houze, *Winchester Repeating Arms Company,* 18.

4. Boorman, *History of Winchester Firearms,* 25, 26 (quote by Brigadier General James Ripley), 24; Williamson, *Winchester,* 50.

5. Sprague, *History of the Thirteenth Infantry Regiment,* 114.

6. Lincoln's Henry is held by the Smithsonian Institution in Washington, DC. See Robert L. Wilson, *Colt: An American Legend,* 15; and Boorman, *History of Winchester Firearms,* 26. Regarding Marsh breech-loaders, see Robert V. Bruce, *Lincoln and the Tools of War,* 117.

7. Houze, *Winchester Repeating Arms Company,* 18, 19.

8. Boorman, *History of Winchester Firearms,* 21; Houze, *Winchester Repeating Arms Company,* 23.

9. Williamson, *Winchester,* 49.

10. Houze, *Winchester Repeating Arms Company,* 43.

11. Boorman, *History of Winchester Firearms,* 22; Williamson, *Winchester,* 49, 460.

12. Houze, *Winchester Repeating Arms Company,* 63.

13. *Emory Report* 50, no. 11 (November 3, 1997) http://www.emory.edu/ EMORY_REPORT/erarchive/1997/November/ernovember.3/11_3_97Bellesiles. html.

14. Benjamin T. Henry believed Winchester swindled him and John Pearson, a technician who worked for Colt who claimed to have invented the revolver. William N. Hosley, *Colt: The Making of an American Legend,* 16.

15. For references to Samuel Colt and military long arms, see Hosley, *Colt: The Making of an American Legend,* 50.

16. Williamson, *Winchester,* 59.

17. *New York Times,* January 24, 1879, 6.

18. Houze, *Winchester Repeating Arms Company,* 73, 75.

19. Williamson, *Winchester,* 84.

20. *New York Times,* August 31, 1881, 5.

21. Houze, *Winchester Repeating Arms Company,* 36.

22. Ibid., 64 (Winchester Repeating Arms Company advertisement).

23. Williamson, *Winchester,* 460.

24. Isaiah Taber, cabinet photograph of Sarah Winchester, circa 1872, HSJ.

25. Richard L. Legault, *Trends in American Gun Ownership*, 12.

26. M. L. Brown, *Firearms in Colonial America: The Impact on History and Technology, 1492-1792*, 126.

27. Stephen P. Halbrook, *The Founders' Second Amendment Origin of the Right to Bear Arms*, 28-32.

28. Advertisement, reproduced in Houze, *Winchester Repeating Arms Company*, 64.

29. James Donovan, *A Terrible Glory: Custer and the Little Bighorn, the Last Great Battle of the American West*, 118.

30. Ibid., 188.

31. James Welch, *Killing Custer: The Battle of the Little Bighorn and the Fate of the Plains Indians*, 170.

32. Charles E. Chapel, *Guns of the Old West*, 248.

33. Legault, *Trends in American Gun Ownership*, 19.

34. George Madis, *The Winchester Book Silver Anniversary Edition*, 641.

35. Legault, *Trends in American Gun Ownership*, 20.

36. Chapel, *Guns of the Old West*, 247.

37. Wilson, *Colt: An American Legend*.

38. Williamson, *Winchester*, 83.

39. Arrival: New York, 1872, National Archives Microfilm serial: M237, Microfilm roll: M237_365, line 47, list number 1008; passenger Lists of Vessels Arriving at New York, New York, *Batavia*, 1820-1957, www.ancestry.com.

40. Williamson, *Winchester*, 77.

41. Wilson, *Colt: An American Legend*, 101.

42. Houze, *Winchester Repeating Arms Company*, 129.

43. Theodore Roosevelt, *Hunting Trips of a Ranchman; Sketches of Sport on the Northern Cattle Plains*, quoted in Boorman, *History of Winchester Firearms*, 70.

44. 1875 Winchester catalog; Wilson, *Colt: An American Legend*, 55.

45. For a full description of small-arms ammunition, see Berkeley R. Lewis, *Small Arms Ammunition at the International Exposition Philadelphia, 1876.*

46. Houze, *Winchester Repeating Arms Company*, 101.

47. Alfred Heller, "Philadelphia 1876 Centennial International Exhibition," 59.

48. Williamson, *Winchester*, 69.

49. Frederick Jackson Turner, "The Problem of the West," The Atlantic Monthly, September 1896. Online source: http://www.theatlantic.com/past/docs/issues/95sep/ets/turn.htm.

CHAPTER 4, THE WINCHESTER FORTUNE

1. Architectural historian Elizabeth Mills Brown attributes the design of the Winchester home to the architectural firm McKim, Mead & White, but this firm was not in existence yet when the home was built in 1866-1868.

2. New Haven Preservation Trust, http://nhpt.org/index.php/site/district/prospect_hill_historic_district/.

3. *Benham's New Haven Directory and Annual Advertiser for 1869-70* (New Haven: 1869), 117.

4. SLW to Jennie Bennett, May 15, 1898, Bennett Family Papers, CHS.

5. For part of the twentieth century, the Davies house was owned by the Culinary Institute of America as a training ground for chefs. In 1970, Yale University purchased the Davies house and its seven acres, but the house sat empty until 2001, when the Betts family donated $5 million to renovate the house, which is currently known as the Betts House, for Yale's Center of the Study of Globalization. The Winchester house was home to the senior Winchesters until their deaths, when their daughter and son-in-law, Jennie and Thomas Bennett, made their home there. Jennie died in 1920 and Thomas in 1930. Within two years of Thomas's death, the house was razed to make way for Yale's Sterling Divinity Quadrangle, designed by the architectural firm Delano & Aldrich. www.yale.edu.

6. U.S. Census, New Haven County, Connecticut, 1860 and 1870.

7. Hosley, *Colt: The Making of an American Legend,* 73.

8. Houze, *Winchester Repeating Arms Company,* 63.

9. Heller, "Philadelphia 1876 Centennial International Exhibition," 60.

10. Julie K. Brown, *Making Culture Visible: The Public Display of Photography at Fairs, Expositions, and Exhibitions in the United States, 1847-1900,* 72.

11. Williamson, *Winchester,* 77-80; Houze, *Winchester Repeating Arms Company,* 9-10, 25, 69-70.

12. For a detailed account of the Bey incident, see "An Exploded 'Torpedo,'" *New York Times,* February 4, 1878, 7.

13. Williamson, *Winchester,* 463, 466, 460.

14. Connecticut Probate Court, New Haven District, New Haven Probate Records, vol. 166, p. 45, Sarah Pardee, LDS microfilm #1405965.

15. *New Haven Palladium,* December 11, 1880.

16. Hotchkiss, *Winchester Notes,* 256.

17. *New Haven Register,* December 11, 1880, 1.

18. Williamson, *Winchester,* 77.

19. New Haven Land Records, vol. 341, pp. 333-338, LDS microfilm #1405534.

20. SLW financial records book, Leib Collection, HSJ.

21. *New Haven Daily Palladium,* March 8, 1881.

22. Funeral expenses are listed in the New Haven District probate record (Connecticut Probate Court, New Haven District, New Haven Probate Records, vol. 167, p. 185, LDS microfilm #1405965). Evergreen Cemetery has records on the William and Sarah Winchester family plot.

23. SLW to Jennie Bennett, May 14, 1898, Bennett Family Papers, CHS.

24. Connecticut Probate Court, New Haven District (Genealogical Society of Utah, Salt Lake City, 1984, microfilm #1405965 and #1405966).

25. Connecticut Probate Court, New Haven District, vols. 166-67, p. 46 (Genealogical Society of Utah, Salt Lake City, 1984, microfilm #1405965).

26. Connecticut Probate Court, New Haven District, Land Records, vol. 340, p. 339, for Leonard M. Pardee's transfer of his interest in the houses on Orange and

Eld streets (Genealogical Society of Utah, Salt Lake City, 1984, microfilm #1405965 and #1405966).

27. SLW to Jennie Bennett, May 14, 1898, Bennett Family Papers, CHS.

28. Connecticut Probate Court, New Haven District, New Haven Probate Records, vol. 167, p. 185, LDS microfilm #1405965.

29. Converse managed Sarah Winchester's financial affairs until he died in 1889, when she began keeping her own accounts. See, for example, William Converse to SLW, April 30, 1888, and May 16, 1888; see also Edward B. Rambo to William Converse, April 17, 1888, and A. Roman & Co. to SLW, June 16, 1888, all in Leib Collection, HSJ.

30. Ibid., 83.

31. Thomas Bennett to Jennie Bennett, June 8, 1881, Bennett Family Papers, CHS.

32. New Haven Directory (New Haven: Price & Lee, 1893).

33. See, for example, Braude, *Radical Spirits,* 10–55.

34. Susy Smith, *Prominent American Ghosts,* 33; Emily Mace, "Haunted by Tourists: Spirits of Spiritualism at the Winchester Mystery House," 30n10.

35. SLW to Charles Morris, December 16, 1909, Leib Collection, HSJ.

36. SLW to Jennie Bennett, June 11, 1898, Bennett Family Papers, CHS.

37. *General Hospital Society of Connecticut Centenary, 1826-1926,* 78.

CHAPTER 5, A CALIFORNIA DREAM

1. New Haven city directories to the middle 1890s.

2. Charles Nordhoff, *California for Health, Pleasure, and Residence: A Book for Travelers and Settlers,* 18–19.

3. E. S. Harrison and San José Board of Trade, eds., *Homes for a Million,* 17.

4. Mary Carroll and her husband, Frank, came to California from New Haven to work for Winchester in 1886. Mary Carroll, quoted in Melick, "Sevenscore Gables," 39.

5. Henry Ward Beecher, quoted in *Santa Clara County, California* (San José: Board of Trade) 1, no. 1 (September 1887).

6. Susan Tolman Mills, *Rebuttal of Homer Sprague's "To My Friends,"* 5-6.

7. Homer B. Sprague, *To My Friends,* 1.

8. Homer B. Sprague, newspaper clipping, 1885, Archives and Manuscripts, Yale University Library.

9. Sprague, *To My Friends,* 32-33.

10. Ibid., 13.

11. *Boston Transcript,* March 23, 1918.

12. Eugene Sawyer, *History of Santa Clara County, California,* 1372. Rambo was known to family members as "Ned," and eventually his brother would work for Winchester. In 1967, Ned's nephew, Ralph Rambo, authored a small booklet about Winchester entitled *Lady of Mystery.* It remains the most accurate depiction of

the woman to date.

13. Harrison and San José Board of Trade, *Homes for a Million,* 19.

14. The Electric Light Tower was severely damaged during a storm on February 8, 1915. Repairs had not been made as of December 3, 1915, when the tower was toppled by another storm. See Linda S. Larson, *San José's Monument to Progress: The Electric Light Tower.*

15. New Haven city directories and U.S. Census, New Haven County, Connecticut, 1900, 1910, and 1920.

16. Daniel Hruby, *Mines to Medicine: The Exciting Years of Judge Myles O'Connor, His Hospital and the Pioneer Physicians of the Santa Clara Valley,* 66.

17. *San Jose Mercury,* January 9, 1894, 2.

18. Santa Clara County, Deeds, Book 106, p. 238, March 22, 1888.

19. *San Jose Mercury,* August 12, 1887, 3.

20. The Los Altos History Museum proposes that Winchester recycled the window, removing it from her house and installing it in Belle's.

21. Edward B. Rambo to William Converse, April 17, 1888, Leib Collection, HSJ.

22. Ibid.

23. A. Roman & Co. to SLW, June 16, 1888, Leib Collection, HSJ.

24. Richard Joncas, David J. Neuman, and Paul V. Turner, *The Campus Guide,* 17.

25. David Starr Jordan, *Days of a Man, Being Memories of a Naturalist, Teacher, and Minor Prophet of Democracy,* 1:365.

26. Joncas, Neuman, and Turner, *Campus Guide,* 25.

27. Jane Stanford to SFL, May 7, 1899, box 2, folder 4, Leib Collection, SUA.

28. *San Jose Mercury Herald,* December 27, 1924, 1.

29. There are letters between Winchester and Leib in the private Halberstadt Collection (in possession of April Halberstadt), in the Leib Collection at the History San José Archives, and in the Leib Collection at the Stanford University Archives.

30. SFL to SLW, April 7, 1906, Halberstadt Collection.

31. Leib Carriage House, National Register of Historic Places, #1980000866.

32. Hannah Moore Everett, "Memories of an Oldest Child Written for the Grandchildren and Great Grandchildren of Evelyn Moore Furst by Her Daughter," 79.

33. Gunther Nagel, *Iron Will: The Life and Letters of Jane Stanford,* 144 (emphasis in original).

34. Elna Leib Wright to Jane Stanford, October 17, 1901, in possession of Marian Leib Adams.

35. Receipt for Anderson Prune Dipper for $90, 1891, box 3, folder 17, Leib Collection, SUA.

36. Luther Burbank to SFL, 1904, and July 16, 1906, box 3, folder 3, Leib Collection, SUA.

37. Receipt for automobile purchase in Halberstadt Collection; Luther Burbank, *Why I Am an Infidel.*

CHAPTER 6, LABYRINTH

1. Winchester Mystery House brochures incorrectly state that Winchester purchased a house on the property in 1884. It was 1886. See also Thompson and West, *Historical Atlas Map of Santa Clara County, California,* 1876.

2. Jeanette Watson, *Campbell, the Orchard City,* 99.

3. William T. Snead, quoted in William Cronin, *Nature's Metropolis: Chicago and the Great West,* 340.

4. *Final Report of the California World's Fair Commission Chicago, 1893,* 34.

5. Ralph Rambo, *Lady of Mystery,* 14 (quotation); Winchester Mystery House, tour script, "Additional Information," 2006, p. 10.

6. *San Jose Mercury Herald,* January 1, 1892.

7. Receipts from a subscription to *Architectural Record,* Leib Collection, HSJ.

8. SLW to Jennie Bennett, June 11, 1898, Bennett Family Papers, CHS.

9. Katerina Rohner, interview with the author, September 10, 2009.

10. Tad Burness, *The Vintage House Book: Classic American Homes, 1880-1980,* 30.

11. SLW to Jennie Bennett, May 14, 1898, Bennett Family Papers, CHS.

12. Ibid.

13. Ibid., June 11, 1898.

14. Hosley, *Colt: The Making of an American Legend,* 139; *San Francisco Chronicle,* June 19, 1887, 13.

15. Everett, "Memories of an Oldest Child," 75, 76.

16. Ibid., 65, 75.

17. *San Jose Evening News,* July 31, 1899, 8; Nancy Newlin, *The Gem of Edenvale,* 38.

18. In 1899, the Hayes home burned to the ground. It was rebuilt and finished in 1905 as an eclectic mix of Queen Anne, Mediterranean, and Italian Revival styles. It maintained its original general layout. Hayes Mansion, National Register of Historic Places no. 1975000481; Haas-Lilienthal House, no. 1973000438; Leib Carriage House, no. 1980000866; Winchester House, no. 1974000559.

19. *San Jose News,* October 11, 1897.

20. Cronin, *Nature's Metropolis,* 340.

21. Winchester Mystery House, tour script, "Additional Information," 2006, p. 19; Merle H. Gray, "The Workshop of a Woman Architect."

22. SLW to Jennie Bennett (emphasis in original), May 14, 1898, Bennett Family Papers, CHS.

23. Ibid., June 11, 1898.

24. A map of Santa Clara County dating from the 1890s, which can be found in the California Room of the Martin Luther King Jr. Main Library in San José, identifies each farm by location and acreage.

25. SLW to SFL, October 27, 1905, box 11, folder 11, Leib Collection, SUA.

26. SLW to SFL, November 4, 1905, box 11, folder 11, Leib Collection, SUA.

27. SLW to SFL, October 27, 1905, box 11, folder 11, Leib Collection, SUA.

28. L. S. Bahusen on behalf of Judge Robert E. Doan to SLW, n.d., Leib Collection, HSJ.

29. Amaury Mars, *Reminiscences of the Santa Clara Valley and San José: With the Souvenir of the Carnival of Roses Held in Honor of the Visit of President William McKinley, Santa Clara County, California, May 13-14-15, 1901,* 72.

30. Houze, *Winchester Repeating Arms Company,* 170.

31. Rambo, *Lady of Mystery,* 9.

32. Ancestry.com. *California Voter Registrations, 1900-1968* [database online]. Provo, UT: USA: Ancestry.com Operations Inc., 2008 (original data: State of California, Great Register of Voters, Sacramento, CA: California State Library); SLW to Jennie Bennett, May 14, 1898, Bennett Family Papers, CHS.

33. *San Jose Evening News,* October 3, 1902, 4, 5.

34. *San Jose Evening News,* November 1, 1902, 1.

CHAPTER 7, DAYDREAM OR NIGHTMARE

1. *Mountain View Register Leader,* April 13, 1895.

2. See, for example, Hansen daybook, March 15, 1915, and September 25, 1915, Hansen Collection, HSJ.

3. *San Jose Mercury,* January 1, 1892, 26.

4. *Final Report of the California World's Fair Commission Chicago, 1893,* 32.

5. Williamson, *Winchester,* app. F, 463.

6. *San Jose Daily Mercury,* April 18, 1896, 7, and May 6, 1896, 3.

7. *San Jose Evening News,* December 7, 1897, 2.

8. *Los Altos Star,* August 5, 1908.

9. *San Jose Evening News,* March 6, 1901, 7.

10. *San Jose Evening News,* October 7, 1901, 4.

11. Neither Isabelle Merriman nor Sarah Winchester identified herself in public records as "housewife," but Daisy did. For Winchester, see for example San José city directories, 1890s, where she is listed as an "orchardist," and U.S. Census, San Mateo County, California, 1910, where she is listed as "head of household." For Isabelle Merriman, see same and voter-registration records, 1912-1920; for Daisy after her marriage (Marion I. Marriott), see census records 1910 and 1920 and voter registration 1912-1930, where she calls herself a housewife.

12. *San Jose Evening News,* February 7, 1899, 3.

13. "Changes Flow of Gossip with a Marriage License," *San Francisco Examiner,* June 17, 1901; "Jesse and His Marriage License," *San Jose Evening News,* June 17, 1901, 4.

14. Ibid.; "Mr. Adel and Miss Cain Have Been Married," *San Jose Evening News,* June 18, 1901, 3.

15. *San Jose Mercury,* April 1, 1903.

16. *San Francisco Chronicle,* July 24, 1903, 10.

17. *Mountain View Register,* February 13, 1904, 3.

18. *San Jose Evening News,* August 25, 1903, 5.

19. At the time, the area was known as Fair Oaks, then, somewhat later, Menlo Park. It was incorporated as Atherton in 1923. For the sake of clarity, "Atherton" is used here.

20. Dominga Atherton's estranged daughter-in-law, Gertrude Atherton, was a best-selling American novelist. She had eloped with Dominga's son, George Atherton, resulting in a bad marriage. Among Gertrude Atherton's most popular books was *The Californians* (1898), set in Valparaiso Park, the old Atherton Estate.

21. *Redwood City Democrat,* October 3, 1903; Phyllis Moulton Merrill, "Memories of Atherton: Oral History Transcript," BANC MSS 75/57 C, 1971, Bancroft Library, University of California, Berkeley.

22. Michael Svanevik and Shirley Burgett, *Menlo Park beyond the Gate,* 49.

23. Ibid., 64–65.

24. Sewall Bogart, *Carolands, Hillsboro: The Imperious Survivor,* 15. The Carolans sold their polo field in 1915, but their enormous "Carolands" mansion built in Hillsborough after the earthquake was decorated and finished with the finest that money could buy and art dealers could import. Frank Carolan never approved of his wife's attention to the mountaintop estate, and the couple's marriage disintegrated. In an intriguing similarity to Winchester's house, in 1939 the *San Francisco Chronicle* reported that Carolands "has remained through the years a strange sort of sepulcher without even a ghost to haunt it for although the place was furnished it was never [to that point] occupied" (October 1, 1939, "People" sec.).

In the years since, the polo pavilion has succumbed to development as part of Burlingame High School. Willis Polk had designed a French-style pavilion, almost an exact duplicate, for Charles Baldwin. When the Baldwins sold their pavilion, the Carolans bought it. It survives today on De Anza College campus in Cupertino, California. The Baldwin house is also on the De Anza College campus and is listed on the National Register of Historic Places, no. 1972001552.

25. *San Mateo Times,* August 6, 1904, 1.

26. Two sources give conflicting measurements. Burton Klose claimed the boat's size was forty feet by sixty feet in a handwritten notebook titled "The Winchester Ark." Frank Stanger's 1967 drawing and sketch of Winchester Ark put it at about fifteen feet by twenty-five feet. Both are in the collection of the San Mateo County History Museum Archives, Redwood City, California.

27. *San Mateo,* pamphlet, 1902, San Mateo County History Museum Archives, Redwood City.

28. Fay Hansen, interview by Burton Klose, and Burton Klose, from a description his parents—who had been guests on the boat—gave him, 1971, tape recording, San Mateo County History Museum Archives, Redwood City.

29. SLW to SFL, July 21, 1905, box 1, folder 11, Leib Collection, SUA.

30. SLW to SFL, August 4, 1905, box 1, folder 11, Leib Collection, SUA.

31. SLW to SFL (emphases in original), July 21, 1905, box 1, folder 11, Leib Collection, SUA.

32. Santa Clara County, Deeds, Book 206, p. 624, February 10, 1898.

33. Florence Fava, *Los Altos Hills: The Colorful Story.*

34. *San Jose Mercury and Herald,* October 30, 1905, 12.

35. SLW to SFL (emphasis in original), November 16, 1905, box 10, folder 4, Leib Collection, SUA; SLW to SFL, November 8, 1906, HSJ.

36. Hale to SFL, May 24, 1907, Halberstadt Collection.

37. Clark's receipt to Winchester, HSJ.

38. Los Altos, California, Chamber of Commerce website, http://www. losaltoschamber.org/community_profile.html.

39. SLW to SFL, August 4, 1905, SUA.

CHAPTER 8, GUNS, GUILT, AND GHOSTS:
THE FIRST COMMENTARIES ON SARAH WINCHESTER'S ODD HOUSE

1. *San Jose Evening News,* March 29, 1895. This is the first known article.

2. *San Jose Evening News,* March 29, 1895.

3. Ibid.

4. *San Jose News,* October 11, 1897.

5. *San Jose Evening News,* October 9, 1897, 1; *San Jose Evening News,* October 11, 1897, 1.

6. Gray, "Workshop of a Woman Architect," 6; *San Jose Evening News,* October 11, 1897, 1.

7. Legault, *Trends in American Gun Ownership,* 28-29.

8. Gray, "Workshop of a Woman Architect," 6.

9. St. Paul's Episcopal Church, Burlingame, California, record of Sarah Winchester's funeral in 1922, states Winchester's affiliation.

10. Sawyer, *History of Santa Clara County,* 701; *San Jose Mercury Herald,* November 27, 1916, 3.

11. *San Jose Evening News,* September 15, 1891, 3.

12. Clay, *The Spirit Dominant,* 97.

13. *San Francisco Examiner,* August 13, 1915, 3.

14. Merrill, "Memories of Atherton."

15. *San Jose Mercury Herald,* January 10, 1909; Gray, "Workshop of a Woman Architect," 6.

16. Williamson, *Winchester,* 463.

17. SLW to SFL, January 22, 1906, box 10, folder 4, Leib Collection, SUA.

18. SFL to SLW, April 7, 1906, Halberstadt Collection.

19. Charles Richter's research in 1958 showed a reading of 8.3 magnitude for the 1906 earthquake, but current research indicates that the magnitude ranged between 7.7 and 7.9.

20. *Campbell Interurban Press,* April 27, 1906, 2.

21. "Memories of the 1906 Quake," *Country Almanac,* April 16, 1986, 13.

22. SFL to SLW, May 4, 1906, HSJ; receipts, box 3, folder 20, Leib Collection, SUA.

23. Fred A. Marriott, in Weldon Melick, "Sevenscore Gables," 157.

24. Minnie Hall, quoted in Henry Calloway, "Taking the Mystery Out of the Mystery House," 5.

25. Mitchell Postel, *Peninsula Portrait: An Illustrated History of San Mateo County,* 42.

26. SFL to SLW, May 4, 1906, Halberstadt Collection.

27. SFL to SLW, January 20, 1906, Halberstadt Collection.

28. SFL to SLW, March 31, 1906, Halberstadt Collection.

29. SFL to SLW, June 28, 1906, Halberstadt Collection.

30. Harry Pollack to Burton Klose, note, July 31, 1972, Burton Klose Collection, San Mateo County History Museum Archives, Redwood City.

31. El Camino Real, or the King's Highway, is the path laid out by the Spanish in the eighteenth century. It has been variously called the Old San Francisco Road, the County Road, and the San José—San Francisco Road. This is the road Winchester would have traveled between Atherton and Burlingame. The two properties were about fifteen miles apart.

32. Measured by Burton Klose, 1971, "The Winchester Ark" (notebook with drawing of the houseboat and sketches and notes on the sea-retaining wall, which, although partially submerged, was still visible when Klose measured it), Klose Collection, San Mateo County History Museum Archives, Redwood City.

33. Ed Bakewell, interview by Burton Klose, n.d., tape recording, Klose Collection, San Mateo County History Museum Archive, Redwood City.

34. Dan Sheehan to Burton Klose, note, n.d., Klose Collection, San Mateo County History Museum Archives, Redwood City.

35. San Mateo County Superior Court, Sarah L. Winchester, Plaintiff, E. W. McLellan et al., Defendants, January 20, 1909.

36. SLW to SFL, February 11, 1907, Leib Collection, HSJ.

37. Millie Lewis Sargent to SFL, n.d., box 3, folder 14, Leib Collection, SUA.

38. *San Jose Mercury,* January 10, 1909.

39. Ibid., October 26, 1909, 5.

40. Hansen daybook, 1908, Hansen Collection, HSJ.

41. "Sells Her Mansion and Defies Spirits," *San Francisco Examiner,* November 8, 1911, 1.

42. Gray, "Workshop of a Woman Architect," 8.

43. Ibid., 6.

44. Gray, "Workshop of a Woman Architect," 6.

45. Ibid.

46. Harry Borchers, quoted in Joe Custer, "Mystery Shrouds One-Time Spirit Haven."

47. Melick, "Sevenscore Gables," 39.

48. Fred Larsen, quoted in Dean Jennings, "The House That Tragedy Built"; Ted Hansen to Helen Arbuckle, May 10, 1972, Arbuckle Collection, CHC.

49. *San Jose Mercury Herald,* August 5, 1925, 1.

CHAPTER 9, HEALTH AND WELFARE

1. Leib Collection, HSJ.

2. For example, Winchester gave houses to Fred Larsen, the Hansens, and the Carrolls. She loaned the Nishiharas a house, and they became renters after she died. Winchester gave Misa Hirata some cash, but no property.

3. Hansen daybook, Hansen Collection, HSJ.

4. Elmer Jensen, quoted in Bruce Spoon, "Sarah Winchester and Her House: How a Legend Grows," 17.

5. Houze, *Winchester Repeating Arms Company,* 160.

6. *Mountain View Register Leader,* February 18, 1916, 1.

7. *San Jose Evening News,* September 2, 1910, 3.

8. Ibid., September 14, 1910, 8; June 5, 1910, 6; *San Jose Mercury and Herald,* June 5, 1910, 6.

9. *San Jose Evening News,* June 28, 1910, 5; July 7, 1910, 5.

10. *San Jose Mercury and Herald,* March 5, 1911, 12.

11. *Daily Palo Alto Times,* September 14, 1912, 1; "Child's Mother Voluntarily Relinquishes Claim and Consents to Adoption," *San Jose Mercury,* September 24, 1912.

12. "Child's Mother Voluntarily Relinquishes Claim," *San Jose Mercury,* September 24, 1912.

13. Santa Clara County, Deeds, Book 389, p. 361.

14. *San Jose Mercury,* September 13, 1912, 8.

15. SLW to SFL, November 14, 1908, Leib Collection, HSJ.

16. Minnie Hall, quoted in Calloway, "Taking the Mystery Out of the Mystery House," 4.

17. Mary Carroll, quoted in Melick, "Sevenscore Gables," 39.

18. SLW to Jennie Bennett, June 11, 1898, Bennett Family Papers, CHS; Corrective Eating Society receipt, Leib Collection, HSJ.

19. Harry Borchers, in Custer, "Mystery Shrouds One-Time Spirit Haven."

20. SFL to Robert E. Payne, July 11, 1912, Leib Collection, HSJ; Merrill, "Memories of Atherton."

21. SFL to SLW, October 8, 1909, and February 27, 1909, Leib Collection, HSJ.

22. SFL to SLW, March 20, 1911, and September 1, 1911, Leib Collection, HSJ; Hansen daybook, January 5, 1911, Hansen Collection, HSJ.

23. *San Francisco Call,* June 10, 1911, 11; *New York Times,* June 12, 1911, 6.

24. *San Jose Mercury Herald,* June 11, 1911; July 16, 1911, 6.

25. *San Jose Mercury and Herald,* January 1 and 2, 1910.

26. Henrietta Sivera Noé to John Hansen, May 17, 1941, Hansen Collection, HSJ.

27. Timothy Lukes and Gary Okihiro, *Japanese Legacy: Farming and Community Life in California's Santa Clara Valley,* 19.

28. U.S. Census, San Mateo County, California, 1910. This census record lists Winchester's staff of seven household servants at Atherton.

29. U.S. Census, Santa Clara County, California, 1910, and San Mateo County, California, 1910.

30. Gray, "Workshop of a Woman Architect," 6.

31. Receipt signed by F.A. Marriott, March 26, 1909, Leib Collection, HSJ.

32. Hansen daybook, April 20, 1911, Hansen Collection, HSJ.

CHAPTER 10, CHANGING FORTUNES

1. SLW to Charles Morris, December 16, 1909, Leib Collection, HSJ.

2. SFL to SLW, March 16, 1910, Leib Collection, HSJ.

3. SFL to SLW, June 22, 1907, Leib Collection, HSJ.

4. *San Jose Mercury,* October 16, 1907, 5.

5. *San Mateo Times,* June 9, 1904.

6. *Menlo Park Progress,* August 29, 1907.

7. Marjorie Pierce, "She Played Musical Homes," 4S.

8. SFL to SLW, October 5, 1908, Leib Collection, HSJ.

9. Hahn photographs for Panama Pacific, 1915, number 114, Winchester home at Atherton, San Mateo County History Museum Archives, Redwood City.

10. Canceled checks and receipts for subscriptions are in the Leib Collection, HSJ.

11. Ruth Crocker, *Mrs. Russell Sage: Women's Activism and Philanthropy in Gilded Age and Progressive Era America,* 3.

12. See, for example, grantor or grantee indexes for San Mateo County and Santa Clara County, 1886-1922, for records of dozens of Winchester's purchases and sales.

13. *Redwood City Democrat,* October 26, 1911.

14. *Burlingame Advance,* June 6, 1912, 4; San Mateo County, Deeds, Book 212, p. 24.

15. Herb Lauter and Ralph Smith, interview by Burton Klose, tape recording, Klose Collection, San Mateo County History Museum Archives, Redwood City.

16. SLW to SFL, October 14, 1908, Leib Collection, HSJ.

17. SFL to SLW, October 5, 1908, Leib Collection, HSJ.

18. SLW to SFL, October 3, 1908, Leib Collection, HSJ.

19. Leib Collection, HSJ.

20. *General Hospital Society of Connecticut Centenery, 1826-1926.*

21. Ibid., 47.

22. SFL to Eli Whitney, December 16, 1909, Leib Collection, HSJ.

23. *General Hospital Society Centenery,* 69-71.

24. Ibid., 71.

25. Thomas Bennett to SLW, April 5, 1918, Leib Collection, HSJ.

26. *General Hospital Society Centenery,* 73.

27. The *General Hospital Society Centenery,* p. 71, states that the William Wirt Winchester Hospital was formally dedicated on May 18, 1918. This must be in error since Thomas Bennett wrote to Winchester on April 5, 1918, stating that the hospital had been formally dedicated the day before, on April 4.

28. Thomas Bennett to SLW, April 5, 1918, Leib Collection, HSJ.

29. SFL to SLW, June 20, 1918, box 1, folder 11, Leib Collection, SUA.

30. *San Francisco Examiner,* April 9, 1917, 1.

31. Ibid., August 13, 1915, 3.

32. Ibid.

33. *San Jose Mercury Herald,* June 10, 1916, 12.

34. SLW to SFL, January 26, 1915, Leib Collection, HSJ.

35. SLW to SFL, July 12, 1917, HSJ.

36. Wilson, *Colt: An American Legend,* 155.

37. Thomas Bennett to SLW, August 18, 1918, Leib Collection, HSJ.

38. Thomas Bennett to SLW, April 5, 1918, Leib Collection, HSJ.

39. Kidder, Peabody & Company to Thomas Bennett, telegram, August 1, 1918, HSJ.

40. Williamson, *Winchester,* 264.

41. Ibid., 265.

42. Ibid., 270; Bennett to SFL, May 1919, Leib Collection, HSJ.

43. SFL to SLW (emphasis in original), April 6, 1921, Leib Collection, HSJ.

44. Ibid.

45. Isabelle Merriman death record issued by Santa Clara County and funeral expenses, Klose Collection, San Mateo County History Museum Archives, Redwood City; Wakefield, "A Tribute to the Memory of Isabelle C. Merriman"; Deed, Leib Collection, HSJ.

46. Clyde W. Blackmun to SLW, June 26, 1917, Leib Collection, HSJ.

CHAPTER 11, TRAPPED IN A MISTAKEN LEGACY

1. Misa Hirata never cashed the check. In 1971 it was among a number of items that were recovered from a robbery. Perhaps Hirata had kept it as a keepsake.

2. Sarah Winchester death record issued by Santa Clara County, Klose Collection, San Mateo County History Museum Archives, Redwood City.

3. Clyde Wayland to Helen Arbuckle, Winchester notes, Arbuckle Collection, CHC.

4. Sarah Winchester death record issued by Santa Clara County, Klose Collection, San Mateo County History Museum Archives, Redwood City.

5. *San Jose Mercury,* September 7, 1922, 1.

6. Tinney & Sons funeral record, Klose Collection, San Mateo County History Museum Archives, Redwood City.

7. Minnie Hall, quoted in Calloway, "Taking the Mystery out of the Mystery House," 4.

8. Superior Court of California, Santa Clara County, Probate Case #12772, Sarah L. Winchester, Disbursements.

9. Alta Mesa Cemetery (Palo Alto) Records, Klose Collection, San Mateo County History Museum Archives, Redwood City.

10. Superior Court of California, Santa Clara County, Probate Case #12772, Sarah L. Winchester.

11. Evergreen Cemetery records, New Haven, Connecticut.

12. *San Francisco Chronicle,* October 7, 1922, 1.

13. Santa Clara County, California, Superior Court, Sarah L. Winchester, Will dated March 23, 1920.

14. Ibid.; Superior Court of California, Santa Clara County, Probate Case #12772, Sarah L. Winchester, Disbursements.

15. Ibid.

16. Superior Court of California, Santa Clara County, Probate Case #12772, Sarah L. Winchester, Disbursements.

17. Santa Clara County, California, Superior Court, Sarah L. Winchester, Will dated March 23, 1920.

18. Superior Court of California, Santa Clara County, Probate Case #12772, Sarah L. Winchester, decree settling thirteenth and final account and report of Wells Fargo Bank & Union Trust Company, Trustee, and Instructing Trustee, p. 7.

CHAPTER 12, CAPITALIZING ON SPIRITS: THE MYSTERY HOUSE

1. *Burlingame Advance,* December 19, 1924.

2. *San Mateo News Leader,* August 2, 1923.

3. SFL to John Hansen, November 16, 1922, Leib Collection, HSJ.

4. *Palo Alto Times,* May 20 and June 29, 1923.

5. SFL to John H. Hansen, November 16, 1922, Leib Collection, HSJ.

6. Probate record, Klose Collection, San Mateo County History Museum Archives, Redwood City.

7. Hansen daybook, 1922, Hansen Collection, HSJ.

8. Winchester Mystery House, tour script, 1996 (revised 2003); SFL to John Hansen, November 29, 1922, Leib Collection, HSJ.

9. Ruth Amet, "Mystery Novel Atmosphere Dominates Web of Rooms," 8.

10. James Perkins, quoted in Calloway, "Taking the Mystery Out of the Mystery House," 6.

11. Frank Faltersack, "The Strangest House in the World," 486.

12. Obituary of James Perkins, *San Jose Mercury,* January 19, 1948.

13. *Oregon Daily Journal* (Portland), November 3, 1924, 8.

14. Jake Batsell, "One Less Mystery." The current owners are several descendants of John and Mayme Brown. Although the *San Jose Mercury News* printed an article in 1997 disclosing their names, in deference to their wishes their names are not reprinted here.

15. Batsell, "One Less Mystery."

16. Melick, "Sevenscore Gables," 39; clipping, n.d., Hansen Collection, HSJ.

17. Melick, "Sevenscore Gables," 39; Shozo Kagoshima, interview with the author, August 28, 2008.

18. Henrietta Sivera Noé to John Hansen, May 17, 1941, Hansen Collection, HSJ; Henrietta Sivera Noé, quoted in Calloway, "Taking the Mystery out of the Mystery House."

19. Minnie Yeager Hall, quoted ibid.

20. Rebecca Smith, "Colleagues Remember Promoter of Winchester Mystery House."

21. Ibid.

22. Kagoshima, interview with the author, August 28, 2008.

23. Gray, "Workshop of a Woman Architect."

24. Kagoshima, interview with the author, August 28, 2008.

25. SLW to Jennie Bennett, June 11, 1898, Bennett Family Papers, CHS.

BIBLIOGRAPHY

Amet, Ruth. "Mystery Novel Atmosphere Dominates Web of Rooms." *San Jose Mercury Herald,* May 27, 1923, 8.

Atherton, Gertrude. *The Californians.* New York: Grosset and Dunlap, 1908.

Atwater, Edward E. *History of the Colony of New Haven to Its Absorption into Connecticut.* New Haven, CT: privately printed, 1881.

Batsell, Jake. "One Less Mystery." *San Jose Mercury News,* April 26, 1997.

Blake, William Phipps. *History of the Town of Hamden, Connecticut.* New Haven, CT: Price, Lee, 1888.

Bogart, Sewall. *Carolands, Hillsboro: The Imperious Survivor.* San Mateo, CA: San Mateo County Historical Association, 1991.

Boorman, Dean K. *The History of Winchester Firearms.* New York: Lyons, 2001.

Braude, Ann. *Radical Spirits: Spiritualism and Women's Rights in Nineteenth-Century America.* 2nd ed. Bloomington: Indiana University Press, 2001.

Brown, Elizabeth Mills. *New Haven: A Guide to Architecture and Urban Design.* New Haven, CT: Yale University Press, 1976.

Brown, Julie K. *Making Culture Visible: The Public Display of Photography at Fairs, Expositions, and Exhibitions in the United States, 1847-1900.* Australia: Harwood Academic Publishers, 2001.

Brown, M. L. *Firearms in Colonial America: The Impact on History and Technology, 1492-1792.* Washington, DC: Smithsonian Institution, 1980.

Bruce, Robert V. *Lincoln and the Tools of War.* New York: Bobbs-Merrill, 1956.

Brush, John Woolman. *A History of the First Baptist Church in New Haven, 1816-1966.* New Haven, 1966.

Burbank, Luther. *Why I Am an Infidel.* Girard, KS: Haldeman-Julius, 1926.

Burness, Tad. *The Vintage House Book: Classic American Homes, 1880-1980.* Iola, WI: Krause Publications, 2003.

California World's Fair Commission. *Final Report of the California*

World's Fair Commission. Sacramento, 1894.

Calloway, Henry. "Taking the Mystery Out of the Mystery House." *Trailblazer* 24 no. 3 (August 1983).

Chapel, Charles E. *Guns of the Old West.* New York: Coward-McCann, 1961.

Clay, Louisa Johnson. *The Spirit Dominant: A Life of Mary Hayes Chynoweth.* San José, CA: The Mercury Herald Company, n.d.

Coit, James B. *History of the Second Connecticut Volunteers,* http://www.ct.gov/mil/cwp/view.asp?a=1351&q=270360.

Crocker, Ruth. *Mrs. Russell Sage: Women's Activism and Philanthropy in Gilded Age and Progressive Era America.* Bloomington: Indiana University Press, 2006.

Cronin, William. *Nature's Metropolis: Chicago and the Great West.* New York: W. W. Norton, 1991.

Custer, Joe. "Mystery Shrouds One-Time Spirit Haven." N.d. Clipping, Hansen Scrapbook, Hansen Collection, History San José Archives, San José, California.

Dexter, Franklin B. *Historical Catalogue of the Members of the First Church of Christ in New Haven, Connecticut (Center Church) 1639-1914.* New Haven, 1914.

Dickens, Charles. *American Notes.* New York: St. Martin's, 1985.

Donovan, James. *A Terrible Glory: Custer and the Little Bighorn, the Last Great Battle of the American West.* New York: Little, Brown, 2008.

Everett, Hannah Moore. "Memories of an Oldest Child Written for the Grandchildren and Great Granchildren of Evelyn Moore Furst by Her Daughter." Unpublished manuscript, 1961. In possession of Marian Leib Adams.

Faltersack, Frank. "The Strangest House in the World." *Wide World Magazine* (April 1929): 486.

Fava, Florence. *Los Altos Hills: The Colorful Story.* Woodside, CA: Gilbert Richards, 1976.

General Hospital Society of Connecticut Centenary, 1826-1926. New Haven, CT: Tuttle, Morehouse and Taylor, 1926.

Gittings, Catherine. "The Lady and the Ark." *Sunset,* November 1916, 2.

Gray, Merle H. "The Workshop of a Woman Architect." *San Jose Mercury and Herald,* July 16, 1911.

Halbrook, Stephen P. *The Founders' Second Amendment Origin of the Right to Bear Arms.* Chicago: Ivan, 2008.

Harrison, E. S., and San José Board of Trade, eds. *Homes for a Million.* San José, CA: E. S. Harrison and Charles Oberdeener, 1887.

Heinz, Bernard. *Center Church-on-the-Green.* Pamphlet. New Haven, CT:

First Church of Christ, 1976. http://www.newhavencenterchurch. org/documents/CCNH_Bicentennial_publication.swf.

Heller, Alfred. "Philadelphia 1876 Centennial International Exhibition." In *Historical Dictionary of World's Fairs and Expositions, 1851-1988,* ed. John E. Findling and Kimberly D. Pelle. New York: Greenwood Press, 1990.

Hoadly, Charles J., ed. *Records of the colony and plantation of New Haven, from 1638 to 1649.* Hartford, CT: Tiffany, 1857.

Hosley, William N. *Colt: The Making of an American Legend.* Amherst, MA: University of Massachusetts Press, 1996.

Hotchkiss, Fanny (Winchester). *Winchester Notes.* New Haven, CT: Tuttle, Morehouse and Taylor, 1912.

Houze, Herbert G. *Winchester Repeating Arms Company: Its History and Development from 1865 to 1981.* Iola, WI: Krause, 2004.

Hruby, Daniel. *Mines to Medicine: The Exciting Years of Judge Myles O'Connor, His Hospital and the Pioneer Physicians of the Santa Clara Valley.* San José, CA: O'Connor Hospital, 1965.

Ives, Charles L. "Statistics of the Class of 1852 of Yale College." New Haven, CT: Ezekiel Hayes, 1855.

Jackson, Helen Hunt. *A Century of Dishonor: A Sketch of the United States Government Dealings with some of the Indian Tribes.* New York: Harper, 1881.

———. *Ramona.* Boston: Roberts Brothers, 1884.

Jacobus, Donald Lines. *The Pardee Genealogy.* New Haven, CT: New Haven Colony Historical Society, 1927.

Jennings, Dean. "The House That Tragedy Built." *Coronet,* May 1945.

Joncas, Richard, David J. Neuman, and Paul V. Turner. *The Campus Guide.* New York: Princeton Architectural Press, 1999.

Jordan, David Starr. *Days of a Man, Being Memories of a Naturalist, Teacher, and Minor Prophet of Democracy.* Vol. 1. New York: World Book, 1922.

Kennedy, Helen Weber, and Veronica K. Kinzie. *Vignettes of the Gardens of San José de Guadalupe.* San Francisco, 1938.

Knight, J. "An Introductory Lecture to the Course of 1849-50, in the Medical Institution of Yale College." *The American Journal of the Medical Sciences* by Southern Society for Clinical Investigation, 1850, pp. 436-441. Digitized May 8, 2007.

Larson, Linda S. *San José's Monument to Progress: The Electric Light Tower.* San José, CA: San José Historical Museum, 1989.

Legault, Richard L. *Trends in American Gun Ownership.* New York: LFB Scholarly Publishing, 2008.

Lewis, Berkeley R. *Small Arms Ammunition at the International*

Exposition Philadelphia, 1876. Smithsonian Studies in History and Technology 11. Washington, DC: Smithsonian Institution Press, 1972.

Lukes, Timothy, and Gary Okihiro. *Japanese Legacy: Farming and Community Life in California's Santa Clara Valley.* Cupertino, CA: California History Center, 1985.

Mace, Emily. "Haunted by Tourists: Spirits of Spiritualism at the Winchester Mystery House." Unpublished manuscript, 2006, in author's possession.

Madis, George. *The Winchester Book Silver Anniversary Edition.* Brownsboro, TX: Art and Reference House, 1985.

Mars, Amaury. *Reminiscences of the Santa Clara Valley and San José: With the Souvenir of the Carnival of Roses Held in Honor of the Visit of President William McKinley, Santa Clara County, California, May 13-14-15, 1901.* San Francisco: Artistic, 1901.

Maynard, Preston, and Marjorie B. Noyes, eds. *Carriages and Clocks, Corsets and Locks: The Rise and Fall of an Industrial City—New Haven, Connecticut.* Hanover, NH: University Press of New England, 2004.

Melick, Weldon. "Sevenscore Gables." *Holiday* (February 1947): 39.

Merrill, Phyllis Moulton. "Memories of Atherton: Oral History Transcript." BANC MSS 75/57 C, 1971. Bancroft Library, University of California, Berkeley.

Mills, Susan Tolman. *Rebuttal of Homer Sprague's "To My Friends."* Pamphlet, 1886. Special Collections and Archive, Mills College.

Morse, Jedidiah. *The 1797 American gazetteer, exhibiting in alphabetical order, a much more full and accurate account of the civil divisions, rivers, harbors, Indian tribes, &c. on the American continent....* Facs. of first ed., with prefatory note by Margaret Sparks. Knightstown, IN: Bookmark, 1979.

Nagel, Gunther. *Iron Will: The Life and Letters of Jane Stanford.* Stanford, CA: Stanford Alumni Association, 1975.

Newlin, Nancy. *The Gem of Edenvale.* San José, CA: Renasci, 1994.

Nordhoff, Charles. *California for Health, Pleasure, and Residence: A Book for Travelers and Settlers.* New York: Harper, 1874.

Osterweis, Rollin G. *Three Centuries of New Haven, 1638-1938.* New Haven, CT: Yale University Press, 1953.

Paige, Lucius R. *List of Freemen of Massachusetts, 1630-1691.* Baltimore: Genealogical Publishing Company, 1978.

Pierce, Marjorie. "She Played Musical Homes." *San Jose Mercury News,* July 22, 1973, 4S.

Postel, Mitchell. *Peninsula Portrait: An Illustrated History of San Mateo County.* Northridge, CA: Windsor, 1988.

Rambo, Ralph. *Lady of Mystery.* San José, CA: Rosicrucian Press, 1967.

Roosevelt, Theodore. *Hunting Trips of a Ranchman; Sketches of Sport on the Northern Cattle Plains.* Illus. A. B. Frost, R. Swain Gifford, J. C. Beard, Fannie E. Gifford, and Henry Sandham. New York: G. P. Putnam's Sons, 1885.

Rydell, Robert W., John E. Findling, and Kimberly D. Pelle. *Fair America: World's Fairs in the United States.* Washington DC: Smithsonian Institution, 2000.

Sawyer, Eugene. *History of Santa Clara County, California.* Los Angeles: Historic Record Company, 1922.

Scott, Kenneth, and Rosanne Conway, comps. *Genealogical Data from Colonial New Haven Newspapers.* Baltimore: Genealogical Publishing Company, 1979.

Simmons, C. H., Jr., ed. *Plymouth Colony Records.* Vol. 1, *Wills and Inventories, 1633-1669.* Camden, ME: Picton Press, 1996.

Smith, Rebecca. "Colleagues Remember Promoter of Winchester Mystery House." *San Jose Mercury News,* February 9, 1997.

Smith, Susy. *Prominent American Ghosts.* New York: World, 1967.

Spoon, Bruce. "Sarah Winchester and Her House: How a Legend Grows." Master's thesis, San José State University, 1951.

Sprague, Homer B. *History of the 13th Infantry Regiment of Connecticut Volunteers, during the Great Rebellion.* Hartford: Case, Lockwood, 1867.

——. *To My Friends.* Pamphlet, San Francisco, 1886.

Starr, Kevin. *Americans and the California Dream, 1850-1915.* New York: Oxford University Press, 1973.

——. *Inventing the Dream: California through the Progressive Era.* New York: Oxford University Press, 1985.

Svanevik, Michael, and Shirley Burgett. *Menlo Park beyond the Gate.* San Francisco: Custom and Limited Editions, 2000.

Thompson and West. *Historical Atlas Map of Santa Clara County, California.* San Francisco: Thompson and West, 1876.

Turner, Frederick Jackson. "The Problem of the West," *Atlantic Monthly,* September 1896. Online source: http://www.theatlantic.com/past/docs/issues/95sep/ets/turn.htm

Turner, Paul V., Marcia E. Vetrocq, and Karen Weitze. *Founders and the Architects: The Design of Stanford University.* Stanford, CA: Stanford University Department of Art, 1976.

Twain, Mark and Charles Dudley Warner. *The Gilded Age.* New York: Oxford University Press, 1996

Vital Records of New Haven 1649-1850, pt. 1. Hartford, CT: Connecticut Society of the Order of the Founders and Patriots of America, 1917.

Online database: New England Historic Genealogical Society, 2007.

Wakefield, Anne Whitney. "A Tribute to the Memory of Isabelle C. Merriman." *San Jose Mercury Herald,* June 18, 1920.

Watson, Jeanette. *Campbell, the Orchard City.* Campbell, CA: Campbell Historical Museum Association, 1989.

Welch, James. *Killing Custer: The Battle of the Little Bighorn and the Fate of the Plains Indians.* New York: W. W. Norton, 1994.

Wickson, Edward J. *The California Vegetables in Garden and Field: A Manual of Practice with and without Irrigation for Semitropical Countries.* San Francisco: Pacific Rural Press, 1897.

Williamson, Harold F. *Winchester, the Gun That Won the West.* New York: A. S. Barnes, 1952.

Wilson, Robert L. *Colt: An American Legend.* New York: Abbeville Press, 1985.

INDEX

—◄ ►—

Abbas, Abdul Baha, 144
abolition, 16, 17, 20, 21, 31, 44, 71, 89,
    217n20. *See also* slavery
Adams, President John Quincy, 16
Adel, Grace, 127, 190. *See also* Linscott,
    Grace Adel
Adel, Jesse, 127, 128, 225nn13–14
Adobe Creek, 99, 135, 136
adoption, 169, 170, 171, 229nn11–12
Agnew Asylum for the Insane, 92, 154
Alameda, CA, 208
Alameda, The (San José), 93, 103
Albany, NY, 61, 183
Alcatraz, 127
Alta Mesa Cemetery (Palo Alto, CA), 194,
    198, 200, 231n9
Altos Land Company, 137
Alvarado, Governor Juan, of Mexico, 99
American Repeating Rifle Company, 63
*Americans and the California Dream,
    1850–1915* (Starr), 83
American Society for the Prevention of
    Cruelty to Animals (ASPCA), 21. *See
    also* animal welfare; anti-vivisection;
    and Humane Society
Amet, Ruth, 208, 209, 216n5, 232n9
Amistad incident, 1, 15, 16, 18
ammunition, 39, 46, 58, 61–63, 90, 182,
    190, 193, 195, 220n45
Anderson Prune Dipper, 104, 223n35
"Angels of Light," 142
animal welfare, 167. *See also* American
    Society for the Prevention of Cruelty
    to Animals (ASPCA); anti-vivisection;
    and Humane Society
anti-vivisection, 96, 184. *See also*
American Society for the Prevention
    of Cruelty to Animals (ASPCA); animal
    welfare; Humane Society
Architectural Record, 107, 182, 224n7
architecture: award from Yale, 81; *El
    Sueño,* 97; French neoclassical, 132;
    Gothic style, 11, 67, 92, 97, 110;
    Mission-revival, 101, 181; in New
    Haven, 11, 21, 67; Queen Anne-style,
    110, 113, 181, 224n18; Romanesque-
    style, 110; in San José, 92, 107; and
    Sarah Winchester, 68, 81, 115, 122,
    143, 164, 172; Stanford University,
    101; styles, 11, 110; and William
    Winchester, 68, 153
"ark." *See* houseboat
Armsmear, 45,
art glass windows, 6, 108, 109
Atherton, CA, 5, 129–31, *146*, 150,
    153–55, 163, 172–75, 177, 178, 180,
    181, 183, 194, 196, 198, 199, 206,
    210, 225n19, 226nn20–21, 227n14,
    228n31, 229n28
Atherton, Dominga de Goni, 129, 225n20
Atherton, Faxon Dean, 129, 131
Atherton, Gertrude, 225n20
Atherton woods, 181
Atwater, Edward E., 28, 216n5
Austin, Henry, 67

B. Altman & Company, 182
"backity back," 208
Bahaism, 144
Bakewell, Mrs., 160, 162, 228n33
Baldwin, Ella and Charles, 3, 132, 226n24
Baldwin, Roger Sherman, 16

Baltimore, MD, 17, 23, 25, 26, 28, 45, 75
Banner of Light, 80
Barker, Mr. E.A., 207
Barnett, T.C., 207
Bates, Hannah, 23
Batsell, Jake, 209, 232n14
Bayshore Highway, 183, 206
Beecher, Hazel, 202, 203
Beecher, Louise, 37
Beecher, Reverend Henry Ward, 85, 222n5
Benjamin H. Merriman & Company, 36
Bennett, Hannah Jane "Jennie": correspondence with Sarah L. Winchester, 78, 111, 115, 121, 215n3, 217n19, 218n23, 219n34, 221n4, 221n23, 222n28, 222n31, 222n36, 224n8, 224nn11–13, 224nn22–23, 225n32, 229n18, 232n25; death, 193; early life, 18, 27, 30, 32, 68; family, 75, 79, 195; finances, 69, 192; marriage, 49, 60, 79; philanthropy, 81, 82, 186. *See also* Winchester, Hannah Jane "Jennie"
Bennett, Hope, 79
Bennett, Thomas Gray: anxious over son's health, 191; attends Sarah Pardee's funeral, 73; Civil War service, 60; counsels Sarah L. Winchester, 77, 80, 85; dines with Sarah L. Winchester, 79; finances of Winchester Repeating Arms Company, 191–93; gift to mother-in-law, 81; letters to Sarah L. Winchester, 187, 191, 217n19, 230n25, 230n27, 230n28, 230n37, 230n38, 231n39; marriage, 27, 60; named executor for William W. Winchester, 76; as officer of Winchester Repeating Arms Company, 49, 61, 79, 99, 191, 195; outlives Sarah L. Winchester, 200; recruits William Mason, 62; relationship to Colt, 62; relationship with John Browning, 62; relationship with William Converse, 61; upon the death of Oliver F. Winchester, 74–75
Bennett, Winchester, 79, 191, 193
Bergh, Henry, 21, 217n30

Berkeley, CA, 94
Bey, Captain Edinboro, 71, 72, 221n12
billboards, 211, 212
Bishop, Jeremiah A., 74
Blair Undertakers, 75
Blanchard, the butcher, 169
Bogie, James, 181, 198, 199, 201
Bogie, Sarah, 181, 198, 199, 201
Bohemian Club, 132
Brett, Mary Ann Winchester, 25, 218n9
Brewer, Reverend William A., 134, 184, 198, 199
Brewster's Park, New Haven, 33
Bridgeport, CT, 41, 43, 44, 46
Brown, Augustus, 74
Brown, David R., 67
Brown, Edna May, 208
Brown, John H., 207, 208, 209, 210, 211, 232n14
Brown, Mayme, 208, 209, 210, 211, 232n14
Brown, Mildred, 208
Browne, Francis, 8
Browning, John, 62
Bryan, William Jennings, 120
Buffalo Bill Cody. *See* Cody, William
Buffalo Bill Historical Center, Cody, WY, 49, 50, 51
Buffalo Bill's Wild West, 62, 64, 213
Burbank, Luther, 104, 223n36
Burlingame, Anson, 157
Burlingame Advance, 206, 230n14, 232n1
Burlingame Country Club, 132
Burlingame Park, *147,* 157, 160
Burnham, Daniel, 156
Burns, grandfather [Daniel], 10
Burns, Polly Morehouse, 10
Burns, Ralph, 10
Burns, Sarah W. *See* Pardee, Sarah W.
"Byde a Whyle," 181

Cahawba, 33
Cain, Katherine, 127
California for Health, Pleasure, and Residence, 84, 211, 222n2
California National Guard, 127, 189

California State Humane Association, 168
California State Normal School (today's San Jose State University), 92
California Supreme Court, 170
California Tourism Hall of Fame, 212
Calvinism, 36
Camp Fremont, Menlo Park, 188
Campbell, CA, 92, 93, 120, 144, 155, 224n2, 227n20
Campbell School District, 93
Canadian Mounties, 64
Carolan, Francis, 131, 132, 176, 226n24
Carolan, Harriet Pullman, 131, 132, 176, 226n24
Carroll, Frank, 94, 95, 132, 160, 162, 165, 171, 179
Carroll, Mabel, 171
Carroll, Mary, 162, 171, 222n4, 229n17
Center Church, New Haven, 8, 11, 12, 67, 193
Central Park, New York, 101
Century of Dishonor, A (Jackson), 59
Chandler School, 137
Chauncy B. Peck's shirt manufactory, 28
Cheney, Doctor, 75
child welfare, 21, 167, 169
Chinese, 57, 92, 94, 107, 175
cholera epidemic (1832), 12, 13
Chynoweth, Mary Hayes, 113, 138, 143, 144, 176
Chynoweth, Thomas, 113
City Bathing House (New Haven), 15, 17, 18, 111
Civil War: Bull Run, VA (1861), 33–34; Chaffin's Farm, VA (1864), 60; conscription, 32–33; Fort Sumter, 33; Gettysburg, PA (1863), 35; Irish Bend, LA (1863), 40; Second Connecticut Infantry, 33; Thirteenth Connecticut Infantry, Company H, 34; Twenty-eighth and Twenty-ninth Connecticut Volunteers, 60
Clark, Walter A., 137, 226n37
Cody, William, 62, 63, 213
Cody Firearms Museum (Cody, WY), 63
Coleman, Maria O'Brien, 130
Collegiate and Commercial Institute,

New Haven, 60
Colt, Elizabeth, 45, 79, 112
Colt, Samuel, 2, 41, 44, 45, 58, 70
Colt's firearms. *See also* Patent Fire-Arms Manufacturing Company, 2, 46, 63, 64
Comstock Lode, 3, 130, 132
Congregationalism, 10, 11, 141
Connecticut State Legislature, 42
Connecticut State Normal School, 89
Connors, Chuck, 213
Constantinople, 41, 42, 65, 71
consumption, 33, 79, 96. *See also* tuberculosis
Converse, Mary A. Pardee, 2, 14, 37, 72, 80, 82, 87, 202
Converse, William Ware: collaborates with Thomas Bennett, 61; counsels Sarah L. Winchester, 80, 85, 98, 216n19, 222n30, 223n21; death, 99; death of wife, 87; executor of Oliver F. Winchester's estate, 77; executor of William W. Winchester's estate, 78-79; hired by Oliver F. Winchester, 61; marketing skills, 62; marriage to Mary A. Pardee, 20, 202; Orange Street house, 72; president of Winchester Repeating Arms Company, 49, 75, 79; works for Leonard Pardee, 34, 37
Coons, Adam, 80
Corliss Centennial steam engine, 71
Coronet magazine, 210
Count Five, 212
Coyote Point, 131
Cozza, Margaret. *See* Marriott, Margaret
Crocker, Ruth, 182, 230n11
Crockers, the, 131
Croft, Samuel, 23
Crossways, 132
Crossways Farms, 132, 133, 160
Crowley & Pederson Harbor Boats and Barges, 133
Crystal Beach Resort, 208
Crystal Palace Exhibition, London, 1851, 19
Custer, General George, 58, 59, 220n29
Custer's Last Stand, 59
Cuvillier, V.P., 125

Cypress Lawn Cemetery (Colma, CA), 96, 167, 184

Davies, Alice (daughter of John M. Davies), 68
Davies, Alice (wife of John M. Davies), 68
Davies, Charlotte, 68
Davies, Cornelius, 29, 41, 42, 43, 68, 74
Davies, John M., 26, 28, 29, 42, 48, 61, 66, 67, 70
Davis, Reverend William W., 202
Davis, Sarah Antoinette "Nettie" Sprague, 37, 185, 202
Dehar, Allen, 82
Delmas, Delphin, 102, 112
Dickens, Charles, 7, 216n1
Diel, widow, 99
Diel land, 99, 102
Disneyland, 211
Domkee, Sarah. See Pardee, Sarah Domkee
Donner Expedition, 94
Dye, Ann Rebecca Winchester, 18, 25, 27, 30, 31, 32, 35, 36, 74
Dye, Charles (baby), 31, 35
Dye, Charles Brockway, 27, 30, 31, 35
Dye, Oliver "Ollie" Winchester, 27, 31, 35, 61, 77-78, 78-79, 185
Dye, William Winchester, 35

Earthquake of 1906. See San Francisco Earthquake of 1906
East Palo Alto, CA, 159
El Camino Real, 130, 147, 160, 180, 228n31
El Monte Canyon, 135
El Sueño 97, 123-25, 134-37, 153. See also Merriman ranch
Electric Light Tower (San Jose), 93, 222n14
Emancipation Proclamation, 32
Emerson, Ralph Waldo, 11
entertainment industry, 64, 213
enunciator, 177
E. Remington & Sons, 63
Evergreen Cemetery (New Haven), 36, 38, 73, 74, 75, 200, 210, 218n9, 221n21, 231n11
Exchange Building (New Haven), 27
Exclusion laws, 167

Fair Oaks, CA. See Atherton, CA
Fanning, Mrs. Wesley, 143
Farrand, Beatrice, 186
First Baptist Church, 22, 216n10
First Federal Trust Company, San Francisco, 185
First Methodist Church, New Haven, 67
First National Bank, New Haven, 190
First National Bank, San Jose, 104
First Spiritual Union, 142
Fleishhaker, Delia, 183
Flood, James, 130
Fogarty Repeating Rifle Company, 63
Foothill Expressway, 137
Ford Model T, 176
Foute, Reverend Robert C., 128, 129
Fox, Kate, 11, 141
Fox, Margaret, 11, 141
Franciscans, 83, 93
Franco-Prussian War, 46
Frémont, Jessie Benton, 126
Frontier Village, 211

Gale, Margaret. See Marriott, Margaret
Gallaher, Reverend Doctor H.M., 74
Gardner's Sanitarium (Belmont, CA), 189, 190
General Hospital Society of Connecticut, xviii, 185, 201, 203, 204, 222n37, 230n20, 230n 23, 230nn26-27
George W. Tinney & Sons Mortuary (Palo Alto, CA), 197, 200, 231n6
Gerard, Estelle L.: children of, 37, 168, 198, 203; death of, 96; divorce, 74; early life, 14, 17, 18, 19, 21, 217n21; illness, 95, 172; in San Francisco, 95; marriage, 36; mother's estate, 74, 77; move to California, 86, 94
Gerard, George Leonard, 86, 94, 95, 96, 198, 202, 203
Gerard, George Lyon, 36, 37, 74
Gerard, Sarah "Saidee" Louise, 37, 86, 94-96, 120, 198, 201. See also Ruthrauff,

Sarah "Saidee"
ghosts, 6, 80, 138, 162, 163, 202, 209, 212, 213, 222n34
Gilded Age, 69
Gilded Age, the, 3, 69, 71, 106, 182, 230n11
Glennon, Frank, 195
Golden Gate Park (San Francisco), 107, 148
Gold Rush (California 1849), 3, 47, 83, 84, 86, 92, 102, 129, 154
Goodyear, Eli, 9
Goodyear, Sally Pardee, 9, 15
Gorham Manufacturing Company, 187
Grace Church, San Francisco, 128
Grace Hospital Society, 205
Grace-New Haven Community Hospital, 205
Grant, President Ulysses, 71, 118
Gray, Merle H., 141, 164, 212, 224n21
Great Depression, 195

Haas-Lilienthal house, San Francisco, 112, 114, 224n18
Hahn, A. G. C., 146, 230n9
Hale, Oliver A., 134, 135, 136, 137, 226n36
Hale's Department Stores, 134
Hall, Edward E., 74
Hall, Minnie Yeager, 171, 210, 227n24, 229n16, 231n7, 232n19. *See also* Yeager, Minnie
Halleck Building, San Francisco, 131
Hamden, CT, 2, 9, 19, 58, 63
Hamm, John, 91
Hamm land, 91, 117
Hansen, Carl, *149, 151, 152,* 171, 174
Hansen, John, *149,* 150 173, 174, 177, 178, 199, 201, 206, 207, 210, 225n2, 228n40, 229n22, 229n32, 232n7
Hansen, Nellie *149,* 174, 175, 178, 199. *See also* Zarconi, Nellie,
Hansen, Richard, 149, 152, 215n2
Hansen, Theodore "Ted," *149, 151, 152,* 165, 171, 174, 228n48
Hansen family, *149,* 171, 176, 178, 187, 195, 198, 201, 214

Hargis wheat ranch, 91
Harrison, President Benjamin, 118
Hart, Brooke, 210
Hartford, CT, 2, 41, 44, 45, 112
Hartford Evening Press, 44
Harvey, Doctor Samuel C., 186
Hawley, Joseph R., 44, 71
Hayes, Everis, 176
Hayes, Jay, 176
Hayes, Mary. *See* Chynoweth, Mary Hayes
Hayes brothers, 121, 138, 176
Hayes Mansion, 113, 224n18
Hebe, Greek goddess of youth, 106
Henry, Benjamin T., 39, 40, 41, 42, 43, 44, 46, 140, 215n1, 219n14
Henry Repeating Rifle Company, 42
Henry's repeating rifle, 39, 40, 43, 44, 58, 63
Hill, Andrew P., 55, 182, 197, 198, 199
Hill, Reverend Benjamin, 10, 12, 13, 21, 31, 36, 37
Hillhouse, James, 67, 68
Hillhouse, James A., 67, 68
Hirata, Misa, 175, 177, 196, 201, 228n, 231n1
Historic Families of America memorial (Washington, DC), 119
Hobart, Virginia "Ella." *See* Baldwin, Ella
Hobart, Walter S., 3, 132
Hollis Street Congregational Church, Boston, 23
"Holy Rollers," 169
Hopkins Grammar School, 8, 22, 217n1
Houdini, Harry, 209
houseboat, *xvi,* 3, 52, 133–34, 147, *148,* 153, 158–63, 176, 183, 184, 206, 216n5, 226n26, 226n28, 228n32
Houze, Herbert, 168, 218n18, 218n20, 219n1, 219n3, 219n7, 219n10, 219n12, 219n18, 219n21, 220n42, 220n46, 221n8, 224n30, 229n5
Humane Society, 168, 169, 206, 217n20. *See also* American Society for the Prevention of Cruelty to Animals (ASPCA); animal welfare; anti-vivisection
Hunting Trips of a Ranchman

(Roosevelt) 62, 220n43

Industrial Revolution, 1, 9, 10, 70
International Expositions: 3; California
    Mid-winter International Exposition
    (San Francisco, 1894), 107, 133;
    Centennial Exposition (Philadelphia,
    1876), 63, 70, 71, 220n47, 221n9;
    Columbian Exposition (Chicago,
    1893), 106, 107, 114, 156, 224n4,
    225n4; Glasgow (1901), 3; Panama
    Pacific (San Francisco, 1915), 146,
    182, 230n9
Interurban Electric Railway, 134, 135,
    136, 137, 180
Ives, Doctor, 35, 36

Jackson, Helen Hunt, 59
Jackson, President Andrew, 13
Japanese Tea Garden, 148
Jesuit priests, 93
Jordan, David Starr, 103, 223n25

Kagoshima, Shozo, 210, 212, 232n22
Kaiser Wilhelm, 188
Kidder, Peabody & Company, 191, 192,
    193, 231n39
King, Nelson, 43, 74
Kohne, Henry, 162, 184
Kohne, Ida, 162, 184

La Amistad. See Amistad incident
Laederich, John, 117
Laederich, Luisa, 117
Laederich family, 117, 176
Laederich farm, 117
Laine, Judge, 98, 99
Lakota Sioux, 58
Lane, Katherine, 8
Larsen, Fred, 165, 177, 178, 228n48
lawlessness, 59, 60, 84
Lee, Doctor Helen, 172, 174
Leib, Elna, 103, 104, 223n34
Leib, Lida, 102, 103, 112, 113
Leib, Roy, 165, 194, 198, 206
Leib, Samuel Franklin "Frank": advisor
    to Jane Stanford, 101, 103, 154,

223n27; appointed to the bench, 104;
    as quoted on Sarah L. Winchester,
    5; comments on Winchester's
    Atherton house, 181; counsels Sarah
    L. Winchester on finances, 179,
    184, 185, 190, 194, 201; counsels
    Sarah L. Winchester on finances
    of the Winchester Repeating Arms
    Company, 192-94, 231n42; earnings
    from Sarah L. Winchester, 102,
    136, 194; friendship with Burbank,
    104, 223n36; funeral of Sarah L.
    Winchester, 198, 199, 200; hired by
    Winchester, 99; illness, 153; letters
    from Sarah L. Winchester, 52, 117,
    118, 135-37, 153, 161, 224nn25-27,
    226nn29-31, 226n 35, 227n17,
    228n 36, 229n15, 230n16, 230n18,
    230nn34-35; letters to Sarah L.
    Winchester, 102, 126, 154-55,
    223nn29-30, 227n 18, 227n22,
    227nn26-28, 228n29, 229nn21-22,
    229nn2-3, 230n8, 230n17, 230n29,
    231n43; makes contributions on
    behalf of Sarah L. Winchester, 186,
    188, 230n22; member, board of
    directors of railroad, 135, 137, 180,
    226n36; member, Stanford board
    of trustees, 101; negotiates with
    Winchester's dentist, 173, 229n20;
    orchardist, 104, 223n35; partnership
    with Delmas, 102; partnership with
    Judge Laine, 99; personal attributes,
    102; portrait, *145;* relationship with
    Sarah L. Winchester, 105, 173, 188;
    title searches for Winchester, 157, 158
Leib Carriage House, 103, 114, 223n31,
    224n18
"Leibheim," 103, 112, 113
Leland Stanford Junior College. *See*
    Stanford University
Lenzen, Jacob, 107
Leonard Pardee & Company, 18, 19, 20,
    31
lever-action rifles, 44, 62, 63, 64
Lewis & Maycock Undertakers (New
    Haven), 200

Lick Observatory, 92, 93, 104

Lincoln, President Abraham, 31, 32, 33, 41, 73, 157, 219n6

Lincrusta, 108

Linden Towers, 130

Linscott, Grace Adel, 190

Little Sure Shot. *See* Oakley, Annie

Llanada Alavesa, 90, 91

Llanada Villa, 52, 56, 91, 93-96, 107, 109, 110, 113-15, 118, 126, 138, 142, 149, 151, 154-56, 159, 162, 171, 174-75, 178, 180, 198, 199

Los Altos, CA, 54, 97, 125, 137, 183, 225n8, 226n33, 227n38

Los Altos Star, 125, 225n8

Louis Comfort Tiffany, 109, 210

Mace, Emily, 80, 222n34

Maine: incident, 121

marasmus, 36

Marin County, 133

Marriott, Frederick, 128

Marriott, Frederick "Fred" A., III, 128, 129, 130-33, *147*, 151, 156, 157, 166, 170, 171, 176, 177, 189, 195, 198, 227n23, 229n31

Marriott, Frederick, Jr., 128

Marriott, Margaret, 151, 170, 171, 177, 189, 190, 195, 198, 200, 203, 229nn10-13

Marriott, Marion I. "Daisy" Merriman, 4, 5, 37, 52, *55*, *56*, 86, 97, 109, 115, 120, 121, 123, 126-33, *147*, 157, 165, 170, 171, 174, 175, 177, 187, 189, 190, 194, 195, 198, 199, 200-203, 207, 225n11

Marsh, Risley, 203

Marsh, William, 203

Marsh breech-loading rifles, 41, 219n6

Mason, William, 62

McGraw, D.F., 121

McKee, Joseph, 107

McKinley, President William, 118, 119, 120, 224n29

McLean, Anita, 202, 203

McLean, Sarah, 202, 203

McLellan, Edgar W., 160, 161, 162, 228n35

Meade, Doctor Euthanasia, 95, 96, 172

Menlo Park, CA *See* Atherton, CA

Meridian School, 93, 171

Merrill, Maud, 175

Merrill, Phyllis Moulton, 144, 226n21, 227n14, 229n20

Merriman, Isabelle C. "Belle" Pardee: associated with Humane issues, 167-171, 217n20, 217n30; at *El Sueño,* 97-98, 123-127, 129, 134, 223n20; attributes, 4, 19; beats German sympathizer, 188; birth and childhood, 14, 17, 18, 21, 217n21, 218n32; to California, 86, 94; children, 37; death, 194, 231n45; given a house by mother, 76-77; kidnaps mental patient, 189; marriage, 36; mother's funeral, 73; named in Sarah L. Winchester's will, 202-3; in Palo Alto, 166; portrait, *54*; registered Democrat, 120, 225n11; relationship with Sarah L. Winchester, 96, 165, 185, 187; and religion, 144; remains sent to New Haven, 220; restraining order against, 136; trust fund cut, 190

Merriman, Louis, 36, 37, 86, 94, 96, 97, 98, 124, 125, 129, 136, 166, 167, 202, 218n32

Merriman, Marion I. "Daisy." *See* Marriott, Marion I. "Daisy" Merriman

Merriman, William W., 37, 86, 94, 97, 123, 171, 202, 203

Merriman ranch. *See also El Sueño,* 123, 134, 135, 153, 166, 180, 183

Methodist College of the Pacific (today's University of the Pacific, Stockton, CA), 92

Mexican War of 1846, 84

Miles, Martha, 8

Milford, CT, 9, 10, 131

Mills College, 86, 87, 88, 89, 94, 217n29

Mills, Susan Tolman, 87, 88, 222n6

Mission Santa Clara, 93

Mitchell, Doctor, 75

Mockbee, Jacob, 124

Morgan, J.P., 187

Mormonism, 10

Morris, Charles, 80, 179, 222n35, 229n1
Morris & Merwin law firm, New Haven, 80
Moulton, Frank, 130, 155, 180, 181, 183
Mountain View, CA, 4, 97, 98, 124, 125, 134, 136, 169
Mountain View Register, 129, 225n1, 229n6
Mountain View Road District, 136
Mount Hamilton, 92, 104
Muir, John, 119

Nakano, Mr., 175, 178
National Association for the Advancement of Colored People, 167
National Register of Historic Places, 103, 114, 223n31, 224n18, 226n24
New Haven, CT, fire 1837, 15
New Haven Arms Company, 39-42
New Haven City Hall, 67
New Haven Colony, 7
New Haven County Superior Court, 205
New Haven Green, 7, 8, 11, 12, 16, 17, 21
New Haven Hospital. *See also* Yale-New Haven Hospital, 186, 187, 204
New Haven Palladium, 32, 73, 221n15, 221n21
New Haven Register, 182, 218n7, 218n12, 221n17
New Haven Water Company, 73
New York Herald, 182
New York Hotel, 71
New York Times, 32, 46, 72, 173, 217n28, 219n17, 219n20, 221n12, 229n23
New York Tribune, 192
Niagara Falls, 208
Nishihara, Ida Winchester, *151*, *152*, 176
Nishihara, Ito, *152*, 175, 176, 177
Nishihara, Ryoichi, 152, 175, 176, 199
Nishihara, Tommie, *151*, 175, 176, 178, 199, 201, 204, 228n2
Noé, Doctor Amon T., 210
Noé, Henrietta Sivera. *See* Sivera, Henrietta
Nordhoff, Charles, 84, 211, 222n2
North Church, 11
Northern California Attractions

Association, 212
Northern Cheyenne, 58

Oakland, CA, 86, 87, 217n29
Oakley, Annie, 62, 64, 213
O'Connor Sanitarium, 167, 223n16
Olin (Corporation or Industries), 49, 195
Olmstead, Frederick Law, 101
Orkney, Miss, 118
Ottoman Empire, 46
Overland Monthly, 96
Oyama family, 175, 178

Pacific Manufacturing Lumber Company, 93, 108
Page, George, 113
Palo Alto, CA, 54, 131, 134, 135, 153, 166-71, 174, 176, 189, 190, 194-98, 200, 203, 217n20
Palo Alto Hospital, 174
Palo Alto Humane Society, 168
Panama Canal Act, 1902, 159
Pardee, Antoinette. *See* Sprague, Antoinette "Nettie"
Pardee, Enos, 9, 24
Pardee, Estelle L. *See* Gerard, Estelle L. Pardee
Pardee, George, 7, 8, 9, 24, 57
Pardee, Governor George, 104
Pardee, Hazel Beecher, 203
Pardee, Isabelle C. *See* Merriman, Isabelle "Belle" Pardee
Pardee, Joel, 9, 24
Pardee, Joseph, 8, 9, 24
Pardee, Leonard, 9, 11-13, 14, 15, 17, 19, 20, 22, 24, 31, 37, 38, 61, 72, 202
Pardee, Leonard Morehouse, 14, 15, 33, 76, 202, 221n26
Pardee, Louise Beecher, 37, 202
Pardee, Mary Augusta. *See* Converse, Mary A. Pardee
Pardee, Sally Murray. *See* Goodyear, Sally Pardee
Pardee, Sarah Catherine, 37, 202
Pardee, Sarah Domkee, 14, 37
Pardee, Sarah E., 12, 13, 202
Pardee, Sarah Lockwood. *See* Winchester,

Sarah Lockwood
Pardee, Sarah W.(Burns), 2, 10-13, 37, 72, 73, 74, 76-77, 202, 221n14
Pardee, Thomas, 9, 24
Park, Alice, 168
Parkinson, J. F., 125, 166
Pasture, The (Burlingame, CA), 131, 153, 184, 206
Patent Fire-Arms Manufacturing Company, 41, 45, 62
patents, 9, 26, 28, 39, 60, 63, 215n1, 218n11
Payne, Doctor Robert, 172, 173, 229n20
"Peacemaker," 64
Peninsular Railroad Company, 137
Perkins, James, 209, 232n12
Philippine Islands, 121
phylloxera, 124, 137
Pierce-Arrow, 177, 195, 203
Pierson, Arthur and Sophie, 117
Polk, Willis, 132, 226n24
Prince Albert, 19
Progressive causes, 120
Prohibition, 121, 165
Prominent American Ghosts, 80, 222n34
Prospect Hill, 32, 35, 45, 46, 48, 69, 82, 195, 220n2
Prospect Street, 18, 46, 48, 66, 68, 74, 75, 77, 79, 81, 110, 115
Prout, Mary, 203, 204
"Psychotic Reaction," 212
Pullman, George, 131
Puritanism, 7, 8, 10, 11
Purves, Alexander, 82
Pyrenees, 91

Queen Victoria, 1, 19, 21, 132
Quinnipiac River, 8, 10, 11

Ralston, William, 57, 131
Rambo, Edward "Ned," 90, 91, 92, 94, 98, 99, 174, 222n29, 223n21
Rambo, Ralph, 120, 222n12, 224n5, 225n31,
Ramona (Jackson), 59
Rancho San Antonio, 99

Rebello, Bill, 211
Rebuttle of Homer Sprague's 'To My Friends,' by Susan Mills, 89, 222n6
Red Cross, 126
Redwood City, CA, 159, 181, 226n21, 226nn26-28, 228n30, 228nn32-34, 230n 9, 230n13, 230n15, 231n45, 231n2, 231n4, 231n6, 231n9, 232n6
Reighley family, 133
Renault limousine, *145,* 177
Revolutionary War, 10, 19, 58, 216n9
Richard II (Shakespeare), 109
Richardson, Mr., 23
R. M. Niagara, 28
Roberts, George, 142-44
Roberts, Nancy, 142-44
Roberts Spiritualist Temple, 142-43
Robinson, Leoni, 82
Rockefeller, John D., 70, 187
Roedel, Mr. & Mrs. P.M., 128
Roosevelt, President Theodore, 62, 63, 119, 120, 187, 220n43
Royal Band of Mercy, 184
Russia, 71, 190, 191
Ruthrauff, Henry "Harry," 168, 184
Ruthrauff, Sarah "Saidee," 168, 184, 203, 204, 206

Sachem's Woods, 67
Samuel C. Winchester & Company, (Baltimore), 28
San Andreas Fault, 154
San Francisco Bay, 47, 87, 90, 131, 133, 147, 157, 159, 163
San Francisco Bay Area, 96, 153, 154
San Francisco Call, 173, 229n23
San Francisco Chronicle, 112, 128, 200, 225n16, 226n24, 231n12
San Francisco Earthquake of 1906, 4, 55, 138, 154-59, 163, 165, 173, 180, 182, 183, 227n19
San Francisco Examiner, 127, 128, 162, 225n13, 227n13, 228n41, 230n30
San Francisco News Letter, 128, 129, 131, 147, 176, 195
San Francisco News Letter Wasp, 128
San José City Hall, 92

San José Convention and Visitors Bureau, 212

San José Daily Mercury, 124, 225n6

San José Evening News, 127, 216n4, 224n17, 225nn33-34, 225n7, 225nn9-10, 225nn12-14, 225n18, 227nn1-6, 227n11, 229nn7-9

San José Hospital, 201

San José Jubilee Committee, 126

San José Los Gatos Interurban Railway Company, 136. *See also* Interurban Electric Railway

San José Mercury, 121, 124, 127, 209, 216n6, 223n17, 223n19, 225n3, 225n6, 225n15, 228n38, 229nn11-12, 229n14, 230n4, 231n5, 232n12, 232n14

San José Mercury Herald, 107, 138, 153, 164, 194, 208, 217n30, 223n28, 224n6, 226n34, 227n10, 227n15, 228n49, 229n6, 229n10, 229nn24-25, 230n33

San José News, 110, 224n19, 227n4

San José Relief Fund, 155

San Mateo County, 128, 129, 176, 225n11, 227n25, 229n28, 230n9, 230n12, 230nn14-15

San Mateo County History Museum, 146, 226nn26-28, 228n30, 228nn32-34, 230n9, 230n15, 231n2, 231n4, 231n6, 231n9, 232n6

San Mateo County Superior Court, 228n35

San Mateo Times, 133, 226n25, 230n5

Sanford, Lockwood, 15, 134

Santa Clara College, 92, 93

Santa Clara County, 54, 99, 118, 124, 134, 218n32, 222n5, 222n12, 223n18, 224n1, 224n24, 224n29, 226n32, 227n10, 229n13, 229n29, 230n12, 231n45, 231n2, 231n4, 231n8, 231n10, 231nn13-17, 232n18. *See also* Santa Clara Valley

Santa Clara County assessor, 121

Santa Clara County Board of Supervisors, 118, 136

Santa Clara County Hall of Justice, 155

Santa Clara County Hospital, 92

Santa Clara County Humane Society, 169

Santa Clara County Juvenile Court, 170

Santa Clara County Superior Court, 104, 145, 201, 231nn13-17, 232n18

Santa Clara County surveyor, 118

Santa Clara-Los Gatos Road. *See also* Winchester Boulevard

Santa Clara Mission Cemetery, 162

Santa Clara University. *See* Santa Clara College

Santa Clara Valley, 2, 84, 90-92, 99, 104, 113-18, 119, 120, 122, 124, 125, 134, 154, 162, 175, 182, 198, 224n29, 229n27

Santa Cruz Mountains, 93, 182

Santana Row, 117, 183

Santa Rosa, CA, 104, 155

Sausalito, 133

scarlet fever, 12

Schenck, Elizabeth H., 77

Science Press, 182

Scopes & Feustmann of New York, 186

Sealis, Hannah, 22

séance, 80, 100, 142, 143, 153

Sears, Roebuck and Company, 109

Second Great Awakening, 11

Sempervirens Club, 182

Seventh Cavalry U.S. Army, 58

sewing machines, 28, 29, 173

Shakespeare, 90, 109, 114, 115

Sharon, William, 131

Sharps rifles, 33, 40

Sheffield, Joseph, 67

Shelby, Mae, 175

Silicon Valley, 90, 137

Silver Dollar Saloon, 211

Sivera, Henrietta, *152,* 175, 177, 178, 195, 197, 198, 199, 201, 207, 210, 229n26, 232n18. *See also* Noe, Henrietta

slavery, 16, 31. *See also* abolition

Smith, Horace, 2, 39

Smith, Richard, 195, 198

Smith, Susy, 80, 222n34

Southern Pacific Railroad, 134, 137

Spanish-American War, 127, 128, 184, 189

Spencer Repeating Rifle Company, 63

Spencer rifles, 58, 59, 63

Sperry, ND, 74

spirits, 11, 141, 143, 144, 163, 209, 213, 216n11, 218n31, 222nn33-34, 228n41

spiritualism, 1, 10, 11, 13, 100, 141-44, 209, 216n11, 222n34

spiritualist, 80, 138, 141-44, 153, 164, 165, 196, 209

Sprague, Antoinette "Nettie," 13, 14, 18, 20, 32, 34, 37, 86, 87, 88, 89, 90, 94, 185, 198, 202, 203

Sprague, Charles, 37, 202, 203

Sprague, Goldwin, 37, 202, 203

Sprague, Homer Baxter, 20, 32, 34, 37, 40, 86-90, 94, 202, 217n20, 217n29, 218n27, 219n5, 222nn6-10

Sprague, Sarah Antoinette "Nettie." *See* Davis, Sarah Antoinette "Nettie" Sprague

Sprague, William Pardee, 37, 198, 203

Springfield rifles, 40, 59

St. Joseph's Catholic Church (San José), 92

St. Paul's Episcopal Church (Burlingame, CA), 134, 142, 227n9

Stanford, Jane, 100, 101, 103, 142, 144, 154, 176, 223n27, 223n34

Stanford, Leland, 99, 100, 101, 131, 142, 144

Stanford, Leland, Jr., 100, 142

Stanford University, 3, 92, 98, 99, 100, 101, 110, 118, 120, 134, 154, 195, 223n29

Starr, Kevin, 83

Stephens, Elisha, 94

Stern, Louis and Lucie, 181

Stevens Creek, 135

Stewart, James "Jimmy," 51, 64, 213

Stowe, Mr. & Mrs., 142, 144

Strauss, Levi, 181

Strawberry Hill, 107

Sunnyvale, CA, 159

Sunset Limited, 133

Sunset magazine, 96, 163, 184

superstition, 1, 5, 139, 141, 163, 164, 212

Sutori, Filomena, 170

Taber, Isaiah, 57, 196, 219n24

Taft, Robert and Elizabeth, 117

Texas Rangers, 44, 45

Thaw, Harry K., as defended by Delmas, 102

The Alameda. *See* Alameda, The

The Pasture. *See* Pasture, The

"thirteen," reference to the number, 209, 212, 213

Thirteen Ghosts, 212

Thoreau, Henry David, 11

To My Friends, by Homer B. Sprague, 89, 222n7, 222n9

tourism, 6, 84, 114, 162, 207, 209, 210, 211, 212, 213, 222n34

Town, Ithiel, 67, 185

transcendentalism, 1, 10

Transcontinental Railroad, 3, 47

Trinity Episcopal Church (New Haven), 11

True Life Church (San José), 143

tuberculosis, 2, 6, 72, 186, 187, 188, 204, 205

Twain, Mark, 69

Tyler, Brigadier General Daniel, 33

Union Army, 33, 36, 41, 60, 102

Union School (New Haven), 17

Union Trust Company (San Francisco), 201, 203, 232n18

United States Supreme Court, 16, 101, 158

University of North Dakota, 94, 217n

Ushio, Rikitaro, 175

Ushio, Tomo, 175

Valparaiso Park, 129, 225n20

Van Daisem, Doctor Samuel, 174

Vendome Hotel, San Jose, 92

Veterans Administration, 205

Victoria coach, 117, *145*

Visiting Nurses Association (New Haven), 75, 201

Vogue, 182

Volcanic Repeating Arms Company, 30, 39

Volcanic sidearm, 2, 39

Warner, Charles Dudley, 69
Washington, DC, 25, 33, 119, 156
Wasp, 128
Wayland, Doctor Charles, 172
Wayland, Doctor Clyde, 172, 174, 182, 194, 196, 197, 198, 231n3
Wayland, Mrs. Lucy, 201
Wayne, John, 64
Weilheimer, Seligman, 124
Wellesley, as Sprague's model for Mills, 88
Wepawaug River, 9
Wesson, Daniel, 2, 39
White Temple, 142
Whitney, Eli (inventor), 2, 9, 58
Whitney, Eli (president, hospital board of trustees), 186, 230n22
Whitney Arms Company, 2, 9, 58, 63
Wier, S. M., 74
Wilbur, Ray Lyman, 101
Wild West shows, 62, 64, 213
Williams, Harry, 189
Williamson, Harold, 73, 218n16, 218n21, 219n9, 219n16, 219n19, 219n23, 220n38, 220n40, 220n48, 221n11, 221n13, 221nn18-19, 225n5, 227n16, 231nn40-42
William Wirt Winchester Hospital, *xviii*, 6, 187, 200, 204, 230n27
William Wirt Winchester Traveling Fellowship, 81
Winchester, Annie Pardee, 36, 75, 200, 202
Winchester, Ann Rebecca. *See* Dye, Ann Rebecca Winchester
Winchester, George, 30
Winchester, Hannah Bates, 23, 27
Winchester, Henry, 24
Winchester, Jane Ellen Hope: daughter's death, 35; death, 125; estate, 82; family, 17, 25-27, 30, 33; husband's death, 74-75; memorial to, 186; mourns Sarah Pardee, 73; philanthropy, 81; Prospect Hill home, *48*, 193, 195; son's death, 75; travel, 41, 61; wealth, 69, 77, 78, 79, 215n2
Winchester, John (born in England), 24

Winchester, John, 24
Winchester, Jonathan, 23, 24
Winchester, Mary Ann. *See* Brett, Mary Ann Winchester
Winchester, Oliver Fisher: attempted takeover by Benjamin T. Henry, 42-43; attributes as businessman, 25, 42; birth and youth, 23, 24; builds new shirt factory, 29; builds palatial home on Prospect Hill, 2, *48*, 66-68, 195; daughter marries, 60; death, 73; death of daughter and grandsons, 35; duped, 71-72; emulates Samuel Colt, 44-45; establishes New Haven Arms Company, 39; establishes Winchester & Davies Shirt Manufactory, 26-28; establishes Winchester Repeating Arms Company, 43; estate, 77, 78, 78, 79, 215n2; family, 17, 25, 27, 30; friendship with John M. Davies, 29; funeral, 79; grandson named for, 31; hires Benjamin T. Henry, 39; international arms sales, 41, 42, 46, 61; invests in arms industry, 39; lobbies for new gun factory in New Haven, 46; marriage, 25; moves to New Haven and patents shirt collar, 26; philanthropy, 31, 81, 82; portrait, *48*; runs for Lieutenant Governor, 44; seeks government contracts, 40-41, 44, 191; suffers stroke, 73; 195; supports sister's family, 25, 218n9; treasurer First Baptist Church, 22; wealth, 28, 66, 69, 70, 73, 77; will, 77, 82
Winchester, Samuel, 23, 24
Winchester, Samuel Croft, 23, 25, 26, 28, 61
Winchester, Sarah Lockwood, 41, 77; ancestry, 2, 7-10, 24; and arthritis, 5, 37, 84, 96, 144, 153, 164, 172, 196; birth, 1, 7, 15; burglarized, 181; buys real estate, 97, 98, 157, 183; childhood, 1, 11, 14, 16-18, 20, 22; courtship of, 30; death of, 196-97; death of father, 37; death of father-in-law, 2, 72, 73, 74; death of husband, 2, 72, 75; death

of mother, 2, 72, 73, 76-77; death of
sisters, 2, 13, 82, 87, 96, 194; during
Civil War, 32, 35; finances, 2, 69, 74-77,
85, 124-25, 170, 179, 190-93; funeral,
198-99; gives gifts, 81, 177; guilt,
140-41; health, 91, 139, 144, 165,
171, 173-74; heirs of, 6, 38, 202; hires
Leib, 102; husband's estate, 75-79;
infant daughter, 35-36, 38; interest
in architecture and interior design,
66, 68, 69, 71, 97, 153; leaves New
Haven, 82; letters, 52-53; litigation,
125, 135, 161, 180; marriage, 1, 27,
31-32; mental health, 141, 157, 164;
mythology about, 5, 6, 121, 161,
212; named for grandmother, 15;
orchardist, 92, 225n11; pets of, 167;
philanthropy, 82, 126, 182, 186-87,
204; pregnancy, 35; relationship with
Daisy Merriman Marriott, 4, 37, 126,
128, 129, 131; religion, 22, 141, 144;
remains transferred to New Haven
for burial, 200; sits for portrait, 57;
speaks French, 30, 164; spiritualism,
80, 141-44; travels, 47, 58, 65, 71, 79,
80, 86, 90-91
Winchester, William Wirt: ancestry,
22-24; attributes, 32; born, 25; builds
new home, 2, 68; carved likeness, 133;
commissions portraits, 68; death, 2,
72, 75, 79; death of father, 74; death
of infant, 36; death of sister, 35; estate,
79; executors, 78, 79; goes to San
Francisco, 47, 57, 58; health, 28, 69,
72, 79; hospital as memorial to, *xviii*,
6, 187, 200, 204, 205; inheritance, 77,
78, 79, 82; manager of Winchester
& Davies Shirt Manufactory, 2, 28,
29, 39, 41, 42; marriage, 1, 14, 27, 30,
31, 202; nephews named for, 35, 37;
officer of the Winchester Repeating
Arms Company, 60, 75, 79; portrait,
49; travel 28, 71; wages, 61, 79; wealth,
69; will, 76; Yale architectural award
named for, 81; youth, 18, 22
Winchester Amusement Company, 207
Winchester & Company (Baltimore), 23

Winchester & Davies Shirt Manufactory,
2, 18, 22, 26-30, 38, 39, 41, 42, 43, 66,
77, 218n20
Winchester Avenue, Atherton, 206
Winchester Avenue, Burlingame, 206
Winchester Boulevard, San José, 94, 117,
183
Winchester Chest Clinic, 205
Winchester Half Acres, 207
Winchester Mystery House (San Jose), 6,
114, 143, 207, 211, 212, 213, 222n34,
224n1, 224n5, 224n21, 232nn8-11,
232nn14-22, 232n24
Winchester Observatory. *See* Yale
University
"Winchester quarantine," 59
Winchester Repeating Arms Company,
2, 18, 42-49, 58, 60-61, 63-66, 70-72,
77-79, 85, 90, 98, 99, 119, 120, 124,
140, 141, 153, 168, 179, 182, 190-95,
215n2, 218n18, 218nn20-21, 219n1,
219n3, 219nn7-8, 219nn10-11,
219n18, 219n21, 219n22, 220n28,
220n42, 220n46, 221n8, 221n11
Winchester rifle museum, 211
Winchester rifles: Centennial Model
1966, 44; Model 1866, 44; Model 1873,
51, 64; Centennial Model 1876, *50*, 59,
63, 64, 70; Model 1896, 122
Wirt, William, 25, 218n10
Woman's Medical Club of the Pacific, 95
woodworking, 9, 15, 17, 21, 22, 37, 143,
216n8
Wooster Square, 17, 19, 22, 37, 60, 67
World War I, 64, 120, 186, 187, 188, 191,
195, 204
World War II, 204
World's fairs. *See* International
Expositions
Wright, William H., 104
Wright, W. W., 143

Yale, Elihu, 8
Yale, Elizabeth, 8
Yale College. *See* Yale University
Yale National Bank, 73
Yale University, 8, 11, 67, 70, 74, 187,

216n15, 217n27, 222n8; Betts House, 69, 221n5; Jane Ellen Hope Building, 82, 186; Sterling Divinity Quadrangle, 69, 221n5; students, 16, 20, 36, 60, 61; William Wirt Winchester Traveling Fellowship, 81; Winchester Hall, 81; Winchester Observatory, 18, 81, 92; Yale School of Medicine, 186, 205
Yale-New Haven Hospital. *See* New Haven Hospital, 6, 205
Yeager, Minnie, 171. *See also* Hall, Minnie Yeager
Yellow Boy, 44
Yen, Charlie, 175, 178

Zarconi, Nellie, 174. *See also* Hansen, Nellie Zarconi

ABOUT THE AUTHOR

Mary Jo Ignoffo teaches in the history department of De Anza College in Cupertino, California. She is the author of five other books about California history.